Help! I'm a Pastor's Wife

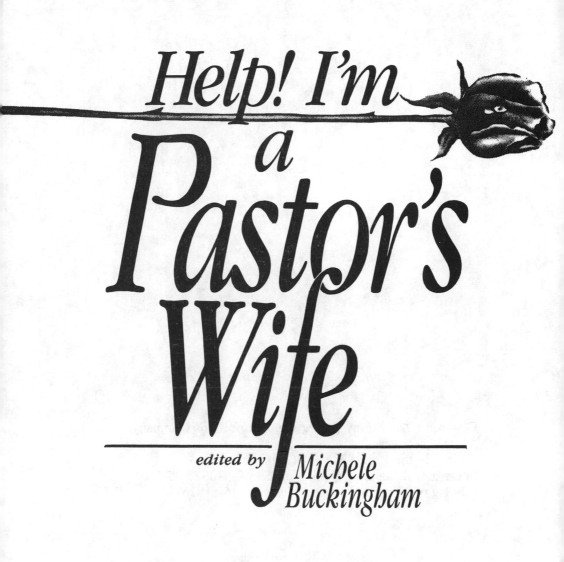

Help! I'm a Pastor's Wife

edited by Michele Buckingham

Creation House
Altamonte Springs, Florida

Creation House
Strang Communications Company
190 N. Westmonte Drive
Altamonte Springs, FL 32714
(305) 869-5005

First Printing, November 1986
Second Printing, June 1987

Contents

Mother

Minister

Introduction

Recently I was eating brunch with two good friends in an Alexandria, Virginia, restaurant.

"I'm editing a book," I told them. "It's called *Help! I'm a Pastor's Wife*."

"What's it about?" asked one friend with a grin. "How to put on the perfect tea party?"

No, *Help! I'm a Pastor's Wife* is not about tea parties. I don't know many pastors' wives who have time for tea parties. These days, pastors' wives are just too busy. They are wives, mothers and ministers—all in one. They fight loneliness, fatigue, insecurity, unfaithful husbands, sickness and death. They reach out to those in need, spreading hope to those who don't know Jesus or who simply need to know Him better. And they fulfill more roles than most of us could ever—or would ever want to—fill.

One has to be called by God to be a pastor's wife.

And each of the 30 pastors' wives who've contributed to this book has responded to that call. In doing so, they have received an extra measure of God's grace.

They have still had their difficulties, their times of darkness and doubt. These women are human. They've struggled, failed and picked themselves up again.

Every woman who reads *Help! I'm a Pastor's Wife* will find someone who understands the problems she faces. Jackie Buckingham lived with an adulterous husband. Marilyn Hickey's rebellious son used drugs. Doris Tomczak suffered low self-esteem because she compared herself to others. Dorothy Jean Ligon's loneliness while her husband was away from home brought anger, self-pity and resentment.

Readers will also discover insight, encouragement and strength, and even something to laugh about.

Help! I'm a Pastor's Wife is not about tea parties. It's about the everyday, nitty-gritty life of pastors' wives—women who have been candid about their weaknesses and their triumphs so that others might benefit.

—Michele Buckingham

Woman

Chapter One
Unrealistic Expectations

---

by Betty (Mrs. Carl) Malz

"Not me!" I hooted. "I don't want to be a pastor's wife!"

"But I'm not a pastor now," said Carl Malz, the man who had just proposed marriage to me. "I'm a returned missionary, on my way to Ellendale, North Dakota, to teach at Trinity College."

"But where is North Dakota?" I shot back. "I'm a Florida girl!"

How could I be reacting so negatively to this man? I was a lonely widow, age 34, living in Clearwater, Florida, trying to raise two young daughters on Social Security. I had prayed for six years that God would supply an honorable father for my children and a husband-lover-companion for me.

Carl Malz was that man. He had been a pastor in Ohio before going overseas. His wife, Wanda, had died of cancer shortly after they returned from the mission field in Egypt and India. He had two married children and a young daughter who had been born in India. He was good, kind, interesting, attractive. I was in love with him.

So why did I feel as if I had stepped one foot on a roller skate and the other on a banana peel?

A lot of my reaction, I think, had to do with the unrealistic expectations I held of what it meant to be a pastor's wife. For that's what I became: three months after our wedding, Carl took on a pastoring job in addition to the teaching he was doing at the college. Where did those expectations come from? Were they the result of having grown up a pastor's daughter? Were they imposed on me by tradition, or by other parishioners? Were they real, or just in my imagination?

My mother was a pastor's wife. She was a good woman who worked hard at her role. But she worried so much about pleasing others and served them with such intensity that she developed ulcers and eventually cancer. She died in her early 50s.

Carl's first wife, Wanda, died at age 51. According to Carl, she suffered from "an overdose of living and loving." She had tried too hard to do more than her share to lighten the load of others. People who had known her called her a "saint."

My mother. Wanda. Both "saints." No one had ever called me a saint. I wasn't sure I wanted them to.

Do the good always die young? I wondered. Do they live 100 years in half the time? Do the hard workers just finish their assignment ahead of schedule? And the really hard question: Did I want to be counted among their number?

There were a lot of difficult adjustments to make in the early years of our marriage. Someone recently asked

Carl, "How long have you and Betty been married?" His answer: "Three wonderful years...but 14 all together."

In those days, it seemed it was not the mountain in our path that made the road almost impassable, but the little rocks in our shoes. There were the little aggravations, the phones ringing, the knocks at the door, people bothering us with little problems while we tried to cope with our own big ones—like how to keep two teenage daughters (one mine, one his) from competing for dates; how to help my youngest daughter overcome her school phobia; how to harmonize Carl's motto for life ("Anything worth doing is worth doing fast!") with mine ("Anything worth doing is worth doing near the beach!"). I felt crowded in our small house, deluged with too many large and unreasonable expectations from the church, the college, relatives and religious peers.

I became depressed. I decided my halo must be square. I think I would have backed out of my marriage and the role of pastor's wife had it not been for my personal pride, the example I would have been setting for the children, and my concern for my Christian witness.

One night, I lay awake for hours, worrying, thinking, praying. I remembered back to my childhood—the year when, as a pastor's daughter, I slept only 67 out of 256 nights in my own bed. The church my father pastored was poor, so when traveling preachers, singers and evangelists passed through, we practiced "open house." There was one night our house was so crowded that I had to take a pillow and four blankets and sleep in the bathtub. It was a short rest since there was only one bathroom, and everyone had to use it at one time or another.

It was exciting to meet so many new and interesting people. But often, the religious celebrities who stayed with us expected mother to wait on them hand and foot. She would always do so without complaint.

Sometimes I heard some of the women in the church criticize Mother for not attending all the church's social functions. I wanted to defend her, but kept my silence. They didn't realize how many miles she put on her accordion to play at nursing homes and jail services, how much she sacrificed to care for her husband and five children, how much effort she put into teaching her Sunday school class, or how much time she spent with various women's ministries on local, state and national levels. Why did she never get the credit she so richly deserved?

Quickly, my thoughts changed from my mother to my first husband. He had been a good man, a steady Christian and a hard worker. But at one point, he became frustrated with me. I had become so involved in church work that I had been neglecting his love and my household duties. I became so "super" that I wasn't "natural."

I realized this one day when he introduced me to one of his business associates. "This is Betty, my part-time wife," he said. "I'm going to buy her a cot and build her a room on the back of the church. It'll save a lot of time and gasoline money."

He spoke jokingly, but his words struck deep. In the following weeks and months, I pulled back from some of the church projects I had gotten involved with simply because others had expected it of me. I devoted more of my time and energy to my family.

Laying awake that night next to my new husband, I thought, Am I falling back into that same rut? Am I so concerned about what people think of me that I'm becoming "super" again without being "natural"?

Another scene flashed before me. Early one morning, just after my first baby, Brenda, was born, the doorbell rang. I glanced out the panel of glass by the front door and saw two ladies from my church, one of them carrying a pink, wrapped box. Hurriedly, I put on my breakfast coat and a little make-up and brushed my hair. I Scotch-taped a pink bow on top of Brenda's head and pulled a pair of ruffled pink panties over her diaper. Finally, I rushed to the door, out of breath. As I opened it, I saw the two ladies driving off down the street in their car.

I waited for several minutes to allow them time to return home. Then I picked up the phone and called them, apologizing for not answering the door sooner.

One lady replied, in a very direct tone, "We wanted to see your new baby, but not badly enough to wait *that* long."

I was crushed. I put Brenda in her crib and flung myself across my bed, face down, arms dangling helplessly over the sides. My fingers felt the warm fur of our family dog, a collie named Missy.

Missy never has anything different to wear, and she's always charming, I thought ruefully to myself. All she has to do is wag her tail and people feel welcome.

I knew, suddenly, that my pride had to go. I had been so concerned with looking perfect and making Brenda look perfect that I had failed to be hospitable. Those ladies wouldn't have cared what the baby had on, if I had just let them in the door!

It was a difficult lesson to learn. I thought I had learned it. Yet here I was, years later, still worried about what other people thought of me.

I lay awake longer and asked myself some questions. Did I really think our church people were so unreasonable as to expect me to be more spiritual, more attractive, more perfect than anyone else? Was it so important to live up to everyone else's expectations, anyway? What were *God's* expectations?

That night I vowed to myself and God that I would be a good pastor's wife. I would use the gifts God had given me and the lessons He had taught me to be approachable and understanding toward others. I would be myself, the natural person God made me to be.

I realized that God uses the ordinary people of this world to do the extraordinary—the Bible records this again and again. God would allow His power to work in me. I would be natural. He would be super.

I also realized that Jesus was "simply profound" because He was so "profoundly simple." I determined to simplify my life. I could not, should not, would not try to do everything to please everyone. In the deep recesses of my heart, I felt God saying: "If you will please Me and your husband, and expect other women to do the same in their families, everything will run more smoothly."

Another thought came to mind: What about the children? My energies had been directed so completely toward meeting other people's expectations that, for quite a long time, I had not given adequate time or good humor to the rest of the family. I misquoted the scripture to myself: "What shall it profit a woman if she gains the whole world, but loses her own *son*?" Were all my efforts to please others causing me to lose those closest to me? Would our children look at me, just as

I had looked at my mother, and say, "I don't want any part in the ministry"?

Something had to change!

The next morning, Carl and I woke before the rest of the family. I lit a candle, put on a pink, ruffled breakfast coat, and built a fire in the fireplace. Over a quiet breakfast, I told Carl about all my thoughts of the night before. Together, we decided that if we couldn't make it, we could never help others make it. If we gave up, no one would listen to him minister. No one would read the books I wrote. We would make it, and we would enjoy it along the way.

That meant, for me, letting go of some of the unrealistic expectations I had for myself as a pastor's wife. It meant no longer falling captive to the unrealistic expectations others placed upon me. It meant being myself—the self God made me.

After the kids left for school and Carl left for the college, I called my father, Glenn Perkins, a minister and Christian statesman. He told me something I have never forgotten: "Betty, maturity is to suffer without complaining, and be misunderstood without explaining."

Later, as I pondered my father's words, I picked up an old daily devotional that my grandfather had given me and opened it to a story about a woman named Elsa Maxwell. When Elsa's father was dying, he called her to his bedside and said, "Elsa, I cannot live. Your mother is already gone. You are only nine and will soon be without parents. You are a homely child, so you will never make it on your looks. I am poor, so you can't make it on my money. You must survive by this legacy I will leave you.

"Number one. Don't worry about 'they' (what 'they'

15

will think, what 'they' would do).

"Number two. Don't collect inanimate objects (things without life).

"Number three. Laugh at yourself before others have a chance to laugh at you."

What wisdom—wisdom for life—I received that day! In the weeks that followed my sleepless night and my resolve to change, I was amazed at the stream of material and helpful advice that flowed to me from unknown sources, or from people who had no idea of my dilemma.

I became hungry to read. God spoke to me through the printed page—even the page of a trade magazine that advised, "Either change your attitude toward your present job, or change jobs." It was settled I could not change jobs, but I prayed that with God's help, I could alter my attitude toward my husband and his position, and relish my own role.

One day I inserted a cassette into our tape player and heard Lillie Knaulls sing, "Every morning I say, 'Yes!'" My heart stirred. I decided to adopt the simple exercise. Now, every morning when I first awaken, before I turn down the covers, I clench my fist, throw my arm upward with gusto and shout out loud, "Yes!" I am saying "yes" to the Lord, "yes" to the day He has planned for me, "yes" to the woman He wants me to become.

Day by day, brick by brick, the wall of unrealistic expectations—my own and the ones others have laid for me—has come tumbling down. I am free now to love my husband and family, to give them my quality time and attention. I am free to enjoy my role as Carl's helpmate, as pastor's wife. And I am free to serve and give to others—not because it is expected of me, but because of the love Jesus has placed in my heart.

Betty Malz was born in Terre Haute, Indiana, in 1929. Her father, an ordained minister, pioneered nine churches. Her mother served as church music director and Sunday school teacher.

Betty's first husband died of a heart condition while Betty was pregnant with their second child. Later, she married Carl Malz, a widower with three children. Carl, a pastor and former missionary, is vice president and campus pastor at Trinity College in North Dakota.

In addition to being a pastor's wife and mother, Betty has been a newspaper columnist and writer. Her articles have appeared in *Guideposts*, *Charisma*, *Christian Life* and other national Christian magazines. She has also authored several books, including the million-seller *My Glimpse of Eternity*, which has been printed in 18 languages.

Chapter Two
When You Move a Lot

by Claire (Mrs. Barron) Brown

During Barron's 15 years as a pastor in the United Methodist Church, we moved on the average of once every two years. It's not that we wanted to. But early on, Barron had an experience with the Holy Spirit, which is probably one of the reasons we were shuffled around so frequently. Besides that, our denominational system required that pastors move anyway—whether they wanted to or not. Through it all, we managed to learn a few things about God and ourselves—though the lessons were not always easy.

It wasn't all bad, though. Granted, moving frequently was hectic and tumultuous, but it was also a great adventure—and a tremendous opportunity to grow. Not only did we get to see and experience the personalities of many different people and places, we also had the opportunity to move closer to a God who is alive, who cares deeply, and who is able to ''work all things together for the good to them that love Him and are called according to His purpose'' (Rom. 8:28).

Our first appointment after Barron graduated from Asbury Theological Seminary in Wilmore, Kentucky, was in Melbourne, Florida, where Barron was the associate pastor of a large church. We were to be there for four years. Both of us had a genuine desire to experience what the early church experienced—miracles, healings and other manifestations of the Holy Spirit. But for the first year in Melbourne, we went without much Spirit-filled fellowship. Finally, out of our own desperate need, we felt led to start a home group where the baptism of the Holy Spirit was taught and spiritual gifts were free to function.

Our little group flourished and we formed strong relationships. These people became our family. Although we went through many struggles, the Lord knitted us together in His love. Together, we ate, took retreats, washed feet, prayed and grew. We grew spiritually as well as numerically. It was not ''church as usual,'' but a living church, the kind we had seen in the Bible. All the while the services in the regular church continued as always, with not much change.

The day came, however, when the senior pastor decided to move. This meant that we had to move also. It wasn't until I was faced with the fact that we were going to have to leave Melbourne that I realized just how emotionally dependent I had become upon the brothers and sisters in the group. Leaving was traumatic. It meant pulling up those roots. But we had no choice. I suppose the break-up of any family is painful; the family of God is no different.

We moved to a church in the Florida Keys where Barron was to become the pastor, fully expecting to repeat our group experience in the new church. All our efforts were without success. I became lonely, frustrated and extremely depressed. We had moved out of a large, lovely home into one that was small and run-down. We had left behind our dearest friends who shared the same vision for ministry. Our new church was filled with strangers who had no idea what we were talking about.

Even though I had a wonderful husband and a precious 3-year-old boy, I was very unhappy. I often cried myself to sleep at night. Ultimately, I sought counseling. I joined a prison ministry and did volunteer work at a hospital, but I could not seem to shake the feeling of being a misplaced Christian, fallen between the cracks.

We moved again. I suppose we thought that if we kept moving, we would eventually find a church that was open to the things of God and that desired to move on spiritually. Unfortunately, it just did not happen. There were always those two or three who wanted to grow and minister, but as a group, each church seemed to be steeped in traditions and closed to New Testament Christianity. For myself, having had the experience of genuine Christianity, I did not want to "play church," or, as the Bible says, "have a form of godliness, but deny the power thereof" (2 Tim. 3:5).

Our next move was to a little country town in Florida. It was a beautiful area, with a vital interdenominational group of women who met regularly for prayer and spiritual edification. The church, however, as we were to discover, thought of Barron and me as radical. Some referred to us as "Holy Rollers." Spiritually, we could not get them to budge.

Barron, who had once been such a lover of people

as well as of God, became very troubled and weary. He developed severe stomach problems. When he had entered the ministry, he was not only a faith-filled Christian, but a dynamic preacher as well. Now he began to question whether or not he had really been called of God. We seemed to meet opposition on every hand. Our ministry appeared so unfruitful. What made it almost unbearable was that we found that people who are not yielded to Jesus can be vicious and cruel. On we moved.

We received word from other pastors who were struggling as we were that some of the denominational officials were opposing us because we were identified as charismatics. One district superintendent warned us that he ''had our number.'' A year later, we were not surprised when we were sent to a dying church in Sarasota, Florida, made up almost entirely of elderly people.

But Barron preached the Word and we worked hard. The church grew numerically for the first two years, but spiritually, it was a house built on sand. We decided to teach New Testament worship on Sunday mornings, hoping to pump some life into the place. Many people were offended and left. It was a difficult time for us, but looking back, I can see that it brought Barron, our two children, Will and Meredith, and me closer to the Lord. Finally, after much prayer, we decided to leave the denomination.

Our last move was a move of faith. It was the most unnerving move of all. We had always lived in a furnished parsonage, and Barron, by this time, had worked his way up to a fairly good salary.

We told our new district superintendent, who had been quite supportive, that we were leaving the denomination. We had absolutely no idea where we would go.

Even though we did not have a lot of support in our local church, we had made many wonderful friends in Sarasota. We had the love and prayers of many of the Spirit-filled pastors in that community and Women's Aglow prayed for us continually. We called friends around the country, including Jamie Buckingham, Karl Strader, Bob Shelly and Gerald Derstine, and asked them to intercede for us. They prayed for us and were a tremendous source of strength and encouragement. I praise God for Christians who genuinely care when you are hurting. This experience has made me want to be more sensitive to brothers and sisters who are going through trials.

We sought the Lord night and day. At first we were not sure the Lord wanted us to remain in full-time ministry. The idea of being a lay person without the responsibility of a church had a growing appeal. Barron started looking for secular work. We prayed that God would open the door through which He wanted us to walk. It was the darkest time in our lives.

After many weeks of futile job-hunting, we heard there was an opening for a pastor to pioneer a new work for the Pentecostal Holiness denomination. I had never heard of the Pentecostal Holiness Church, but they wanted someone to go to the Miami area and start a congregation from scratch. Since we had prayed that the Lord would open the right door (and nothing else had opened), we decided to walk through. It was not an easy thing to do. We had no idea how we would manage on such a large cut in income.

It was really funny how the Lord spoke to us. One night, I had gone to the Christian Retreat in Bradenton, Florida, to get spiritually refreshed. Gerald Derstine prayed with me and told me I was getting ready to take a big step of faith. Around that same time Barron attended an Aglow meeting. Going forward for prayer, he was surprised to hear the speaker prophesy that he would be the pastor of a Spirit-filled church. He was immediately slain in the Spirit.

We said all our good-byes to our friends, packed our U-Haul trailer and were ready to leave. Barron decided to call our realtor to let him know we were on our way. Incredibly, he informed us that we could not move into the apartment we thought was waiting for us because of a two-week wait that was required to be approved by the homeowners' association. What could we do but pray?

That evening, our realtor arranged for us to rent another apartment, sight unseen. But the battle continued. On the lonely trip across the Everglades from Sarasota to Miami, our truck stalled. We were stranded on the side of Alligator Alley. We sat in the hot sun for several hours. It seemed like an eternity.

After the tow truck finally pulled our U-Haul (with "Adventures in Moving" written on the side) up to the apartment, we spent the evening unloading the few possessions we had (it seemed that most of them were Barron's lead-bound books). It was well past midnight when we were able to shut the door behind us and make our beds on the floor. It was a hot and humid night in South Florida and—did I mention?—the air conditioner was on the blink. After collapsing from exhaustion, I managed to smile to myself. I remembered what a minister friend, Judson Cornwall, had once said: "God tells the truth, but He doesn't tell the whole truth. If He did, you would never go anywhere with Him."

Being a Christian does not make us immune to difficulties. In fact, it is just the opposite. Isn't it good to know, though, that when we go through the fire, He is with us? Even though our lives seemed so disheveled, I had an inner peace and believed that we were in God's will. Perhaps that is the way the Hebrew children felt when they were on the way to the Promised Land.

That summer was very lonely because we knew no one. For the first time in our married lives, we were without a church. It was just us and the Lord! We visited different churches in the area, but as soon as we told them we were going to start a church, they became defensive. We did the only thing we could. We drew together as a family and tried to encourage one another.

Barron and I went on an extended fast. I fasted for 23 days, the longest I have ever fasted. Barron fasted for 40 days. He was desperate! We were trying to make some sense out of our jumbled-up lives.

We prayed with our children and together tried to gather strength and encouragement from the Word of God as well as comfort from each other. We praised God together daily. Before my eyes, I saw our little family come together and make Jesus our center. The Lord was doing the same thing in our family that He had done in that home group in Melbourne years before. I was excited! We—Barron, the children and I—were forming our new church in Miami. We called ourselves the Cathedral of the Holy Spirit.

That was the summer of 1985. Since then, we have started over a half-dozen Bible studies and soon hope to begin a Sunday morning worship service.

Yes, I have moved a lot and have known a lot of chaos and turmoil in my life. Admittedly, there were times when Barron and I thought that we were moving around without a purpose and that maybe God had forgotten us. Of course, He hadn't. God never forgets His children. He has such a wonderful plan for each of us. Perhaps Barron and I had to walk through all these things so that we would be prepared for the ministry that was and is ahead. How could we ever comfort someone going through a hard time unless we had known pain ourselves?

As I have learned to trust the Lord, He has not only brought me through, but has blessed my life in so many ways. Through our trials, our children have come to know that Jesus is real and is interested in every aspect of their lives. As young as they are they have experienced the Lord, His miracles and His love. They both love to sing and dance in the spirit, and they trust the Lord with all their little problems. For this, I am especially thankful.

The group in Melbourne will always have a special place in my heart. In the past, when things would get difficult, I would think back to that time in my life and desire to be with that group of believers again. But at last, I can say I have moved not only geographically and spiritually, but emotionally as well. Now, instead of one group, we have several, and hope to have many more in the months ahead. Instead of trying to resurrect old dead Christians, we're giving birth to new ones.

I have learned through our circumstances that my security cannot be in a particular place, a job, friends or even family; my security must be in Jesus. If we have nothing in this world but Him, then we have everything. If we have everything in this world but Him, we have nothing. When we walk with God and love Him with all our hearts, He "shall supply all [our] needs according to His riches in glory in Christ Jesus" (Phil. 4:19).

In the Christian life we are, or at least should be, always moving and growing, becoming more and more like our wonderful Lord. I don't think it matters whether you live in one place for a decade or have a different house each year, as long as you are trying to follow Him and serve Him the best you can. The people I feel sorry for are those who are incapable of moving, reaching up, touching Jesus and becoming all they can be.

This new ministry is deeply fulfilling as I see the hand of God at work. Perhaps our problem before had been that we were always trying to build on someone else's foundation. "Unless the Lord builds a house, they labor in vain" (Ps. 127:1). The Cathedral of the Holy Spirit has a long way to go, but I know the Lord holds it in His beautiful and loving hands. Perhaps, God willing, I will find out what it is like to stay for a while in one place.

Claire Brown was born in 1948 in Weisbaden, Germany, but grew up in Jacksonville, Florida, where her father was the area director of elementary education and her mother a teacher. The only daughter among four children, Claire was led to the Lord at age 20 by one of her brothers.

Claire met her husband, Barron, in 1970 at a Spirit-filled, interdenominational prayer meeting. They were both youth directors—Barron at a Methodist church and Claire at a Presbyterian church. After their marriage, Barron pastored in a number of Methodist churches throughout Florida. He and Claire now pastor the Cathedral of the Holy Spirit, a new Pentecostal Holiness church in the greater Miami area.

The Browns have two children, ages 12 and 8.

Chapter Three
Unclogging the Channels of Communication

---

by Nancy (Mrs. Curry) Vaughan

I was in the kitchen cooking breakfast for the family when the telephone rang. Who would be calling at such an early hour? I wondered, sending up a quick prayer that it was not some kind of emergency.

"Hello?" I asked, tentatively.

"Nancy, this is Jim." Immediately I recognized the voice of our close friend who heads up a conference ministry in the East. We chatted a moment or two about the weather and the children. I expected him at any moment to ask to speak to Curry, my husband.

He never did. Instead, he continued, "I'm calling to ask if you would pray about being a part of the program for our women's conference this coming October."

My heart sank. I felt as though a 100-pound bag of cement had been laid on my head. My whole body shook with anxiety.

Why me, Lord? I thought. You know I have diffi-

29

culty communicating to a group, especially a large one.

Of course, the Lord already knew this. He also knew that I would not turn down the invitation.

For years, I have struggled with this matter of communication. This one area, perhaps more than any other, has been my greatest weakness. It has also been the area I've worked hardest to develop.

Next to my husband, I am a mouse. Curry is a lion— an outgoing, gregarious man who has no trouble communicating his thoughts and feelings or confronting someone with a problem. For years I consoled myself with the thought that "opposites attract" and that my role was to be a helpmate from the sidelines. Even during our dating years, when Curry was a cadet at West Point, I chauffeured him on weekends from church to church so that he could give his testimony to whomever would listen. I followed along meekly, staying far away from the platform.

But during my 23 years with Curry, I've learned something: every pastor's wife will have times when she must communicate publicly. This doesn't necessarily mean she will be asked to speak often or long. But because her husband is in the public eye, she is, too. She will be given opportunities to share Jesus with various groups—opportunities the average woman will not have—simply because she is the pastor's wife. How important, then, to develop a few skills and overcome the fear!

Twice in recent weeks I've been called up to the platform during a worship service to speak, with no advance notice either time. In the first instance, our senior minister simply decided the congregation needed to hear from the pastor's wife. I went forward and spent 10

minutes or so giving a brief testimony of how I became
a Christian, how Curry and I met and married, and how
it was that God called us to settle down in Melbourne,
Florida, after years of travelling the world with the
Army chaplaincy.

While many of my close friends in the church knew
the story, I had never shared it with the entire assembly.
So often, a congregation gets to know a pastor very well
because they listen to him speak every Sunday, but few
get to know the pastor's wife. I appreciated the sensitiv-
ity our senior minister showed in giving me an opportunity to ''be known.''

In the second instance a few weeks later, Curry called
me forward at the beginning of his sermon.

''Nancy, I want to ask you a few questions,'' he
began. I gulped, and the congregation laughed at my
unease. They were laughing *with* me, and I knew they
empathized!

''What has been the main thing that has kept our marriage going for the past 23 years?'' he asked. I thought
a moment, then began to tell how, from the beginning
of our dating relationship, Jesus has been our center.
Curry brought me to Christ on our first date! He asked
me two or three more questions and used my answers
as the foundation for his message.

Many years ago, I would have been embarrassed,
tongue-tied and probably a little upset with those responsible for putting me on the spot. How good it was to
be, well, not quite comfortable, but enough at ease with
myself and with God to share with my church family.
Only prayer, practice and a willingness over the years
to trust God for strength, not to mention the words, has
brought me to this place of relative ease with the public

platform.

I've learned something else, too. As important as it is for a pastor's wife to learn to communicate publicly, it is even more important for her to learn to communicate with her husband and family. Pastoring is a unique job. It is a communicative job. In order to do it well, all channels of communication need to be open—between pastor and congregation and between the members of the pastor's family. A blockage between husband and wife, or between parents and children, will mess up the whole communication system and make the pastor ineffective in the church.

For the first five years of our marriage, I listened to Curry as he poured out his heart to me, sharing his innermost thoughts and feelings, his visions and dreams. I sat quietly beside him, infatuated with his every word—but also longing to share some of the deep areas of my own life. Somehow, I never could seem to get the words out. The deeper my feelings, the less able I was to speak them.

I suppose Curry could have done more to draw them out of me. But it was not really his fault. It was mine. Our communication was clogged, and I was the one responsible for the stoppage.

Many times I cried out to God, "Help me open up to my husband!" But no change came. Then in 1968, at the height of the Vietnam War, Curry was ordered to serve as an Army chaplain with the 173rd Airborne Brigade. He would be gone—separated from me and his two small daughters, seven-month-old Julie and two-year- old Virginia—for 12 months. I was devastated but knew he had to obey.

Before his departure for Saigon, Curry asked me to

make a promise. Would I record a 15-minute tape each day, sharing all of the thoughts and feelings going through my mind in his absence? When the tape was full, would I send it to him? I said yes. It seemed a simple request.

For the first week or so, it was easy to fill the tape. The Army had moved our family to California. Our surroundings were new and different, and our everyday activities seemed exciting. But as the second week rolled around, I found I had said just about everything there was to say about the beauty of the hills surrounding San Francisco, the thrill of driving across the Golden Gate Bridge, the taste of the sourdough bread at Fisherman's Wharf, and the serenity of the sailboats maneuvering gently in the bay.

Suddenly, I was hit by a realization: the one I loved so much was in a dangerous war zone, yet here I was sharing things that could have no possible meaning to his life and work among the troops! Curry was sharing Jesus with these fighting men and women, many of whom would never return home. He didn't need a soliloquy on the culture in San Francisco. How could I be so shallow?

I began to look deep within myself and prayed for help in communicating to Curry about things that truly mattered—things that would give him love, hope and strength for the day ahead. Within a few days, I found myself, for the first time in my life, being transparent before him, even though we were separated by thousands of miles. God truly did a work in me and in our marriage, through those simple tapes, that has carried through to the present day.

True communication between husband and wife, I've

learned, comes through a willingness to be transparent before one another, sharing our weaknesses and failures as well as our successes and triumphs. I was afraid to admit to Curry, "I'm not perfect." I was afraid if I opened up to him, he would criticize me. But I've learned to trust him. He will love me even in my imperfect moments. And when criticism does come—well, so does an opportunity for growth, if I'll accept it positively.

Of course, communication problems did not end when Curry came home from Vietnam. There were still lessons to learn.

Many times, our channels got clogged through simple stubbornness—sometimes Curry's, sometimes mine. Both of us like to be right. The simple words, "I'm sorry—I was wrong," can bring healing and renewal to any situation, yet they've often been the hardest words for Curry, or me, to get out of our mouths.

For a while, we played a dangerous game called "gunny-sacking." If Curry said something hurtful to me, I wouldn't react. With great composure, I'd simply add a "stone" to my "gunny sack." After several episodes of unkindness or neglect on Curry's part, my gunny sack would begin to get very full. Inevitably, the day of reckoning would come. Curry would say one small, insignificant thing and BOOM! I'd lower the gunny sack over his head.

Slowly, we've learned a different way of dealing with disagreements and hurtful words. We simply talk, talk, talk until we understand each other. The sooner we get a problem resolved, the better. Our guideline has become the biblical adage, "Don't let the sun go down on a misunderstanding." We've had a lot fewer bruises and bumps to nurse since we've put away the gunny sacks.

Good communication with each other has not always been easy to achieve. But our efforts have been worth it. The same goes for communication with our children.

Perhaps for some, there is an easy, natural flow of communication between parent and child as the years pass. But for Curry and me, and I imagine for many others as well, communication with a child at one stage or another becomes clogged. This was the case for us as Julie entered the teenage years.

We moved into an old, turn-of-the-century home in Fort Riley, Kansas, the summer before Julie's ninth grade. She joined the swim team and the tennis team and seemed eager to begin her final year of junior high school. She appeared perfectly content through the fall and had many friends. We thought everything was going along just fine.

In October I flew East for a few days. When I returned late one evening, Julie was anxious to show me what she and her father had done in my absence: they had moved all of Julie's bedroom furniture to the "servant's bedroom" in the attic. She was so excited about the prospect of being alone, away from the rest of the family—her first real sense of independence.

Unknown to us, however, in her isolation Julie began to listen to rock music—the kind we did not approve of. She spent more and more time alone. She told us she was doing homework, but in reality she was listening to the radio. Our conversations became fewer and fewer. Our oldest daughter, Virginia, tried to tell us we had a problem, but when we asked her what it was, she couldn't be more specific.

Curry and I became concerned. Julie was no longer the happy, carefree junior high student we had known a month or two earlier. She was distant, uncommunicative. We prayed for the situation, asking for wisdom and the right words to help us deal with the barrier that had grown up between us.

Lying in bed late one snowy December night, I distinctly heard a door in the house close. Footsteps on the staircase followed. Julie's gone to the kitchen to get something to drink, I thought. I snuggled back into my pillow.

Suddenly, a loud bang reverberated from the garage—the unmistakable sound of the car trunk being slammed shut.

The thought came instantly to my mind, She's running away! How can she do this when she knows we love her?

Curry leapt from the bed, grabbed his robe and flew down two flights of stairs to the garage. The car was still there. He opened the trunk and found Julie's suitcase, packed for travel. But where was Julie?

Curry cannot explain to this day why he did what he did next. Surely the Lord was leading him. Rather than return through the garage, he went out another door into our backyard and rounded the house. He walked up the front sidewalk, thickly lined with snow-tipped shrubs. As he placed his hand on the front screen door, he heard a faint sound to his left. He turned and looked into the bushes. There sat Julie, curled tightly into a ball, her head tucked between her legs.

''Come on, Julie, let's get out of this cold,'' Curry said. Almost until morning, Julie, Curry and I sat around the kitchen table, talking.

"Why?" we asked, over and over. "We love you so much. What have we done wrong?"

Her reply was the reply of any young girl her age: "You just don't understand."

"Understand what? We want to understand."

Round and round we went. Finally, in the midst of our anguish, there came a glimmer of light. Then a stream.

In Julie's desire to grow up and have independence, she had isolated herself from her family. At 13, she was unable to handle the emotions she felt. Her desire to "make it on her own" had taken its toll. The dam within her broke and the tears flowed. We cried together. We shared our feelings with one another. And most important of all, we prayed together.

We turned the whole ugly experience over to the Lord and asked Him to renew our hearts and restore our family. We agreed that we would work together to rebuild, stone by stone, the bridge that had been broken through lack of communication.

The next day, Julie moved back to her old room. As we carried the heavy furniture down the staircase, we laughed together. It felt so good to be a family once again.

In the months that followed, Curry and I asked ourselves many times what we could have done to have avoided the situation. We agreed that we were wrong to have allowed Julie to isolate herself. We should have recognized that our youngest daughter was at a critical point in her life. Instead of blindly assuming that all was well, we should have talked about things that really mattered to her—the pressure of making good grades, the desire to please her new peers, the fear that perhaps she was weird because her father was a pastor and she believed in Jesus.

Communication is the key. It was the key to our relationship with Julie. It is the key to our own relationship—Curry's and mine. It is the key to our relationship with the church.

Whether on a public platform or in a one-on-one conversation with a husband, child or friend, a pastor's wife must learn to communicate, and to unclog the channels of communication from time to time. It is not an easy task, but it is an important one. The benefits will last a lifetime—and beyond.

Nancy Vaughan was born in 1943 in Gainesville, Texas, the daughter of a U.S. Army officer. She also married an Army officer—Curry Vaughan—her brother's classmate at West Point. As the daughter and then wife of a military man, Nancy moved an average of once every 16 months for 43 years.

An Army chaplain, Curry pastored chapels in the United States, Korea and Germany. After retiring from the military, he became senior pastor at the Tabernacle Church in Melbourne, Florida. The Vaughans have been in Melbourne for over three years—the longest they've stayed in one place.

Nancy graduated from Marjorie Webster College in Washington, D.C. She has worked in secretarial and administrative positions in many of the cities in which she's lived.

The Vaughans have two daughters, ages 18 and 17.

Chapter Four
Living in a Glass House

by Devi (Mrs. Larry) Titus

Christmas was past and a new year had just begun. We were excited. Not only was the year new, but our lives, too, seemed new and fresh. My husband, Larry, had resigned a secure position as a church music director to fulfill the desire of both our hearts—to spread the gospel. Now we were evangelists, young, eager and anxious to see God move in our midst.

We willingly made the necessary adjustments—traveling frequently, staying in other people's homes, adapting to their schedules. Larry spent the mornings in prayer, the afternoons in study. We held meetings in the evenings and prayed with people until late into the night. Our infant daughter, Trina, learned to sleep wherever her pallet was laid.

As my birthday approached, we scheduled a set of meetings in my hometown. How exciting to see our "revival" sign on the old church lawn, blooming along with the red tulips! The first few meetings were challenging, exciting, fruitful—God was doing a real work in the hearts of the people. With great anticipation, we looked forward to our second week of services.

My birthday came—a wonderful day spent with my parents, my husband and my daughter, in the glow of a successful revival. With the $25 Mom and Dad gave me, I set out on Saturday to buy a new dress. Money was tight for Larry and me. New dresses didn't come often. I wanted to pick one that was just right.

The perfect dress was waiting for me on a $10 sale rack. I still remember it—pink crepe with full ruffled sleeves. It fit perfectly, except for the hem. That was not surprising. I wore a size 5 and stood 5'8'' tall. All my dresses had to be lengthened. Mom promised to take out the hem for me, just as she had done dozens of times when I was growing up.

That Sunday morning I felt very special. I groomed myself meticulously, arranging each large barrel curl so that not a hair was out of place. At church, many people complimented me. "You have a beautiful glow on your face," they said. I thought to myself, It must be the pink dress.

Larry preached that morning with dynamic ease. It was obvious the Holy Spirit was present. Many in the congregation responded to his message.

After the service, however, the pastor asked Larry to come to his office.

"I'm concluding the meetings this evening," he said. "You'll not continue into a second week as we had previously planned."

Larry was caught by surprise. Hadn't the crowds increased each night? Weren't large numbers being saved?

"Pastor, is there a reason why?" he asked softly.

The pastor's reply was concise. "Your wife's dress is too short," he said.

When Larry repeated the conversation to me, I was devastated. I had never been the victim of such scrutiny before! Larry reassured me and encouraged me as best he could, but I was not easily comforted that day. It was my first, rude awakening to the fact that by marrying a preacher, though homeless, I had moved into a glass house.

A life of ministry is a life in the public eye. That brings both problems and privileges. I've learned I can't have one without the other. But I can choose to be motivated by one or the other.

Psychologists tell us our behavior is definitely altered when we know we're being evaluated. Either we try to do what we think is expected of us, or we try so hard to maintain our individuality that we exaggerate our normal behavior. I've been guilty of both at one time or another. Neither fully represents being "crucified with Christ...not I that live but Christ that lives within me."

Each of us has unique gifts, talents and personalities that are the result of God's handiwork in our lives. Though we must be sensitive to others, we should never lose focus of our personal identity and calling.

"...Why is my freedom judged by another's conscience?" Paul laments in 1 Corinthians 10:29. Obviously, it's possible to accommodate another's conscience and conviction and lose our own. If our behavior is to change, it should be altered from inward, not outward, pressures. The former improves our character; the latter destroys our self-worth.

Every time I looked at my pink dress, I was reminded

of my embarrassment and horror that Sunday in my hometown. I wanted to give the garment away, as if I could get rid of the memory that simply. I determined that I would wear all my dresses down to my ankles from that day forward.

Fortunately, Larry stopped me. "I want you to keep the dress," he said. "Wear it with dignity and joy."

I did. Amazingly, no one else was ever offended by it. Thanks to my husband's quiet wisdom, I saw that I didn't have to throw away my personal taste for the sake of another's bias.

No, being in the spotlight is not easy. Another pastor's wife told me recently that she'd like to write a book called "Why Does a Pastor's Wife Have to Go Through Hell to Get to Heaven?" The language is strong but the question is one we've probably all asked.

We do many things to protect ourselves and our families from public scrutiny. I've done them. I've also come to reject them.

Oftentimes we build walls around our house to keep the slings and arrows of criticism from shattering the glass. We become secretive and withdrawn, no longer feeling comfortable enough to tell a friend about the vacation we are planning or the new carpet we hope to buy. Such innocent, personal tidbits always seem to be used against us.

"How can the pastor's family afford such a grand holiday? We must be paying him too much."

"How can they think of buying a new carpet? That's not very spiritual."

"You'd think a pastor's family would give its money to the poor rather than spend it on luxuries."

It's easy to become driven by the desires or directives

of others who always think they know God's will for our lives better than we do. We get stuck between a rock and a hard place—we are in the ministry and so cannot withdraw fully, yet we are fearful when we come out from behind our wall.

Somehow, we must find a way to remain vulnerable. Otherwise, ministry will lose its joy. We'll become isolated, lonely, unhappy and unfulfilled.

Just after Larry and I had accepted our first pastorate, we stopped by the home of a pastor friend to share the excitement of our new appointment. The pastor and his wife had been a major influence in our lives and ministry. We respected them highly. As usual, before we left that afternoon, he offered some fatherly advice. We perked our ears and listened intently.

"Kids, don't get too close to your people," he said. "They'll hurt you. Don't let them come into your home, or they'll interfere with your family life and criticize your personal life."

I could tell Larry was disturbed by his words. I was too. We thanked the two of them for their hospitality and politely excused ourselves.

As we began the two-day trip to our new home, all was quiet in the car. Trina, now 3 years old, had fallen asleep. Larry and I were both engrossed in thoughts about our friend's advice. Finally, I broke the silence.

"Larry, do you agree with the instruction we just received?" I asked.

"No," he answered slowly. "I don't think so."

"Well, neither do I."

As we talked, we found that we both had trouble with the idea of separating public and private lives so completely. How could we truly help people and remain aloof? We concluded, finally, that we would choose a different course. We would choose to touch people where they hurt—and let them touch us as well, even if it hurt.

The pastor was right about one thing—it has been painful. But God has seen us through and has blessed us and our ministry. The fruit we've seen could never have been planted, much less sown, from behind a protective wall.

Sometimes we don't build walls—we just bullet-proof our houses. We decide that nothing is going to penetrate to our hearts. Many times I've said to myself, I'm tired of being hurt! Chin up and bottom lip jutted out, I've thought, No one's going to hurt me like that again!

But what is my alternative? I cannot harden my heart to the pain of criticism, rejection and unkind words without finding all of my emotions becoming hard. When we shield ourselves from hurt, we shield ourselves from love as well. We lose our ability to respond to our husbands, our children, our neighbors, church members—even the Lord. The best we can do is to remain vulnerable, love others with the love Jesus gives, and let God fight our battles for us.

Living in a glass house is not easy. But despite its problems, public ministry does carry certain privileges, too. Sometimes I've taken these for granted—or failed to notice them at all. When the going gets tough, however, it always helps to "count my blessings."

For example, I have become a more disciplined person— physically and spiritually—because of my public calling. As the pastor's wife, I am set up to be an example to the flock. The definition of "example" is "to act in such a way as to arouse the imitation of others." How can people imitate me unless they watch me and evaluate me? Recognizing this basic principle of discipleship has helped to change my attitude toward the scrutiny I receive. It has also enforced a discipline in my life that I would probably not have had otherwise.

When someone drops by my house unannounced, they often hint that they want a personal tour of my entire home. This fact used to upset me greatly—but it also forced me to clean the dishes after each meal and pick up the house at the end of each day. Today, I don't resent the impromptu tours or grumble, "It's none of their business how I keep my house!" Rather, I appreciate that I've become a disciplined housekeeper with a clean, tidy home that I love to show off to guests.

It is discipline that produces personal growth and development in increased proportions. How thankful I am, then, that I have had to be disciplined!

Another privilege is that of recognition. After ministering in the same church for 12 years, Larry and I resigned the pastorate and moved to a community in another state where we were just part of the congregation. We attended all services regularly, and Trina, a teenager by then, got involved with the youth group. For the first time in her life, she was not a pastor's daughter. It seemed to me that this was a good time in her life to experience being a Christian without the added pressure of being a "P.K."

One afternoon, I commented on this to Trina. Her reply surprised me. "Mom, it's not a pressure being the pastor's daughter. It's a privilege."

Together, we began to identify and discuss all of the privileges we had enjoyed in the pastorate of our previous church. I had to admit I missed them. People knew our names, even when we didn't know theirs. We were often given seats of honor— the head table at a banquet, a special row of seating, a reserved parking space. Our expenses at conferences and retreats were prepaid. Our household repairs were frequently taken care of by members of the congregation at no charge. In all of these ways and more, God extended our resources and made us feel special.

As I've grown older and have continued to count the blessings of public ministry, I've come to appreciate the greatest privilege of all—fulfillment. As pastors and pastors' wives, we plant seeds in people's lives and see them grow and bloom. Nothing could be more satisfying.

Over the years, Larry and I have invited about 30 young men and women to come live in our home for a time. Our purpose has been to disciple them by allowing them to observe us on a day-to-day basis. They've seen our strengths and our weaknesses. They've seen what it's like to live in a glass house. And now some of them have chosen to live in glass houses of their own.

When I hear of the growth in their lives and ministries, of the blessings they have experienced in their families and businesses, I am overcome with gratitude. I'm so glad that I've endured the petty problems and can now enjoy the abundant privileges of my calling.

So look on! Evaluate me, scrutinize me. Criticize me if you feel you're justified.

And if you see me following Christ, then follow me.

Devi Titus was born in 1947 in Salinas, California. Her father was the meat cutter and her mother the clerk in the only grocery store in their small town of 300. The family attended the community's only church where, from the age of 12, Devi played the piano. Later, her father became the church's pastor.

Devi met her husband, Larry, at a youth camp when she was 13 years old. They were from different towns and began writing to each other when she was 15. They were married two years later.

Larry has been a pastor since 1968 and is senior pastor at Christ Community Church in Camp Hill, Pennsylvania. In addition to their pastoral duties, he and Devi have been involved in the evangelizing and discipling of thousands of young people.

Devi is the founder and developer of the nation's first full-color magazine for Christian women, *Virtue*. She and Larry have two children and two grandchildren.

Chapter Five
I'm Important, Too

by Doris (Mrs. Larry) Tomczak

I didn't just wake up one morning feeling bad about myself. Low self-esteem doesn't appear overnight. The unwanted vine sends out shoot after shoot until, one day, its green tangle obscures the garden path. In the same way insecurity takes root and grows, almost unnoticed, until one's self-esteem is lost in a tangle of confused emotions and false images.

For me, insecurity took root as a little girl. Introverted and shy, I felt lost in the crowd, unable to find my niche in our family of eight children. Most of my early memories are of a pregnant mother who was forever cooking and cleaning and folding mountains of diapers—and of a father who worked in the day and went to school at night. When Dad *was* home, he was usually studying, tucked away in a bedroom that was cramped by two cribs. Neither of them had much time for me.

My parochial school was even more crowded than my

home. As a 5-year-old, I shared first grade with 80 other students, sitting two to a seat. I was too petrified even to ask questions. In second grade, my fear grew. My teacher was a classic, crack-thewhip type of ex-nun with Dutchboy bangs and tightly curled hair. She marched around the classroom waving a 12-inch paddle that seemed like an extension of her arm.

One day the boy sitting in front of me said he'd skipped breakfast. To kid him, I stroked one forefinger across the other, indicating "shame, shame." Suddenly, the teacher barrelled across the room and slugged me in the shoulder. I cried out in pain. But my deepest hurt was inside. The experience was devastating—the kind that goes so deep and does so much damage that a sensitive child spends years and years recoiling from the effects. I became full of fear: afraid of teachers, afraid of classrooms, afraid of groups, and as the years to follow would bear out, afraid of people in general.

My poor self-image worsened in high school. Feelings of inadequacy and self-hatred taunted me daily. I became obsessed with what others had that I didn't. I compared my looks, talents and popularity with other girls, always coming up short. The popular girls had long, thick, sunstreaked hair, like the "surfer" image that was "in" at that time. I agonized over my boring, brown hair, so thin that my ears poked through despite all my efforts to give it body.

Besides scraggly hair, I had linebacker shoulders developed from swimming. And then there was my nose. It was huge. The more I contemplated the mirror, the more depressed I became.

I watched the school cheerleaders enviously. They seemed to embody perfection—thick, blond hair, cute figures, sexy uniforms. They bounced down the school hallways in a bevy of boisterous excitement. They were always surrounded by a pack of handsome varsity football players. In my eyes, they had it all. What did I have? Three tomboyish girlfriends from the field hockey team, a rare date now and then and a AA bra cup!

In college, I rebelled. I tried desperately to be anyone but "me." Drinking, smoking marijuana and promiscuous sex became my new lifestyle. It was the only way I knew to be "accepted." I fought constantly with my parents. Finally, my father asked me to move out of the house. He said I was a bad influence on my brothers and sisters. In my heart, I knew he was right.

For the next year, I tried to hide from my self-condemnation and guilt by partying, drinking and having romantic flings. I took Valium to calm my nerves. But things only got worse.

Meanwhile, my parents were changing. Each time I went home for a visit, it was more and more obvious that something was different about them. One day, I asked them what it was.

"We've given Jesus Christ control of our lives," Mom explained. "He is changing us, and we are experiencing a wonderful new life."

Even though my first reaction was skeptical, a spark was ignited deep inside me. For a while, I resisted the flame that was growing in my heart. But soon I agreed to attend a few Christian meetings. I observed the people, listened to them and wondered, "Could Jesus really make a difference?"

I wrestled with this question for six weeks. Finally, I realized that I had made enough of a mess trying to run my own life. Jesus *had* to do a better job. On March

13, 1972, I accepted the Lord and asked Him to make me the kind of woman He wanted me to be. Whatever that was, it would surely be an improvement.

Shortly afterwards, I attended a Basic Youth Conflicts seminar conducted by Bill Gothard. There, my eyes were opened to the cause and effect of my poor self-image. I learned that the low self-esteem I'd battled with for so many years was a common problem for women. (Dr. James Dobson calls it the number one cause of female depression.) I saw that a major cause in my own case— the part that couldn't be attributed to upbringing or environment—was the way I habitually compared myself to other girls. I was tormented over my hair, my shoulders and my nose— features that were simply a part of the "me" that God specially created. Yet my self-consciousness made me miserable.

God began renewing my mind with Scripture verses that warned against comparing myself to others and against conforming to a world system which overemphasizes outer beauty. God had created me carefully and beautifully. My quieter personality, thin hair, broad shoulders and large nose were not defects, but special marks of His loving craftsmanship. It gave me tremendous peace to realize He designed me exactly as He wanted me to be. Slowly but surely, the self-destructive attitudes that had fed my low self-esteem dissipated.

I saw that my heavenly Father wanted me to be unique—different from every other woman—because He had a special plan for me to fulfill. I was specifically designed to reflect the character of Jesus to the world around me. Perhaps God had limited my outer beauty to develop the Christlike, inward character He wanted me to have. Little by little, I was freed of the selfish preoccupation that had blinded me to the needs of others. Self-consciousness gave way to a genuine love for the people I came into contact with from day to day. I had such motivation! What Jesus had done in me He could do in them!

When I married Larry Tomczak, a nationally recognized minister, I was 24 and had been a Christian for four years. By that time, God had placed me well on the road toward a healthy self-love. But ahead lay many life situations through which that road was to be further traveled.

Larry was in demand as a speaker. The beginning days of our marriage were dotted with trips to churches and cities I had never visited before. I had never even been on an airplane before the wedding. I was not only a new bride, I was a wide-eyed cross-country traveler. My days and weeks were filled with excitement.

They were also filled with insecurity. Overnight, I'd moved from comfortable obscurity to being the wife of a prominent Christian leader. I was introduced everywhere to large audiences and to men of God who had nationally known ministries. I was thrust into the company of wives who had been in ministry for 30 years. I was overwhelmed and intimidated. What could I possibly talk about with Derek Prince? Or with his wife, for that matter? I wondered if the other leaders and their wives doubted my ability to be a true helpmate to Larry. I felt so inadequate.

Frequently, I had to remind myself of Larry's wise advice on our first trip. As our plane was landing that day in Georgia, he turned to me and said, "Doris, don't see yourself as a leader's wife. We're here as servants." Then he reminded me of the scripture on which he had based his entire ministry: "Let him who is the greatest among you become as the youngest, and the leader as the servant."

They were Larry's words, but it was Jesus speaking to my heart. Jesus was to be my example in relating to people. He did not come to be served but to serve, and to lay down His life for His friends. How liberating that understanding proved to be! As we traveled from conference to conference, I looked for opportunities to uplift or pray for my new friends. I had little time for self-preoccupation. It was such a joy to serve.

Larry made another good suggestion: rather than dwell on my feelings of intimidation, I should take the initiative and arrange to have lunch with some of the more experienced pastors' wives. Once again, I felt complete release from my anxiety as I tried this humble, God-given approach. With notebook in hand, I joyfully took the position of learner rather than leader. I gleaned much from these seasoned women of God who were delighted to impart something to a young newcomer in whose shoes they'd once walked.

As our ministry developed and grew, I couldn't help but notice the special endowments of other leaders' wives. Some were polished public speakers like their husbands. Others were writing books and tracts. I had none of these talents. God had taught me about not comparing myself to others, but the temptation was ever before me.

I sought the Lord for help and direction. Eventually, I discerned that God's plan for me in those first years of marriage did not include embarking on my own public ministry. Rather, He wanted me to develop excellence within my present sphere. A broader ministry could come later.

Larry agreed that my focus needed to be on deepening my relationship with God through prayer and study and on enriching our marriage by allowing plenty of time for communication, homemaking and physical intimacy. I needed to devote myself to becoming an efficient helpmate. I had much to learn.

I saw myself as building a deposit for later withdrawal. As Larry said, "We're responsible for the depth of our ministry— God is responsible for the breadth."

I knew how to make hamburgers, hot dogs and meatloaf, and Larry taught me how to wash perma-press clothes. I stumbled through menu planning and grocery shopping. I knew nothing of time management, so we were perpetually late to meetings. Sometimes I couldn't see how I'd ever be on top of managing our little two-bedroom apartment.

As often as I could, I reminded myself that I was new at this kind of life. It would take time to feel competent. Larry was patient. Every new wife, he said, had to start as a learner and eventually improve. I soon found that as I developed skill and confidence in the areas of marriage, homemaking and personal devotionals, my self-esteem grew also. I then had a solid platform from which to offer help and encouragement to other women.

Through the years, as Larry's ministry has developed and changed, this is the pattern the Lord has used to mold me into the woman He wants me to be. At each new place, when I have been willing to seek Him, God has faithfully equipped me to reject the temptation to run from the challenge and simply obey.

At one point, Larry asked me to help meet the needs of the women in one of the churches he was overseeing by discipling several of them as Titus 2:3-5 directs. Inwardly, I groaned. Our first child was only six weeks old and I wasn't feeling on top—spiritually, emotionally or physically. Besides, while I was slightly older than the women he had in mind, I was no veteran saint. I'd gleaned all I could from the older women I'd met in the ministry, but how could *I* disciple others? Where would I begin? Despite all my growth, that familiar insecurity was right there, trying to shoot down one more new endeavor with self-doubt.

Finally, like Peter, I decided to step out of the boat, relying totally on God's grace. I reasoned that since I was focusing my time and energy on the home, it made sense to get acquainted with the other women in settings that involved homemaking. We'd gather at my invitation to do normal, daily things together like washing clothes, shopping or de-boning chicken. We found we had much in common. Many counseling insights flowed out of my heart as we opened up to one another. We discovered that God was eager to meet our deepest needs when we were willing to be vulnerable.

Later, Larry asked me to lead the very first of what became regular women's home meetings in our church. He told me how pleased God was with my willingness to serve the women and that the Holy Spirit was going to give me wisdom and discernment for the new task. He assured me that the women would be uplifted through regular sharing and praying together.

I was sure the meeting would be awful. The women would be bored, my mind would go blank and I'd have no idea what to do next. I wanted to run, to take a quick trip somewhere until the night of the meeting had passed. But I'd only have to face the church the next Sunday and explain. There was no way out!

Sobbing, I cried out to Jesus, "Lord, You've got to help me. I believe this meeting is part of Your will to deepen relationships in the church. You know these women and their needs. So I ask You, with everything that's in me, use me. Use me, Lord, in any way You can to bring the needs of the women to the surface and to meet those needs."

Several hours later, as the last of 35 women who attended got into their cars and drove away, I sat on the sofa exhausted but thrilled at what God had done. He had "shown up" in spite of one obviously inexperienced leader. He had honored obedience, willingness and prayer with His special presence and had flooded us with koinonia, wisdom and unity of heart. I eagerly related to Larry how enthusiastic the women had been and how everyone had gone home uplifted. He smiled. He knew all along it would be that way.

That night I had experienced God in a new way. He had clearly given me divine guidance to handle the meeting. And although it would take many more meetings before I was totally comfortable in leading, I learned then, and would learn more deeply each time thereafter, the importance of trusting in His grace.

I often thought my feelings of inadequacy about leading groups and speaking publicly were proof that I couldn't handle the job or wasn't suited to the task. When I shared these feelings with a more mature leader's wife, however, she assured me that feeling inadequate is normal and even necessary to keep me crying out to God for His strength and guidance. She showed me in the Bible how even David had had feelings of despair: "From my distress I called upon the Lord: the Lord answered me and set me in a large place'' (Ps. 118:5). And Jesus, too, at Gethsemane cried out in anguish, not once but three times.

Realizing this helps me cry out, too, believing God will answer and give me what I need. It's important, as a pastor's wife whose life is constantly touching others, that I have this truth securely under my belt: God comes through in times of need if I'll simply admit my lack and step out in faith.

As I've allowed the normal feelings of fear and insecurity to motivate me to reach out to God, I've found the grace He provides ''sets me in a large place.'' In other words, He increases the level of His anointing in proportion to the increase in task. Whether it's been adapting to a surprise pregnancy, adopting a little Korean girl, relocating our family for anywhere from six weeks to one year to help start a new church, speaking at retreats or writing a chapter for a book, I've found Him to be lavish with up-to-the-minute provision.

The end result is that I've been able to enter into the joy of fulfillment that comes from being used by Him. Rather than giving in to the temptation to escape my situation and abandon responsibility, I've been able to grab hold of God's enabling power and accomplish something that seemed impossible before.

I can still remember the panic that rushed through me six years ago as I overheard Larry on the phone, talking about me to a South African Christian leader: ''Yes, Doris speaks publicly. Three hundred leaders' wives from all over South Africa? Do you want some meetings with the women? Yes, I think she can do it.''

At that point, I had spoken publicly only once. I was numb with disbelief that Larry would even consider volunteering me for such a task!

Larry and I had many late-night discussions over that conversation. He didn't pressure me into ministry, but he did challenge me to respond if God was opening up another door. Finally, after much prayer, study and crying out to the Lord in desperation, I sensed a go-ahead in my spirit and began work on a few basic outlines from which I would speak to the South African women on marriage, self-image and sisterhood.

"Just share from your life," Larry coached. As I kept that in mind, I soon found that I had a larger resource for teaching than I'd realized.

Many obstacles cropped up in the months before the actual trip. I thought more than once about backing out. But preparation for South Africa became a lesson in perseverance. Not only was I pregnant with our second child and suffering from morning sickness, but our house was being renovated. For months I lay on the couch and worked on the outlines, jumping up frequently to run to the bathroom to throw up. Meanwhile, the deafening noise from the jackhammers and bulldozers working just outside constantly frightened our little son, who could only be comforted by having Mommy stop all else and hold him.

As if all this weren't enough, the day before our trans-Atlantic flight Larry received legal papers suing him for $26 million. At a speaking engagement, he had mistakenly repeated some misinformation that had been circulating across America and abroad. (The suit was eventually settled out of court.) Still, we refused to let anything stop us from climbing onto the plane the next day.

Right up to the moment I ascended the platform in South Africa to speak, my morning sickness plagued me.

No sooner had I put on my makeup and prepared my appearance than I threw up again, forcing me to re-do my whole face! But when my teaching sessions were over, woman after woman came up to me and encouraged me. Apparently, my insights, which seemed elementary to me, were revolutionary to them. Once again, I was poignantly reminded of the joy that comes in focusing on others and not on myself.

God was changing me in many ways as more and more responsibility was given to me. He was even changing my attitude toward responsibility itself. That lesson came from Matthew 25, the parable of the talents, in which Jesus tells the faithful slave, "Well done...you were faithful...I will put you in charge of many things." But I was more like the unfaithful servant. I was fearful of responsibility.

Then I began to see that I was often using low self-esteem as an excuse for unfaithfulness. I was settling comfortably into laziness rather than fulfilling the responsibilities God had called me to. Now the Holy Spirit wanted me to stop limiting what He intended to do in my life. He wanted me to fulfill my destiny and become all He intended me to be.

It shocked me that the Lord didn't coddle the timid, insecure servant. Instead He called him "wicked, lazy and worthless," ordering him into "outer darkness." The poor man hadn't murdered anyone. He wasn't involved in adultery. He was simply lazy and unfaithful, not using what God had given him. That man could have been me.

The severity of God's view in this parable sobered me. I recognized that every new responsibility was an opportunity to choose between being a fearful servant, shrinking back, or being a productive contributor pleasing to the Master. At the heart of the choice is trust in God's promise never to burden me down with more than I can handle or more than He can equip me for.

My husband has been a major tool in the hands of God to pull me out of my stubborn insecurity and low self-esteem. Larry has regularly helped me redirect my focus from selfish preoccupation to the needs of others. He visualizes me, through the eyes of faith, as a woman fulfilling her potential in God.

Through Larry's consistent attentiveness and friendship, I have found the loving stability under which I can flourish. He has put building blocks into my self-esteem by valuing my opinion and seeking my input into his life and ministry. He understands that a healthy marriage makes the wife a healthy woman, and he purposely limits his ministry engagements out of town so that marriage and family do not become casualties. His motto: "If it doesn't work at home, don't export it!"

The status of our home life is an important factor in my self-esteem. Worry and tension over unresolved issues at home can make me—and any pastor's wife— feel low about herself. The assurance I have that my "bases are covered," that my husband is happy and my children are properly cared for, gives me freedom from the chronic worry and despair which cancel self-growth.

The church Larry and I are a part of also provides the security that comes from having committed, caring friends. We've placed a high priority on relationships in the congregation. Our marriage and our lives have been greatly enriched by our ability to be vulnerable with a number of other pastors and their wives in the church.

What a miracle Jesus has worked in me! Over the past

10 years, the Lord has enabled me to be free from those waves of insecurity and panic that used to engulf me and move out in faith and confidence to embrace fresh realms of responsibility. Each new experience has stretched me and drawn me closer to the woman of God I am intended to be.

God took an unbeliever who couldn't face a group unless she had a few drinks first and transformed her into someone who, today, can preach about Jesus in the open air to a crowd of university students! The woman who dreaded leading a woman's sharing group now finds it very natural. The lady who, seven years ago, couldn't imagine leading a women's meeting is now rejoicing that her efforts are impacting thousands of others.

Low self-esteem may be common among women, but it doesn't have to last. It doesn't have to cripple forever. We don't have to keep our treasures buried in the ground.

No, low self-esteem is something God wants us to leave behind. He has an image for us to step into—the functioning, glowing woman He's envisioned all along. All we need to do is see her through the eyes of faith.

I know. Just ask me.

Doris Tomczak was born in 1951 in Pittsburgh, Pennsylvania. Her parents, while religious, did not become Christians until they were in their 50s. Seven of their eight children, including Doris, followed them to Christ over the next five years.

Doris met her husband, Larry, at a Catholic charismatic prayer meeting the same week she gave her life to the Lord. They were married four years later.

Larry is an apostolic team leader and one of two founders of Covenant Life Church in the greater Washington, D.C., area. Doris supports him in this ministry and in their ministry of planting New Testament churches across the country. Larry is also editor of *People of Destiny* magazine and a national and international speaker.

The Tomczaks have four children, ages 7, 5, 4 and 3.

Chapter Six
She Who Laughs, Lasts

by Kristy Roberts (Mrs. Milton) Dykes

"Come on, honey. Follow Mommy," I whispered
to my 3-year-old Julie. Nature calls frequently when
you're pregnant and I took Julie's hand to lead her out
of the church service. Because we had sold our building
and were erecting new facilities, our congregation was
temporarily meeting in an old, dilapidated armory. I ac-
cidentally knocked some of the peeling green paint off
the wall of the foyer as I leaned against it and peered
up the long, dark stairway that led to the women's
restroom. I knew from previous trips that the electricity wasn't working. After a moment, I decided to slip
into the nearby men's room. It was a Wednesday night,
I reasoned. The crowd was slim. I hadn't seen anyone
else leave the service. I would be alone. I would hurry.
No one would ever know.

My ever-talkative Julie followed closely as we walked
down the narrow hall. "Now, Julie, Mommy's going

to go into *this* restroom. If anyone comes, you tell Mommy, OK? We'll use this chair to prop the door open so we can at least get a little light. Now, if you hear any footsteps, you tell Mommy, OK? Mommy will hurry,'' I said, thinking out loud more than talking to her. She was busy talking to herself, too, and I learned long ago to tune her out whenever I had something important to do.

We entered the restroom with its long row of doorless stalls. I walked into the first one I came to. ''Now, Julie, you just stand there facing me, and if you hear anything, you just let Mommy know.'' I draped the seat with tissue paper and was almost ready to sit when suddenly, I tuned into my daughter's words.

''I see somebody. I see somebody. I see somebody. I see somebody,'' she repeated over and over.

I glanced under the partition into the next stall and noticed two big feet with trousers around them. Have you ever seen a jackrabbit run? Well, we could have beaten him! I grabbed Julie's hand and darted down the hall and back into the service with lightning speed. Later when I told my husband, Milton, about the incident, he fell to the floor, holding his sides and laughing.

Why, I wonder, do the funniest things happen at the most serious times—like weddings, funerals, baptisms and in restrooms? Having a sense of humor as a pastor's wife is one of the greatest things you can possess. Why? Because you will need it!

There are many frustrating times in church work with which we, as leaders, must learn to cope. There are times when people fail to do their jobs right; times when things aren't done exactly as we'd like them to be done; times when our dreams don't materialize; times when sickness or tragedy strike; even times when people fail you, or hurt you, or attack you. How we deal with these sources of irritation can determine our mental well-being. As Richard Dobbins, noted Christian psychologist, states, "It's not the circumstances in life that can make us or break us, but how we *choose to handle* the circumstances."

Humor helps. According to *Parade* magazine, a six-week study at the University of California proved that students under stress were better able to handle pressure when they were taught the physiological and psychological benefits of laughter. If you've been a pastor's wife for more than a month, you know that the ministry is filled with many stressful situations. So what do you do when these incidents occur? Laugh about them!

Every church seems to have at least one "character" who tends to create stress. Ours was Brother Golden, or "Goldie" as he called himself, a little, old, senile man from the nursing home who attended our services faithfully for several years. Week in and week out, a loving brother in the Lord brought Goldie to church, and Goldie loved coming.

Goldie had bushy eyebrows that bristled out over the large glasses which seemed to cover most of his face. His mouth dropped open in a constant "O." His out-of-date double-knit clothing in mismatched hues hung loosely on his hunched shoulders. His walk reminded me of Tim Conway's slow shuffle on "The Carol Burnett Show." Goldie always got right in a person's face to talk to them and his dragon breath was bad enough to knock them down. If the urge came on him, he would bellow out in his extremely loud, raspy voice in the middle of a service, and although we deeply loved Goldie, we had to learn to do a lot of laughing in dealing with him.

Once, we were having "testimony time." The praise reports were faith-building and exciting and the air was permeated with a spirit of praise and worship to God. Slowly, from his usual spot on the second pew, center section, Goldie rose, twirled around slowly in a complete circle, and came to a stop facing the pulpit.

"If you want to go to heaven
When you D—I—E,
Then put on your coat
And your T—I—E."

Thus having spoken, he grabbed the pew in front of him and plopped down in his seat.

Another time, at the close of an evening church service, my husband called the whole congregation to come and stand in the altar area. We worshipped God, sang in the spirit and danced before the Lord. We were joyful, exuberant, expectant, and Milton led us in a victorious little chorus before we left. Just before he dismissed us, he said, "Does anyone have something exciting from the Lord to share with us before we go?"

Goldie raised his hand high and my husband, with a premonition of what was to come, reluctantly called on him.

"Goldie, do you have something *exciting* to share?" he asked, emphasizing the word "exciting."

"Wel-l-l-l," Goldie drawled, "the worst thang in the world is when you wake up in the mornin' and you cain't remember your name."

Thankfully, the congregation knew Goldie's ways and we laughed inwardly as my husband closed in prayer, asking God to help and bless Goldie.

I'm so glad we used our sense of humor in dealing with Goldie. Oh, we had to call him aside privately many times and instruct him, but we dealt with him in a gentle and loving manner. Goldie's physical problems prevent him from coming to church anymore, but every time I go to visit him in the nursing home, his eyes light up and he says, "My little China doll has come to see me." He takes my hand and leads me to the old upright piano in the social hall and insists I play hymns for him as he sings in his raspy voice. I can do it in the spirit of love because I know I treated him right. And oh, how we treasure the stories we now have about Goldie, our funny little man from the nursing home.

Laughter is good for you. It not only improves your mood, but also your health. Solomon, one of the wisest men who ever lived, said, "A merry heart doeth good like a medicine..." (Prov. 17:22). That means that seeing things, even frustrating situations, from a humorous viewpoint is just as good for us as taking Alka Seltzer when we've eaten a big meal late at night after one of those many ministerial meetings.

In recent years, the health care community has begun to realize that recovery is actually speeded up when humor is part of the medicine. A growing number of hospitals are opening "humor rooms" for their patients, where funny movies and reruns of "Candid Camera" are shown. An unlikely group called "Nurses for Laughter" is now 600 members strong. These nurses wear buttons that read: "Warning: Laughter may be hazardous to your illness." Pastors and their wives, who deal so often with the sick, should remember that warning!

Laughter is also of great value in the pastor's home.

71

The minister and his wife who don't take themselves and the situations of life so seriously are better off. One way my husband, Milton, and I are putting this into practice in our home is by developing a knack for learning and sharing funny stories with guests and at family mealtimes. Our children are even blossoming into expert joke-tellers. It's so very important for pastors' kids to know that Christians can have lots of fun. Most "P.K.s" hear constantly about sickness, need, death and trouble and they need an infusion of lightness and laughter.

Yes, having a sense of humor helps. It helps in a myriad of ways. In a study conducted at Michigan State and Florida State universities, behavioral scientists found that humor could actually help in embarrassing situations. This proved true for my husband recently.

The incident occurred during a wedding. Milton was in his study, waiting with the groom and best man for their cue to enter the sanctuary. At the end of the second song, they were to walk out on the platform. Horror of all horrors, the fear of every man, his zipper broke! He could hear the strains of the first song wafting through the room and he knew he didn't have much time. At first, panic seized him. He slipped off his trousers and he and the groom frantically worked on the zipper, hoping they could somehow fix it.

His embarrassment was acute as he pondered what these men must think of him. "What if I can't go out there and the wedding must be postponed," he thought, aghast. But his marvelous sense of humor came to the rescue. The best man noticed a few extra boutonnieres in a box and upon examining them, found two-inch long straight pins in each one. Amidst laughter and joking, they literally "pinned Milton up" and he performed the ceremony with none the wiser. An embarrassing, once-in-a-lifetime situation (he hopes!) ended on a happy note.

Of course, we know that the Bible is the all-authoritative standard on every subject, even laughter. All through the Bible, we read the words, "merry," "cheerful," "laugh" and "laughter." The word "joy" or its derivatives are mentioned more than 200 times! Even one of the nine fruits of the Spirit is joy. And I know God has a sense of humor. Just look at some of the creatures He made!

Many humorous incidents are found in God's Word. In Matthew 20:20, the mother of James and John came to Jesus asking Him to let her sons sit on either side of him in heaven. I heard one preacher put it this way: "Jesus dealt with a nagging woman humorously when He said, 'I'm sorry but I don't handle that department. You'll have to take it up with My Father.' "

The funniest incident I've come across in the Bible happened when Elijah and the prophets of Baal were trying to call down fire from heaven on Mt. Carmel. You probably recall the story found in 1 Kings 18 when Elijah decided to prove to Israel once and for all that Jehovah was the true God. He and the prophets of Baal built their own altars. The agreement was that whichever god answered by sending fire to light the wood on the altar would be worshipped by all of Israel. Elijah gave the Baal worshippers first chance, and all morning long they called on their gods frantically in orgiastic dances, even cutting themselves with knives and swords. About noon, Elijah's sense of humor got the best of him. "You'll have to shout louder than that to catch the attention of your god!" Elijah scoffed. "Perhaps he is talking to someone, or is out sitting on the toilet, or maybe he is away on a trip, or is asleep and needs to be awakened!'' (1 Kings 18:27, Living Bible).

Learn to see the humor in every situation, especially those you can't seem to change. Life will be much better! When old Mr. Cantankerous calls on Sunday afternoon during your much-needed nap and asks what time church starts that evening (he really knows, but is lonely and just wants to talk), put your sense of humor to work. When Mrs. Starved for Attention goes on and on about her many illnesses and surgeries, look for the light side (but please, not in front of her!) And even when Mr. Lack of Tact attacks you and your integrity, or you hear that he is talking about you behind your back, remember the joy of the Lord. Humor can carry you through some deep waters and dark days of church work.

My husband and I have proved true so many times the scripture ''The joy of the Lord is your strength'' (Neh. 8:10). In the 15 years we have been in the ministry, we have pastored some wonderful churches. God, in His great mercy, saw fit to bless our ministry and each church grew and prospered under our leadership. We built three new buildings in different cities (all to the glory of God) and we can now look back and see lives that were brought into the kingdom while we were there as shepherds. We have been so thankful for His blessings on us and for what He did through us. But through the years, we had a standard line that we joked about at ministerial meetings. ''This church is going down slower than any other church we've ever pastored,'' we'd quip to our minister friends. We'd all laugh over that statement, but it never meant anything to us until recently.

We began pastoring our present church almost seven years ago and the attendance then was approximately 100 people. The previous pastor had some moral problems, so we had major obstacles to overcome. We moved to the town with the intention of bringing God's healing and restoration to a deeply scarred congregation.

Soon, God began to bless. Our attendance increased. We hired a wonderful associate pastor whose lively songleading helped make our services exciting and power-packed. Our minister of music did a superb job and had at least three major musicals a year that attracted hundreds from our community. We began a weekly television ministry (which my wise husband insisted I co-host—a growing experience for me), and we put our Sunday morning services on radio. All seemed to be going well as five wonderful years quickly passed by.

At the beginning of the sixth year, we had our annual week of prayer. Milton and I made a commitment to fast and pray more than we had ever done before. We interceded with God to bless our church, to exalt Him in the community, to save souls and to help our people grow in Him.

Right after this, the church voted to buy new property for expansion. But as soon as we signed on the dotted line, "the bottom fell out." Two deacons and their families left. Other members, for many reasons, quit our fellowship. Before our very eyes, the humorous quip we had repeated to our minister friends began to come true. It was terribly hurtful, but it was also frightening, for we had taken on the project of the new church property. And when you lose almost 100 people, needless to say, it's difficult to pay the bills. Milton and I sank into the depths of despair and depression. "God, haven't we sought You more than ever before? Haven't we obeyed You and believed You to work in this church?" we cried out.

One Sunday night, almost a year later, Milton called me up to the platform.

"Kristy, will you trust me?" he whispered in my ear.

"Yes, certainly, Milton."

He slowly turned to the congregation and with tears trickling down his face, he said, "Folks, I've tried to be a good pastor to you. I've tried to follow God. I know I've obeyed Him and sought Him diligently in prayer. But for some reason, the church is not progressing. I've struggled with this for almost a year now. I've finally come to the conclusion that maybe another man can step in and lead you on to the heights that God has for you. I still love you and have a great burden for this church and this community, but for the reasons I've mentioned, I submit my resignation."

A hush fell across the church, followed by the sound of loud sobs. I saw many people, men and women alike, dabbing their eyes with tissues. Slowly, a man rose from the back of the church.

"I've been in this church for quite a number of years, Pastor. I've seen this church surge forward with the blessings of God, only to be downtrodden by Satan again and again. I've seen your commitment, your love, your faithfulness to us and to God."

He paused, bit his lip, and a tear trickled down his cheek. "Pastor, the reason this church is like it is is our fault, not yours," he said, making a wide sweeping gesture with his hands. "We should've reached out more, been more concerned. We should've prayed more. I ask you to reconsider your decision, and if you'll stay and lead us, we'll help shoulder the burden and get in and work until we see victory."

One by one, the people stood and expressed similar sentiments. Afterwards, the leaders of the church met with Milton and gave him their full support, also asking him to reconsider and to take whatever time he needed to seek God.

For two weeks, we talked little and prayed much. We were buoyed by the people's marvelous expressions of love for us. The cards poured into our mailbox and people sent flowers and brought us baked desserts. Finally, encouraged and strengthened, Milton agreed to keep the pastorate.

And then the annual business meeting came up. In the 15 years we've been in the ministry, we've always called these meetings our annual praise reports, and that's exactly what they've been. We've lifted our hands over and over again and thanked God for His many blessings on us—financial, numerical and spiritual.

But we've found that when times are hard in a church and things aren't going really great, people have a tendency to become disgruntled and nit-picky. And that's what happened that night, although we never expected it. Julie and Jennifer and I drove to church. After getting special permission from the nursery workers to let 7-1/2-year-old Jennifer stay there "just this one time," 11-year-old Julie and I went into the church and knelt down for a 30-minute prayer time before the meeting.

As soon as the financial report was read, a man asked to speak. I knew as soon as he started that the meeting was going to be negative. A small handful of the members took their turns firing questions at Milton and the board of directors about everything from our salary to our integrity.

If I had only known, I would never have let Julie attend

the meeting. We have always tried to keep the negative things of church work from our children, even though it has been hard. Many times we've discussed problem church situations in quiet whispers until we were sure the children were asleep.

On the way home, Julie started crying. "Mom, why did those people do that? I thought they loved us." On and on she went, asking questions, demanding answers. Anger spilled out, only to be replaced with deep hurt. Jennifer sat in the back seat, taking it all in as I did my best to explain the situation gently.

"Even though these few who criticized us made mistakes tonight, we have the love of Christ in our hearts and we are going to be kind to them and love them anyway," I said to the girls. "We will not hold grudges or try and get back at them. We are going to practice the Golden Rule. And besides," I added, "only a handful felt that way. Think of all who stood and said nice things about us."

At home, I gave them a quick snack and after they brushed their teeth, I prayed with them and tucked them into their twin beds.

"But, Mom, are we going to move? They took a vote...," Julie cried.

"I know, honey. But I'm not worried. God cares for us and He loves us and He *will* take care of us."

"But what if I have to leave all my friends? I can't take that, Mom. It would mean a new school...a new neighborhood. Why were they so mean?"

I had to admit that I was hurt, too, and even though I kept reassuring her, I knew I needed special comfort from the Lord, also.

I sat down on the edge of Julie's bed, stroking her

forehead and wiping her tears with a tissue. Suddenly, our second-grader, Jennifer, sat up in bed.

"Mommy, this is nothing but the devil, do you hear me?" she railed out. "The devil, I said," she hollered, her teeth gritted. She balled her little fists, and with a boxer's motions, swung into the air. "Satan, I rebuke you in the name of Jesus. I hate you, Satan, you mean thing. I rebuke you, Satan. Do you hear me?"

From the other twin bed, I began to feel a light-heartedness for the first time that evening. Jennifer jumped out of bed and swung into the air again.

"Take that, Satan. And that," she added, as she spit into the air. "We're not taking anymore off of you. We rebuke you right now, you brat, you." She jumped up and down and then balled her fists again and looked over at me.

"Mommy, we're going to rebuke Satan every night, do you hear?"

Suddenly, Julie sat up and began to laugh—vibrant, bright, giggly laughter—and I joined her. Our bodies shook and tears welled up in our eyes as we watched Jennifer and her antics. Julie swung her feet to the side of the bed and I jumped up and grabbed Jennifer, swinging her around and around as I said, "I'll help you fight the devil, Jennifer." The three of us joined hands and we laughed until we fell to the floor, gripping our sides.

The "peace that passeth understanding" overshadowed both children as I tucked them in a second time. They fell asleep immediately.

When Milton came home a little later, I told him about the incident. He laughed so hard, I thought he was going to roll on the floor. It was a cleansing, sustaining laughter—accompanied by God's healing.

From that moment on, we never worried about our church again. We committed "our people" to God, believing Him to work it all out. He has. We are still there today, and the congregation is once again growing and thriving.

That night we fulfilled Proverbs 18:14: "The spirit of a man will sustain his infirmity; but a wounded spirit who can bear?" In other words, the spirit of joy overcame our troubles, but if we had kept our wounded spirits, who would've been able to bear being around us?

Are you facing a stressful time in your life right now? Are you discouraged? Downhearted? Disappointed in people? Then take heart! Solomon said in Ecclesiastes 3:4: "[There is] a time to weep, and a time to laugh...." Put your weeping behind you. Remind yourself of the past and the great victories God has given you. Look around your congregation. See that person you won to the Lord? Or that one you comforted when death or tragedy struck? Or what about the miracles God performed in provision for that family over there? Be like the Israelites: "Then was our mouth filled with laughter, and our tongue with singing...The Lord hath done great things for us; whereof we are glad" (Ps. 126:3,4). Laugh and laugh hard. And remember: she who laughs, lasts!

Kristy Roberts Dykes was born in 1951 in Jacksonville, Florida. Although her father was not a church-goer, Kristy was given a strong Christian upbringing by her mother, a full-time secretary who found time between home and job to teach Sunday school, visit the sick and take her children to church whenever the doors were open.

Kristy met her husband, Milton, at Southeastern College of the Assemblies of God. They married in 1971 and went into the ministry shortly after Milton's graduation. They have been in their present pastorate, First Assembly of God of Bartow, Florida, since 1980.

In addition to pastor's wife and mother, Kristy is a free-lance writer. She contributes a weekly inspirational column to her local paper and, together with Milton, co-hosts a weekly television program called "Real Life."

The Dykeses have two daughters, ages 11 and 8.

Chapter Seven
Dealing With Criticism

by Carolyn (Mrs. Charles) Simpson

''Sticks and stones may break my bones, but words can never harm me.'' As little girls, my friends and I called this rhyme out with firm conviction. Some other children were calling us ugly names. Back and forth across the backyard fence, our words flew like missiles.

One day, the gang taunting us finally got the message. They arrived fully armed with sticks, stones and anything else they could throw at us—determined, it seemed, to break our bones. At that point we decided the whole situation was out of our control.

Unarmed and outnumbered, we took a new approach. We backed away as slowly as we dared, holding our heads high. We suddenly realized there were more important things to do in life than get hurt. We were ready to end our fight and get on with our lives.

When I was asked to write a chapter on how I, as a pastor's wife, face criticism, I could not help but laugh.

Sometimes laughter can take the sting out of a touchy subject!

I realized I must have become known as someone who has faced criticism and survived. That does not mean I have always dealt with criticism well or wisely. But I *have* been forced to deal with it. And you can't continue to confront criticism without learning a few things.

Perhaps as a child I thought that words could never harm me. Well, I've changed my mind. Words definitely can hurt us. I've seen them hurt feelings and damage reputations—even ruin lives. I've seen hurtful, critical, gossipy words spread far and wide. They've blown like feathers torn from a pillow and carried into the wind, never to be gathered again.

The extent to which criticism has hurt me has depended upon the way I have managed it. I could let it deal me a crushing blow, or I could face it for what it is and get on about the work to which the Lord has called me.

I guess there isn't a pastor's wife in the world who knows exactly what she's getting into when she marries a man called to ministry. I am sure I didn't. I've always been grateful for the many people who've loved and understood me through the years, but I wasn't fully prepared for a few of the experiences that have come my way.

As they do with most pastors' wives, people look at me with unrealistic expectations. Perhaps many women will identify with the little lady in this verse I've written:

Daily works from morn' til night,
Perfect children act just right,
House is always neat and clean,
Company may soon be seen,
Cheerfully at every meeting,

Smiling nicely with her greeting,
Slim, trim and always fit,
Confident and quick with wit,
Thrifty, smart and pretty, too,
Knows the Bible through and through,
Cooks and entertains with zest,
Never worried, never stressed,
Talent, charm and patience, too,
Nothing that she cannot do,
Never existing in real life,
She's the mythical preacher's wife.

The person who has helped me the most in adjusting to being a pastor's wife has been the pastor himself—my husband, Charles. When we were first married he jokingly told me about a pastor who never called his wife by her given name. He always called her "wife." Soon the whole church was calling her "wife."

Charles said when I married him he wanted me to be *his* wife and not the church's wife. This helped to define for me my main responsibilities. Then, through prayer, we have tried to determine just what realistically could be expected of me in the church.

Knowing what I want to accomplish as a pastor's wife helps me when I am criticized. With goals I know where I'm headed and can determine better whether or not I need to change.

Then, when criticism comes, I avoid confusion since I know God has given me a work to do. And if God is pleased with what I am doing, eventually I will be blessed.

In the midst of criticism I try to remember that its main purpose—if it is invalid—is to distract me from doing the will of God. Remember Nehemiah, high up on the wall of Jerusalem? His vision was to rebuild the wall. He was constantly being criticized, ridiculed and threatened. If he had spent much time worrying about what his enemies were saying, he never would have finished the job as quickly as he did.

Nehemiah's job was completed because he was not intimidated by threats and ridicule. He kept his eyes on the thing God had called him to do. I, too, want to keep my eyes on the work for which God has prepared me.

Unjust criticism aimed at pastors' wives comes from the devil. It helps me to remember that. No one wants to slow down the purposes of God as much as the devil does.

The Bible tells us our wrestling is not against flesh and blood, but against powers that are unseen. If criticism keeps me from doing what is right and accomplishing the will of God, then Satan wins a victory in my life.

If, however, I can keep my mind on God's purposes, then God's work can continue unhindered. No matter who tears me down or maligns me, I need to recognize that the devil is the source of the problem—not necessarily the person.

On a number of occasions Charles and I have seen Satan try, through people's words and actions, to "pull us off our wall." Our church has changed through the years as we have sought to follow God's Word. But we have received criticism for these changes, often from "church-going" folks who perhaps fear change.

During one such period, the criticism did not concern me as much as the manner in which it came. I can understand a friend who comes in love and explains how I have offended her, and seeks to understand and help me. However, I have trouble understanding the well-educated, intelligent Christians who have used un-Christian tactics to hurt us.

People lied about our church—people who did not want to take the time to find out the truth. And because more and more people believed the lies, more and more lies were told.

Sometimes the devil overplays his hand. Some of the rumors mushroomed into wild, unbelievable tales. I enjoyed hearing one wide-eyed man report that someone in our church jumped over a pew and flew into a wall.

"Well, that's farther than they fly in most churches," replied Charles dryly.

Then there was the one about a lady from our church who, while rolling on the floor, bit a man on the foot. To that Charles responded, "Oh, she didn't actually bite him on the foot"—which, of course, led the listener to speculate on where she *did* bite him!

As the rumors grew, someone catalogued them in a booklet which they passed around our neighborhood. Christians and non-Christians alike worried about us.

We were remodeling our home, but word got out that we were turning our house into a church building. The builders felt threatened. A high school fraternity used our yard as an initiation site for its new members, driving their cars through the grass and spinning the tires. Our mailbox was torn down repeatedly. One night, three crosses were burned in front of the house.

The words blew like feathers into the wind. We tried to catch them but couldn't.

Our children were becoming upset by all the stories that were circulating about me, their father and the church. How was I, the pastor's wife, able to respond to all of this? Where did I begin? I sought the Lord.

Why were Christians attacking us? It seemed they were totally disregarding the teachings of the Bible. I looked for Scripture verses concerning criticism.

I read 1 Peter 4:12-16 and 2 Timothy 3:12. In these verses I saw that all Christians will be criticized, persecuted or ridiculed. And I shouldn't be surprised when the attacks come.

Next I read about Paul. In his religious zeal he persecuted Christians, thinking he was "doing God a favor." Paul evidently wanted to serve God and yet did not understand that through Jesus, God had done a new thing in the earth.

Understanding Paul helped me understand the perspective of many of our persecutors.

Much of the unjust criticism came from the hearts of those who gave it. Frustration, anger, insecurity and misunderstanding caused people to lash out. Because we seemed to be a threat to these people, we were their target.

And when people spoke good words, they came from the good feelings in their hearts. Those who wanted to find something good said positive things. Those who filled their minds with negative thoughts communicated unpleasant things wherever they went.

At one point, some people said I was a "zombie"—a dead person who only appeared to be alive, whose actions someone else controlled. This was, to say the least, not a very flattering name!

Actually, it was a criticism not only of me, but also of my husband, since he was the one supposedly controlling me. I tried to pass it off as insignificant, but the thought of me as a "zombie" stuck in the back of my mind.

Two weeks later, Charles and I were in a meeting of Christians in Lebanon. Charles was the speaker. As the pastor rose to introduce Charles, he said, "First, I would like to introduce Mrs. Simpson, the *dynamo* behind Brother Charles!" I had to laugh. In two weeks' time, I had gone from "zombie" to "dynamo"! People do speak out of the abundance of their hearts.

It was good to understand why the attacks came, but the next step was to forgive the offenders. It helped that Charles didn't tell me all the bad things people were saying. He didn't get angry or bitter, or recount all the nasty stories, so I found it easier to want to forgive. I probably would have held on to my grievances longer if he had not protected me in this way.

Once, when we attended a large meeting, I was introduced to the wife of a prominent pastor. I remembered that Charles had spoken in their church a few years before. When I mentioned this to his wife, she immediately drew back in her chair and looked at me rather coldly. I continued saying how nice I had heard their church was. Suddenly, she smiled and talked to me.

The change in her demeanor was so dramatic that I tried to figure out why she had not been friendly at first. Then it came to me. Her husband was one of the people who had spoken against us. I had forgotten. She had remembered. But because I had spoken to her in a friendly way, she saw that nothing was held against her. She seemed relieved, and we had a pleasant conversation.

Forgiving is not always easy. Sometimes I thought I had forgiven someone, only to find that I had not. Then I had to go back and truly forgive. I realized it was important to keep my heart open to the Lord. That way, if I needed to do something, I could see it more clearly.

I also needed to take forgiveness one step further. I needed to pray for those who had offended me. Sometimes that was even harder.

Claiming Matthew 5:43-48, I prayed for my enemies. Every time I thought of them, I prayed for them. It was difficult at first but in time became easier. Every now and then I would hear of a new criticism that would hit a friend or loved one. Then I would feel guilty about praying for those who criticized.

But I was always led back to the Scriptures and knew that I must pray. There was something about those prayers that began a healing in me. I really thought I was beginning to love my enemies. Then one day God surprised me.

Quite unexpectedly, Charles and I ran into some of the people who had been speaking against us. They were very friendly and kind. God was prospering them. I had always thought that when such a day came, I would be happy and thankful to God because of my change of heart. Instead, I felt confused and sad—and angry.

How could these people be happy and prosperous when they had never once asked my forgiveness?

I wanted to go and pout in the shade like Jonah. I knew just how the prophet felt. It seemed so unfair. I couldn't understand why I should have to go through the whole process of forgiveness, prayer and soul-searching when they were allowed to act as if nothing had ever happened. ''Why, God?'' I asked.

In time, God answered. When I forgive someone, my action can't be based on whether or not they have repented. Forgiveness is a gift I must give freely from my heart. I may never hear the words, ''I'm sorry.'' But if I can forgive anyway, then the work the Lord has given me can go on and prosper. I can be free to serve God with a clear conscience and an uncluttered mind.

Forgiveness also gives me the opportunity to take the grace God has given me and pass it on to others. Vengeance is not my job. My job is to be found faithful.

The lessons I've learned by being criticized have not been easy. But God has used them to bless me. I understand forgiveness more fully when I forgive. The grace of God becomes more real to me when I extend that grace to others.

Now I know what it feels like to be criticized. I have empathy for those who are put down. When I start to criticize, the words choke in my mouth—I realize their power to destroy.

With Joseph of old, I can say that the evil with which man meant to harm me God used to do me good. Perhaps one day, if you and I persevere, the walls of misunderstanding and distrust can be torn down and we can work together, without criticizing each other, to build the kingdom of God!

Carolyn D. Simpson was born in Chattanooga, Tennessee, in 1940. Her father, a doctor, and her mother, a trained nurse who discontinued her practice to be a full-time mother, raised Carolyn and her sister in a Christian home.

When Carolyn met her husband, Charles, he was already pastor of his first church. Just a sophomore in college, Charles was holding a revival meeting and needed a piano player. A mutual friend recommended Carolyn, then a high school senior. The two were married in 1960.

Charles is senior pastor of Gulf Coast Covenant Church in Mobile, Alabama. He is also a widely traveled Bible teacher and chairman of the board of Integrity Communications.

The Simpsons have three children. Their oldest son is employed with Integrity Communications.

Chapter Eight
Coping With Loneliness

---

by Dorothy Jean (Mrs. William) Ligon

When I married Bill, a young, enthusiastic pastor I met at a Southern Baptist revival, it never occurred to me that I would one day be lonely.

I grew up in the Florida countryside, surrounded by people who knew and loved me—my parents, brothers, aunts and uncles, cousins and church friends. In this extended family I was sheltered, secure. I didn't know what it felt like to be lonely.

My first few years with Bill were exciting. We moved to a large metropolitan city hundreds of miles from my hometown so that Bill could enroll in seminary. I worked to help pay expenses while he went to school. At night, I went to classes of my own to learn how to be a pastor's wife. Life was happy and hectic. No longer was I an inexperienced small town girl. Now I was married, employed and living in the big city.

After Bill's graduation, however, our lives changed

swiftly. We moved into a large pastorate of several hundred people. In a short time, our first son, William Jr., was born.

Suddenly, I was lonely.

Bill was determined to be a successful pastor. I wanted that for him. What I hadn't considered, however, was what that success would require of me. The baby and I had to be fit into Bill's busy schedule, which began at 6 a.m. and often didn't end until 11 p.m.

I thought a pastor's wife was supposed to "understand," so I tried not to complain. But as time wore on, I saw less and less of Bill. I felt as if I had to make an appointment to see my own husband.

I was discouraged and frustrated. Home was not home without Bill. I desperately wanted time with him—unpressured time that was not cut short by the demands of the church. I wanted to know that my needs—and the baby's—were at least as important to Bill as the needs of others. Most of the time, it didn't seem that way.

I made friends on my own, but somehow they weren't much comfort. I felt isolated, rejected, unloved. Self-pity overruled common sense, and I became resentful and angry.

If only I had known then what I know now! God never intended loneliness to control the hearts and lives of His people. Adam was given dominion over all things in the earth, yet God looked at him and said, "It is not good for the man to be alone." We need companionship.

God is a practical God. He didn't want Adam to be lonely, so He created a helpmate for him. He doesn't want pastors' wives to be lonely, so He created pastors—and not only pastors, but also friends. In addition, He gives us guidelines for how to become close to these special people in our lives.

I didn't know these guidelines in my early years as a pastor's wife. From time to time, my isolation and separation from Bill would become unbearable. Bill would try to comfort me. We'd reassure ourselves that we would take time to be together—tomorrow. The feeling of loneliness would subside for a while, only to return with greater intensity at a later date.

Fortunately, God had a schoolroom prepared—a place where He was going to begin to teach me about overcoming loneliness.

Bill was in his third year as senior pastor of a 2,000-member church. He was well on his way to a successful career in the pastoral ministry. Yet both of us began to feel another tug in our hearts which grew stronger each day. God was telling us to leave the pastorate and become missionaries in a foreign country.

It seemed such a drastic change, but we both knew God had spoken. Bill resigned his position, and within a few months we found ourselves, Bill Jr., and our youngest son, John, in Spain.

Far away from home, culture and familiar routine, our family was forced to cling together for support and to depend on God like never before. My prayer life and quiet times with the Lord became essential. I began to find a comfort I had never known simply by being in God's presence. I learned my first guideline: "I no longer call you servants...Instead, I have called you friends" (John 15:15); and, "Surely I will be with you always..." (Matt. 28:20). Jesus was my true friend. He was always there for me. In His presence, my loneliness was lightened.

A second guideline quickly followed. Bill and I

discovered that in order to be effective on the mission field, our work could not come first. It was paradoxical, but true. God and family needed to take priority, otherwise work was draining and fruitless.

This, then, was our guideline: God must come first, then family. Our missions or church work, as important as it is, must come third. Bill and I knew we had struck upon God's plan because we actually accomplished more as missionaries when we kept God and family first than when we rushed to put our missions work above the rest!

The result was that for the first time since our children were born, Bill and I became family-oriented. We depended on each other and the two boys for love, companionship and encouragement. We grew closer together than we had ever been. We traveled together, planned together and worked together. The strength of our relationship seemed, at times, to be essential to our very survival. No longer was I lonely for my husband.

Slowly, I realized that much of my loneliness back home had been caused by my own self-centeredness. I had always expected Bill to do something to meet my needs. I'd thought little about what I could do to help him. But as Jesus taught, a grain of wheat must fall into the ground and die or it will abide alone. Abiding alone is a raw state of loneliness—and that's what I had felt. In Spain, as I focused on how I could serve—not only in the mission field, but in my family—things began to change.

A real breakthrough came when I consciously released Bill from having to meet all my self-centered wants and needs. As I learned to lean more on God, I saw I had been leaning too much on my husband. Bill was meant to be my companion, not the source of my contentment. By my unrealistic expectations, I had bound my husband and denied God His rightful place in my life as the source of my fulfillment and peace. The day I released Bill, I actually gained him as an attentive husband who was willing to meet my needs when he could. What a difference my new attitude made!

Despite the strides I made in my relationship with Bill, I still had days of overwhelming loneliness. This time, I was not lonely for my husband—I was lonely for friends. Bill could not fill that void, just as the friends I made in our old church had not been able to fill the void left by his absence.

Usually outgoing by nature, I was handicapped in Spain. I couldn't speak the language. Culturally, I was a fish out of water. I had trouble communicating even when shopping for groceries in the open markets. Many mornings my heart ached as I looked out the fourth floor window of our apartment to the busy streets below. So many people and not one familiar face! So many conversations, yet no one to talk to!

Eventually, as I continued to study and work with the Spanish churches, the language flowed more easily. But there were still lessons to learn. I took Proverbs 18:24 to heart: "A man that hath friends must show himself friendly." I opened up our home to many who were in need. As I became more confident with my Spanish, I reached out to others. Soon, I had one Spanish friend, then two, then several. Friends from the United States came to visit us, too. My loneliness disappeared.

I carried these lessons back to the States with me when, after six years as missionaries, my family returned home. Bill took on a Baptist pastorate in the state of Georgia. In 1973, we started a new church in Brunswick, the Christian Renewal Center, where we've been to this day.

As I've looked closely at loneliness over the years, I've added a few new guidelines to the list I developed as a missionary, especially with regard to making friends with women in the church and the community. These, too, are based on biblical principles.

First of all, I've learned to be comfortable with women of all ages—young, middle-age and elderly. Some of my best friends are not in my peer group. They may be younger or older than I am, but they are women with peaceful spirits, generous hearts and good senses of humor. I enjoy being around them.

On the other hand, I avoid becoming close to women who are angry and contentious, who are habitual complainers or fault-finders—whatever their age. I don't want to be careful always of what I say in a friend's presence!

I don't believe I have to accept the close friendship of everyone who attends my church. I try to be wise and discerning. Someone who approaches me may be a "wolf in sheep's clothing." I ask myself: Does she show respect for her husband? Is she a committed mother who prays for her children and shows interest in their welfare and behavior? Is she hungry and eager to learn the ways of God?

This doesn't mean I won't get to know people who have problems, or who are in need of ministry. That's another subject entirely. But when I need a close friend—someone I can be open with, pray with, who will accept me as I am and support me in my own low moments—I look for a woman with a servant spirit, who joyfully shares her life with others.

I still get lonely sometimes. A few years ago, I longed to find a Christian woman my age with whom I could pray and study the Bible. God heard my prayers and brought me such a woman. We met weekly, or sometimes more often. We became very close. Soon our little get-togethers grew into much larger gatherings. A number of women who came to study with us became Christians and received the infilling of the Holy Spirit. My friend and I were a great team.

One day, however, she broke the news to me that her husband was being transferred by his employer to another part of the country. They would be leaving in a matter of days.

I was devastated. In my prayers, I raged against God for taking my friend away. But the Lord spoke to me very clearly one morning: ''I am and always will be the best friend you will ever have,'' He said.

I smiled. I knew it was true. God had always been there for me, and He always would be. No friend—not even my husband—could be so faithful.

With God at my side, I don't have to be lonely anymore.

Born in Tallahassee, Florida, in 1937, **Dorothy Jean Ligon** was the oldest of three children. Her family was active in the Southern Baptist church where her father was a deacon.

Dorothy Jean met her husband, Bill, when he came to her church to preach a revival. They continued to communicate and eventually married in 1958.

After pastoring several Baptist churches, the couple went to Spain and served for six years, from 1965 to 1971, as missionaries. In 1973 they founded the Christian Renewal Center in Brunswick, Georgia, where Bill is senior pastor.

Dorothy Jean has been a speaker at various women's retreats and Aglow chapters. She has also spoken at the Southern Baptist Foreign Missions Conference and the National Leadership Conference.

The Ligons have two sons, ages 25 and 21.

Wife

Chapter Nine
Keeping the Fire Burning

by Arlyne (Mrs. Ray) Mossholder

"I will love you longer than forever," the vocalist sang in a clear voice. Ray and I looked softly at each other and smiled. We exchanged rings and a kiss then turned to march down the aisle arm in arm—Mr. and Mrs. Ray Mossholder.

That was 26 years ago. What expectations we had on that day for our new life together! We were sure our marriage would be perfect. We would cherish one another, comfort one another, encourage each other. We would work and play side by side. We would "love each other longer than forever"—the perfect song for a perfect match!

Ray and I had both just graduated from college. After our honeymoon we planned to teach—he in speech and drama at the high school level and I in an elementary school. We settled into a new lifestyle and a new area, developing new friends and activities. The days ahead

103

seemed so romantic and exciting.

But how soon life started to become routine, frustrating, exhausting and just plain ordinary. Problems cropped up at every turn. Ray was a night person. I wasn't. He squeezed the toothpaste tube in the middle. I insisted on rolling it up from the bottom. I liked to keep things in a particular order. He looked at me cross-eyed when I asked him to tidy up.

Our work commitments conflicted. While my school day usually ended at 3:00, Ray needed to go back to the high school many evenings and Saturdays for rehearsals.

We fought. We sulked. Our wedded bliss, so satisfying in the first months of marriage, waned. In my times alone, I sometimes blamed myself. I was inadequate, a failure. Other times, I decided everything was Ray's fault. As we struggled along and the months turned into years, there were many times of despair and hopelessness. A romantic, loving, lasting relationship seemed out of our reach. The song we had chosen for our wedding mocked us.

Finally, it seemed as if our life together was near its end. Where could we turn? Friends encouraged us to seek the Lord for the answer. We agreed. After all, the alternative was divorce, and somewhere deep inside we knew that wasn't what we really wanted.

Thank God He is in the business of healing broken hearts, broken spirits, even broken marriages! When Ray and I turned to God, He immediately accepted us where we were and began to lead us—by His Word, the good counsel and teaching of others, and godly example. He showed us that while we had promised to love each other "longer than forever," the ability to love did not come automatically with the marriage license. As the Word said, we had to "practice loving."

The lessons we've learned—are still learning—haven't been easy. But today, I can honestly say that Ray and I love each other more than ever. More than on our wedding day. We've practiced loving.

How do you practice loving? For Ray and me, practice takes many forms. Sometimes we're silly, laughing together and having great fun. Other times, we're passionate and intense. Sometimes we're tender and quiet, giving each other "space." Other times, we're partners, tackling a project together for the pure joy of working side by side.

It was wonderful to realize, in those early days of putting our marriage back together, that romance is not necessarily the same for each person or couple. When Ray and I paint the house together, I feel romantic. Not many other women do! What I've learned is this: I'm not bound to initiate and respond romantically in the same way as my best friend, my next door neighbor or the woman on the soap opera. I'm not someone else!

Ray isn't someone else, either. He doesn't have to fill the living room with flowers—just because some TV Romeo did—to show me he cares. He has his own ways, and I'm learning to appreciate them.

Hadn't we chosen each other? Our unique characteristics were what attracted us to each other in the beginning. Now we're still those unique individuals—and together, a unique couple. We've had to develop our own unique style of romantic love.

Developing that style has required, first of all, communication. We've had to make the extra effort to tell each other what our needs and desires are. This came easier for Ray—a very verbal and outgoing man—than for me. Not only am I more reticent by nature, but I think I expected Ray to be able to read my mind. When he couldn't, my dissatisfaction became his fault, not mine. But eventually, with the Lord's help and Ray's encouragement, I took more responsibility for my feelings and became more transparent and less afraid to express my needs.

Open communication has been absolutely essential. Some of the things that make me feel cuddly and romantic had been completely unknown to my husband. For example, until we shared our romantic likes and dislikes, Ray had no idea that I felt special when he repaired a light fixture or worked on some other malfunctioning household item. Yet these small activities made me feel protected and cared for. At the same time, it never occurred to me that Ray really liked it when we watched television together. I figured since we weren't talking during the show, it didn't matter if I was there or not. But to Ray, it mattered.

We've also had to accommodate each other. The biblical adage ''Give and it shall be given unto you, pressed down and running over'' applies in every area of life—including romance. As I did things simply for the joy of blessing my husband, he responded in kind. The ''pressed down and running over'' came in as the Lord added His blessing, too.

Accommodation often takes a large dose of self-sacrifice. For example, I love to shop, and Ray will sometimes go with me. We both enjoy browsing through a mall or a few specialty shops. It's relaxing exercise as well as a change of scenery. When I look at women's clothing, however, I know it's not easy for him! But patiently and politely, he gives me his opinion on the outfits I try on. When we find something we both really like, he enjoys buying it for me. How I appreciate him at those times!

In turn, Ray appreciates the things I do for him because *he* loves them—even when I don't. For example, he loves going to baseball games. I, on the other hand, find them boring unless there's a lot of hitting and the score is in the neighborhood of 25 to 23—not too likely if you're watching major league teams. I go anyway and look for the good plays, watch people, enjoy the outdoors, and have a hot dog. The game may not be fun, but being with Ray is.

Sometimes accommodating each other has meant just the opposite—not being together but giving each other space to pursue our separate interests. Ray needs time alone for studying and writing. I need time to express myself creatively through art. We've had to learn to respect these differences and appreciate and encourage each other's special talents.

Most often, though, it has been the little, daily occurrences that add up to the "Wow! He's so romantic!" These things have to be practiced, too. I love it when Ray opens the door for me, walks on the curb side or takes my hand when we're driving. He likes it when I reach over from my side of the car or couch and give him a hug. A wink, a smile, a pat, a squeeze, an unexpected or even expected kiss or hug, a word of endearment—these are small but romantic gestures that have come to mean so much as Ray and I have practiced them.

There are other things, too. When Ray is reading at the office, he will often save an article he thinks will interest me. I also skim the magazines and papers for material that I think would be of importance to him. Sometimes, we give each other little surprise gifts—a card, some flowers, an article of clothing, a record, a book or some silly trinket. The key is we're showing each other that we're *thinking* about each other. We may have separate activities, but our hearts are one.

Having a full bank account isn't necessary for little acts of kindness. Ray and I have learned to be creative. For my birthday one year, he put much care into choosing a coffee mug to add to my collection. It was all he could afford. Now that mug is displayed specially and not used because it is so treasured. Another year, I took Ray out to San Francisco to celebrate our anniversary on spare change I had been putting away for several months. He knew nothing about my little horde and enjoyed the evening all the more because we normally would not have been able to afford it.

I planned the anniversary outing to San Francisco—paid for with nickels, dimes and quarters—because I *knew* Ray had forgotten the date. The old Arlyne would have fumed over his thoughtlessness and made him miserable for forgetting such an important day. The new one simply organized an exciting night out for her husband.

Love covers up the lapses in each other. It was when I decided not to place blame or feel sorry for myself but to concentrate on loving Ray, and vice versa, that great joy was released for both of us.

That evening after dinner, I presented Ray with a little plastic bag tied with a bright red ribbon and a tag that read, "Happy Anniversary." When he opened it, he found all of the change I had collected and an advertisement for a show being performed in the city by our favorite male vocalist. He couldn't have been more surprised or more pleased. We dropped our son Tim at the home of a friend and scooted off to our anniversary celebration—one of the best we've ever had.

As Ray's ministry has expanded, we've had to concentrate on keeping the romance alive. His travels now take him away from home for periods of three or four weeks or more. Absence does not necessarily make the heart grow fonder! When he's ministering out of town or overseas and I'm at home with the children, it's easy to think that separation is "normal." We have to fight against this.

When Ray is traveling he calls or writes every day. It's important that he be constantly informed of the daily home routine, my successes and failures, and the children's needs and activities. It's just as important that the children and I know what he is doing, whom he is with, and the things the Lord is accomplishing in his ministry. He needs to be and feel a part of us, and we need to be and feel a part of him. Usually he calls at a scheduled time, but sometimes he calls when I least expect it—and usually just when I really need to talk to him.

Occasionally I travel with him. These are treasured times when we can be together and I can be more involved in what he's doing. We look for these opportunities even though at times they're not convenient or affordable. The dividends are more than worth the cost.

Two summers ago, for example, I was able to go with Ray to New Zealand and Australia for several weeks of ministry. The schedule was very demanding. We had only two free days completely to ourselves in the entire eight weeks. As soon as we finished one service, Ray would begin studying and preparing for the next one. Still, whenever possible, we would get away for a quick walk, hand in hand. We had a wonderful time simply being near each other—experiencing another part of the world together, ministering together and making new friends.

When Ray is home, we look for moments of togetherness. Often this time has to be planned carefully because Ray's office schedule is full—he's either catching up on all that transpired while he was out of town or preparing for the events that will take him away again.

At least once a month we have "Surprise Date Night." Ray will tell me the day, the time and how to dress—nothing more. We may go to a play, a movie, the beach, out to dinner, for a long drive or any combination of these. Sometimes I am the one who does the planning and surprising. We both eagerly anticipate this special time of talking, relaxing, focusing on each other and just having fun!

While we plan, we also try to be open for an unexpected lunch out, a quick excursion or a quiet time together. Just recently we made a last minute decision to stay home from a church meeting we would normally attend. The children went on without us. We were home alone—such a treat! We listened to a new record that our son David put on for us just before he left. We played a game. We watched a television program. We talked and thoroughly enjoyed each other. It was a special time.

Of course, it's hard to be romantic and loving in the midst of chaos. We've worked hard to make our home a place of retreat, a refuge in which we are physically, emotionally and spiritually refueled. This doesn't mean that our house is expensively decorated—it's not! But it's comfortable and reflects our taste and style. Garage sales, discontinued items, paint, wallpaper, "elbow grease" and loving care have all gone into making our home a pleasant place.

It also doesn't mean that our house is quiet or dull. With children around, how could it be! But we try to set a positive atmosphere with Christian music and carefully selected radio and television programs. Love, joy and laughter emanate so much more freely from this environment.

All of these things, we've learned, are important for developing a loving, romantic relationship. But the final, most important aspect of romantic love is spiritual. Without the Lord in the center of the home, the house is built on sand. The oneness of spirit that comes from worshipping, praying and studying together, and talking and sharing about what the Lord has done and is doing, has been the real glue that has kept Ray and me together.

The Lord has taken us through some happy and exhilarating experiences. He's also walked with us, comforted us and taught us through times of despair. Through it all He's been faithful.

We still "practice loving." We are still learning and refining our own unique brand of romantic love. On our wedding day, our confidence in our ability to love had been cocky, naive. But today, our confidence is in the Lord, who promises to complete the good work He has begun in us.

"I will love you longer than forever" is no longer the dreamy song of two young and naive lovers on their wedding day. It is no longer a song mocking the fragmented lives of a husband and wife on the brink of divorce. It is our song—Ray's and mine—sung in a new hope born of experience, hard lessons learned, victories won, and faith in God's ability to bring it to pass.

Arlyne Mossholder was born to Christian parents in 1936 in Portland, Oregon. She met her husband, Ray, at church when she was a college senior attending San Jose State College in California. The two were married six months later.

Arlyne and Ray are members of the Church on the Way in Van Nuys, California. Founder of Marriage Plus Inc., Ray has been in full-time evangelistic ministry since 1970. His seminars, held throughout the United States, Canada, New Zealand and Australia, teach practical Christian principles for strengthening marriages and healing broken relationships.

Arlyne is a substitute teacher in the local Christian schools. She has spoken at Women's Aglow and other Christian women's meetings.

The Mossholders have three children.

Chapter Ten
Starting Over as Number Two

by Ann (Mrs. Bill) Sanders

"I have a special work that I want you to do."

The word from the Lord caught me by surprise. I was not in prayer. I was not seeking the Lord on any matter. I was simply looking out my kitchen window, silently praising God for the beauty of that warm October afternoon and thanking Him for His faithfulness.

My thoughts ran back over the six years since my husband died, leaving me with three teenage children to raise and a business to manage. Those were difficult years, often marred by anxiety, stress, my own feelings of inadequacy. Yet I always had a strong sense of the Lord's presence during those months of sorrow. How faithful He was to comfort and sustain me!

Now, with my youngest son, Jeff, in college, I was enrolled at Oklahoma State University—an interior design major. I enjoyed the rigors of academic life and looked forward to my new career. But then the Lord broke through on that quiet fall day. He had a different plan. "Ann, you will not be a decorator. I have a special work that I want you to do."

I wondered about God's statement. During the rest of that semester, as I trudged from class to class across that windy and sometimes snowy campus, I kept asking myself, "When is God going to show me what He has in mind?"

It never occurred to me that God's plan would have something to do with Bill Sanders, the founding pastor of Tulsa Christian Fellowship, the church I had been attending for five years. The summer before, Bill's wife, Marty, had died of cancer, leaving him with four teenagers and a 10-year-old son to raise alone. While Bill and the children stood together in great faith and were a testimony of God's peace and comfort in sorrow, it was evident to all who knew Bill that a great void had come into his life. He missed his beloved Marty deeply.

With the rest of the congregation, I wept with and for our pastor. At that point, I knew him—everyone knows their pastor— but he didn't know me, at least not by sight. The congregation was large, and I usually slipped in and out unobtrusively. I lived 35 miles away on the banks of Keystone Lake. Every Sunday I drove into town for church, scooted in on the back row, joined in the worship and praise, then slipped out as soon as the service was over. I was always in a hurry to get back to the peace and quiet of the country.

Who would have thought that one day I would sit beside the man under whose teaching I was being silently nourished!

God spoke to me again a few months later. I was working between semesters for an interior decorator, Shirley

Meeks, who also attended TCF. When Bill contacted Shirley to have an antique loveseat re-upholstered, I went with her to his home to help select a fabric. As the three of us talked, I clearly heard the Lord say, "*He* is the special work I have for you."

He? The pastor? My heart skipped a beat then began to pound wildly. I wanted to run out of the room. Silently, I cried, "Lord, you've got the wrong woman! This is a big mistake!" Bill and Shirley were sitting across from me, calmly discussing colors and textures. They had no idea that something of frightening importance had just occurred in my heart. I sat still, in agony. I couldn't wait for the meeting to end.

I steered clear of Bill over the next few weeks and months. If God meant for us to be together, I figured, He was perfectly capable of speaking to Bill as He had to me. I had no intention of helping Him out.

Of course, help from me was not what God needed. At a Christmas party that December, Bill "noticed" me. A few days later, he called me and we had lunch together. After that, we saw each other many more times. There was no denying it: something was there.

But how could it work? I kept asking myself. Even if my three children accepted Bill and his five accepted me—by no means a sure thing—how would the congregation react? Besides, was I ready, or even able, to jump from my serene country existence into the midst of a busy pastor's life?

In the end, I knew I was just going to have to trust the Lord and find out. Bill loved me and I loved him. We were married the following September.

To my great relief, most of my fears proved groundless. In fact, coming into the ministry as "number two'' has been a relatively smooth transition for me. The bumps and rocks I expected to find along the road have been very few.

Why is this? Several reasons, I think. Having sat under Bill's teaching and preaching for several years, I knew what he believed about family headship and authority, submission, and the discipline of children. From my place in the congregation, I saw how he related to his first wife. I saw how his children loved and respected him. I remember thinking once, before Bill and I started dating, It takes a man who "walks his talk" to command that kind of love and respect from teenagers!

Our children were with us all the way. All eight were happy and excited about our courtship and marriage. I think if I had felt opposition from any one of them, I would have backed off. But only positive words were spoken.

As a couple, Bill and I fasted and prayed about our relationship, wanting to be certain that we were doing what God wanted for both of us. Right up to the day of the wedding, we held the relationship with open hands, saying, "Lord, if this is not Your desire, we are willing to give it up."

I knew I could not expect to replace Marty. I told Bill and the children that I would never try; what I *would* do was love and care for them to the best of my God-given ability. This not only assured them, it released me from the potential bondage of always trying to fill someone else's shoes.

Once a pastor from another church told us that he would never be able to remarry without having his congregation fall apart. Bill and I were surprised at his statement. From the very beginning, we submitted our relationship to the other pastors and elders at TCF and had their full support. Even Marty's best friend, JoAnn Farah, the wife of our associate pastor, Chuck Farah, encouraged us (she has since gone to join Marty with the Lord).

That kind of enthusiasm permeated the church, although there were a few people who thought Bill should remain single. Some felt he was "hurrying" things, that he should wait at least five years before he even looked at another woman. In the end, a small number left the church after his remarriage. But the vast majority of the congregation loved us and rejoiced with us—they even gave us a reception when we returned from our honeymoon.

My life changed drastically after I married Bill. Before the wedding, I had been living in a spacious country home, directing most of my time and energy toward maintaining the house and the yard. My free time was spent floating lazily in our swimming pool. I remember thinking this couldn't be how God wanted me to live out my days. It wasn't.

I moved into Bill's bungalow, which bustled with busy teenagers and an energetic 11-year-old—not to mention a much-in-demand pastor. Telephones rang off the hook and the door-bell chimed constantly.

"It's easy to be an angel when no one ruffles your feathers," I once read on a poster which featured a photograph of a serene white swan floating on a placid lake. Well, there were a lot of feather-rufflers in my new house. As I tried to meet the needs of eight children, each with his or her own unique temperament and personality, as well as the needs of my busy husband and his ministry, the Lord showed me I was not quite the angel I thought I was.

It didn't take me long to realize that I couldn't handle my new, large family in my own strength. I've always believed that God is merciful—He never calls us to a task that He will not give us grace to do. In those early days, however, I couldn't help but wonder if He had overestimated my ability! I can still visualize the mountains of laundry that used to appear like magic each week on the laundry room floor. Sometimes I imagined that some sort of malevolent machine upstairs was churning out dirty clothes, emitting a sinister chuckle with each grease-stained shirt or smelly sock.

I knew from the beginning that my primary calling was to be a helpmeet to Bill. He certainly needed one. Still, we *did* have to spend some time dispelling some of the misconceptions I had about my role as a pastor's wife. For one, I was not Marty Sanders—to Bill or to the congregation. I was Ann Sanders—a totally different person. When Bill asked me to marry him, my reply had been, "How can I? I don't play the piano and my voice is off-key when I make a 'joyful noise.' "

"Where does it say in God's Word that a pastor's wife must play the piano and have a beautiful voice?" he asked.

Of course, I couldn't find the proof text. And eventually I realized that all my new role called for was this: to love the Lord with my whole heart and my husband as myself, and to be willing to do whatever God calls Bill and me to do. Everything else was only stereotype or tradition—molds made by man, not God. My goal became simply to "walk in a manner worthy of the calling with which you have been called, with all humility and gentleness, diligent to preserve the unity of the Spirit in the bond of peace'' (Ephes. 4:1-3).

Sometimes Bill asked me to help him with team counseling. I was willing, but inexperienced. At first I mostly listened, trying to learn from my husband's example. I was always amazed at the patience with which Bill would listen to troubled people as they poured out their souls. When they were done, he always had a few words of wisdom for them. We'd pray, and they'd leave with their burdens lifted and spirits encouraged.

As the years have passed, I've become more and more involved in this kind of helping. As the children have grown up, I've had more time. I've never pushed for a ministry role, however. I've let this aspect of my life unfold as God has enabled me, or as the need has become evident.

The first Bible study I ever held in my home came about because the need was presented to me. A young woman from the church appeared on my doorstep one day and said, "Ann, I'm part of a group of young women who need an older woman to teach us how to be the helpmeet God's called us to be." After realizing with a start that *I* was the "older woman," I agreed to do what I could.

Today, I minister in many ways. Hospitality is one of these. This was not a "natural" gift for me, but as in other things, God has taught me over time to open up my home with joy to serve those He sends. I also go with Bill to make hospital calls and to pray for the sick and dying. I get involved with premarital counseling and help at the wedding rehearsals. Sometimes I speak before various groups—a difficult task that I'm finding a little easier each time.

Looking back, I can see how God has prepared me,

step by step, for the life I now lead. I can more fully understand the apostle Paul when he wrote, "And we know that God causes all things to work together for good to those who love God, to those who are called according to His purpose" (Rom. 8:28, NAS).

God had this "special work" planned for me all along. And, somehow, there's nothing I'd rather be doing.

Born in Eldon, Missouri, in 1935, **Ann Sanders** grew up with two brothers on a small dairy farm. Her mother became a Christian when Ann was 8. Her father did not accept the Lord until he was in his 60s.

Ann's first husband, her high school sweetheart, died in 1971 in a fire at their family business. She remarried in 1978. Her second husband, Bill, was her pastor for five years and a widower. Bill continues as the founder and senior pastor of Tulsa Christian Fellowship in Tulsa, Oklahoma.

Ann has three children from her first marriage and five "inherited" children from her second. Together, the Sanderses have 16 grandchildren.

Ann is president of two corporations started by her first husband and operated by two of their sons. She also initiated a "Titus 2:4" ministry to young wives and mothers at Tulsa Christian Fellowship.

Chapter Eleven
I Didn't Marry a Minister

by Anne (Mrs. Harry) Elver

I had just finished speaking to a ladies' church group.
As I headed out the door, I felt a hand on my arm. I
looked up at a petite woman, a few years older than
me, with salt and pepper hair.

"Your husband left a good career to become a
minister," she said. "That's great, but my husband
would never do such a thing."

"Don't be too sure," I laughed. "Harry and I thought
the same way once. And look where we are today."

She smiled sadly and walked away. I think she really
envied me.

No, I didn't marry a minister. But now I'm a pastor's
wife. And a happy one.

Why did Harry enter the ministry, forsaking his first
career to do so? Like most decisions, it didn't happen
all at once. It was a series of events that led up to the
change. In 1970, a corporation purchased the local

125

shipyard where Harry worked. A management shift followed, producing considerable stress and discord as faithful workers were fired one by one. Harry stayed on, but this increasing pressure made him feel that a job change would be welcome.

The next year, Harry and I both rededicated our lives to the Lord. We began ministering to children in our church and holding a children's Bible study in our community, too. We enjoyed working with youngsters. At the same time, we often thought that extending our ministry to other age groups would be rewarding; we just lacked the opportunity to do so.

The children's work—plus the pressure at Harry's job—combined to prepare us to say yes when the Lord called my husband to enter a small Bible school in 1973. After earning his diploma in 1975, Harry went on to get a college education over the next four years. His seminary work followed next, with graduation in 1985. He is now serving his first non-student church—and I am a full-fledged pastor's wife.

My role as a second career pastor's wife isn't unusual. My peers in this situation are numerous. Recent statistics from Phillips University Seminary where Harry attended reveal that the average entrance age to the school is 35, and this is true of other religious institutions as well, according to the Association of Theological Seminaries. Surely most of these 35-year-olds had earlier careers!

Of course, a husband's ministry always affects his wife, and second-career pastors' wives are no exception. But I do believe the joys and difficulties of being married to a pastor are doubled for me, since I have known life as both a pastor's and a layman's wife.

I lived a reasonably settled life before Harry's career

change. Afterwards, however, life became much more jumbled and hectic, especially during his many years of training for the pastorate. Our denomination encourages pastors to have seminary degrees, and while they are not absolutely required, a pastor lacking one is sometimes professionally handicapped. Harry and I felt he should obtain full educational credentials *especially* since he was entering the ministry as a second career. He would never have time to build the kind of seniority that another man his age would have already built in our denominational structure. He needed every advantage he could get.

I learned early in Harry's schooling that when he was preoccupied with studies, papers or exams, he would get a bit edgy, and I had to assume that it wasn't anything personal if he was moody. In this sense, it was a good thing we had been married for a number of years! I'm sure having a tense spouse would have troubled me much more in the earlier years of marriage. And our social life suffered when Harry was a student; there just wasn't time in his busy schedule to go out. Fortunately, I had memories of more relaxed years to sustain me when the pressures of his schooling climbed. I knew the situation was temporary and could handle it with relative ease.

Harry's studies forced us to move more frequently than I would have liked. Just when I felt at home in a community, we moved. Sometimes this disrupted professional contacts for me that I relished. Also, it was hard for me to help our children adjust to new homes during their teen years. I've known the sadness of leaving loved friends behind many times over.

Frequent moves because of his educational needs also

affected our student ministry. Our churches all knew we would not have a long time with them. This prevented people from forming deep attachments to us. For our part, we were never in one place long enough to see the fruit of God's work through us. Thankfully, ongoing contacts with individuals in our past churches have shown us that we do have lasting fruit in these former pastorates, but it was hard being seed-planters who didn't get to see the crop come in.

In spite of these hardships, Harry's training was not without its blessings. Moving a lot taught me to be content where I am, living one day at a time. It also taught me to reach out to others, to initiate friendships. This lesson was important for me; my introverted nature has received a needed polishing in this area. Moving as often and as far as we have has exposed me to a wide variety of people, churches and communities which has given me an appreciation for the body of Christ at large that I don't think I would have attained otherwise. I might have missed these valuable lessons if I hadn't supported my husband's desire to further his education at a time in life when most men have long finished theirs.

Harry's education benefitted me, too, even though I didn't realize it at the time. Whenever his classes covered a subject I was interested in, I made trips to the libraries to research the topic, just for my own enrichment. Harry enjoyed having me read his textbooks, and he always let me read his papers before he handed them in. I also got to see them after his teachers graded them. I listened to a young seminary wife once as she complained about being home with a baby, stagnating while her hubby was in school being fed intellectually. Listening to her reminded me of how thankful

I was to be a second-career pastor's wife. By the time Harry was a student, my children were in school and I was free to satisfy my curiosity about Harry's studies, go to campus with him to use the library, and read his notes, papers and textbooks. All that has blessed my life as well.

The research I did on my own while my husband was a student forced me to develop skills which are helpful to me now. Today I have a ministry of my own as a writer which I might not have cultivated otherwise. After Harry had been a student for several years, he said I was almost as familiar with his field of study as he was. When I completed my college education later, I was able to use my "second hand studies" in obtaining credit via aptitude testing—one of the greatest rewards of those years as the wife of a pastor-in-training.

Fortunately, my personality, interests and self-identity were well established by the time Harry entered the ministry. This has helped me as I have faced others' unrealistic or tradition-bound expectations of what I should be or do because I am the pastor's wife. For example, in one church, the choir director called on me the day we moved into the parsonage. She informed me that choir practice was that night, and since every pastor's wife before me sang in the choir, I was expected to be there. I thanked her for the opportunity but declined the invitation.

Much to my surprise, the invitation to join the choir was extended again the next week. Once more, I declined. The third time, the director made the invitation in my husband's presence, asking him to tell me to attend choir practice. Harry informed the woman that singing was not one of my gifts nor interests, and that no amount of pressure to turn me into a choir member would work! I've pitied my younger parsonage peers who report yielding to expectations like this against their wishes. The difference between us, I think, is the self-knowledge I brought into my role, borne of age and experience.

Experience before Harry became a pastor also confirmed many of my spiritual gifts, and this has been a tremendous help to me in our new career. Teaching is one of my gifts, and I can easily make room for this talent in our churches. I volunteer for teaching before I am asked, knowing I can function in this way. I've listened to younger pastors' wives tell of becoming overextended when they first enter church work as a minister's mate. But the second-career pastor's wife brings confidence and life experience into her first parsonage, and this has been a blessing to us.

A pastor's wife who is willing can have many opportunities to minister that may not come to the layman's wife. As a second-career pastor's wife with a heart for ministry, I appreciate this fact deeply. I love it when someone calls for Harry and, if he is unavailable, they accept my offer of help. Our people are thankful for my willingness to assist them in emergencies until Harry is available. Once a church lady introduced me as her minister-in-marriage. I didn't mind a bit! I've listened to people's needs, prayed with them and given encouragement many times over. Harry even includes me in premarital counseling sessions. He feels my presence and input add a feminine dimension that enriches the discussions. And several women have told me they like having another woman to talk to about personal matters.

Still, the frustrations are there. As a pastor's wife,

I lack the control over my life that I once enjoyed when I was married to a layman. This shows up in several areas.

For example, finances. Harry's first career paid well. Budgeting as carefully as I must do now just wasn't necessary. I've had to learn to shop only after praying for wisdom! Harry's educational loan payments are difficult, and it troubles me that our retirement benefits border on being inadequate. It is also nerve-wrenching for both of us when his salary and benefits come up for review, since our church structure forces the pastor to be his own champion as far as raises and benefits go. On top of all this, when my children were still at home, I sensed that they sometimes resented seeing their peers with things they did without—a hard realization for a mother who wants the best for her children.

Once I shared just how many items of clothing I had bought for a certain sum of money as a testimony during a ladies' Bible study I led at our church. One woman, Velma, spoke up and said, "It amazes me to see how you manage so well on the salary we pay. When Harry preaches on stewardship, I listen carefully. You two really do seem blessed by the Lord in having your needs met." Velma's words almost floored me. It might aggravate me to have a small budget, but I try to control these feelings. People do notice if a pastor's spouse is blessed and contented with her material status! And a contented spouse who manages finances well is a strong witness to the consistency of her husband's words and life.

Our housing situation is another factor over which I have less control than I used to. We are supposed to be provided with a furnished house, but parsonages in our denomination vary greatly in size, age and condition, and are often furnished with donations from members—in other words, furniture placed in the parsonage rather than discarded. I am actually grateful that none of the churches we've pastored so far has furnished our parsonages as they should! If my fellow pastors' wives don't complain of worn, mismatched parsonage furniture, their next complaint is of inadequate furnishings. Happily, Harry and I have been able to keep and use most of the furniture we chose for ourselves when we owned our own home.

Two problems still arise, however. For one, our moving allowances from denominationally initiated moves aren't sufficient to cover a complete household shift, which includes all our own furniture. Harry and I have a great task when we move; we do the work ourselves and end up paying part of the cost for rental trucks and equipment. Second, I am often frustrated in trying to place my furniture, chosen for a specific home, into rooms that are either too large or too small to fit them.

Of course, the parsonage system isn't all frustration. The challenge of turning a cold, impersonal dwelling into a home that reveals our family's personality compensates somewhat for the lack of control over my housing that I miss. In addition, parsonage living has extended my witness to our congregations. Past home ownership taught Harry and me handyman skills that allow us to maintain and improve our parsonages ourselves. Harry and I have left every parsonage we've occupied in better shape than we found it on moving day, and this satisfies me deeply. I have sensed the pleasure and pride of our people when they see how we improve their property. This, too, is part of our ministry to the flock.

Over the years, I've found the public nature of the pastor's profession to be both a hardship and a blessing. In Harry's first career, he had clearly defined hours, a specified workplace. His job was a regulated part of our lives. The ministry is nothing like that! Since none of our churches has had a church office, much of Harry's work has been done at home. This has produced constantly ringing telephones and doorbells, which I have sometimes resented.

On the other hand, I have heard many women complain because they don't have their husband around the house during the day. Seldom do I worry, like I used to, about getting someone to accept United Parcel deliveries when I am out. I never worry about being home to let a repairman in. And when my children were sick, needed something brought to school or had an errand for me to do, Harry's presence at home was a lifesaver.

On occasion, I do hear parishioners criticize my husband, and this hurts me. I was never exposed to such things with Harry's first, much less public career! But on the plus side, people do keep up with their pastors and are most helpful when they sense our needs. When I was ill, our congregation prayed for me, brought food for my family, offered to help and expressed their love in many tangible ways. There have been unexpected birthday, anniversary and Christmas presents from our people that make me realize just how blessed I am to be the object of their love and esteem. Harry's first employer wasn't a bad one to work for, but the company never had these "spouse benefits"!

Being a pastor's wife has also doubled my joy in my

family. People share with me from time to time the victories they have experienced in the Lord as a result of Harry's ministry. How happy that makes me, and how proud of my husband! One time my friend Vicki called and asked if I knew what the congregation was saying about my son. "I can't imagine," I said, bracing myself. "What?"

"They're talking about how he found that $10 bill in the school trash can and returned it to the owner," Vicki announced. "His honesty and character reflect well on you, and I wanted to let you hear it," she added. My maternal pride, love for my friend and pleasure at receiving such a telephone call about one of my children had never been greater!

An unanticipated blessing has been the closer bond Harry and I have experienced in our marriage. I love it when he comes out of his office at home and with a sly grin asks, "Would you like lunch out with someone who loves you?" Often I accompany him on pastoral duties just so we can talk in the car without the interruption of the telephone or the doorbell. Our marriage was good before he became a pastor, but being in the ministry has united us even more, and the freedom to control our time has allowed us to cultivate our relationship in all areas.

The abstract, unquantifiable results of pastoring can sometimes discourage Harry, as it does most pastors. This is hard for me to handle. In his first job, he was able to see a ship taking shape. The areas he supervised and later inspected at each step of the way kept him going. But the minister must often plant seeds which don't grow quickly.

A man recently left our church. He told Harry he

realized every pastor was different and that these differences aren't character faults, but he didn't care for
his style of preaching. I sensed my husband's disappoint-
ment and tried to comfort him. "No one pleases
everyone all the time. It's not personal," I told him.

Harry accepted my words, and I hope I helped him.
But on the heart level, I grieved just as deeply as he
did. It's difficult for me to remain emotionally objec-
tive to happenings in the church when my husband's
self-esteem is involved. And knowing that Harry's time
in the ministry before retirement will be shorter than
a first-career pastor's, I long for him to see fruit—
perhaps quicker than it usually develops.

Just the other day, someone asked me if I would give
Harry my blessing if he had to re-make the decision to
enter the ministry. I quickly said, "Yes!" I think most
second-career pastors' wives would agree. Wives in my
position have known another life, and the frustrations
of the ministry may occasionally tempt us to look back.
I have certainly had to fight this from time to time. But
I have resolved to use the personal assets I brought into
the ministry as fully as I can, while letting my position
as pastor's wife polish my character in needy areas. The
annoyances of my role aren't without redeeming value,
and the joys don't show up often enough to make the
position of "pastor's wife" an idol or pedestal for me.

Having experienced life before the ministry, I know
I appreciate its blessings all the more. I may not have
married a minister, but I thank God I'm a pastor's wife!

Anne Elver was born in 1942 in Newport News, Virginia, and was raised in a Christian home. She met her husband, Harry, while both were in high school. They were married in 1960.

Pastoring is a second career for Harry, who was a middle manager in the shipbuilding industry for more than 15 years before he resigned to attend Bible school. He is pastor of the United Methodist Church of the Good Shepherd in Yukon, Oklahoma.

A non-traditional adult student for many years, Anne is working toward a degree in adult education, with the goal of teaching at the junior college level. She has been a free-lance writer since 1980 and is also a speaker, teacher and workshop leader for pastors, their families and those interested in non-traditional adult education.

The Elvers have three children, ages 25, 22 and 19.

Chapter Twelve
Encouraging Your Man

by Betty (Mrs. Fred) Price

The primary ministry of the pastor's wife is that of encouragement. She may have many callings. She may be a mother, the church accountant, the choir director, a prophet, a teacher or even an evangelist. But she has no greater ministry than that of being an encourager to the man of God she married.

Pastors are human—just ask their wives! They have their times of weakness, doubt and discouragement, just like other men. Their jobs are not easy. On a daily basis, they deal with hostile critics, chronic complainers, ambivalent leaders and a host of other people and problems—not to mention the devil himself. No wonder pastors sometimes feel like throwing in the towel.

But they don't (usually). They allow God to minister encouragement to them, and they are revived. How does He do this? Three ways: through the Word of God, the Holy Spirit and the pastor's wife.

Fred and I were married on March 29, 1953. Within two months, he became a Christian and felt a clear call to the ministry. That's when my own ministry of encouragement began.

We joined a Baptist church near our home. Fred worked a full-time job and spent most of his free time studying the Bible, memorizing scriptures and attending services. He joined a young ministers' class. He was serious about becoming a minister and devoted himself to learning everything he could about his new faith.

I had grown up loving God and was excited about Fred's plans to enter the ministry. Unfortunately, neither his parents nor my parents shared that excitement. They offered no help or encouragement. My support and Fred's own determination filled in the gap.

Within two years, Fred was hired as the assistant pastor of our church. He didn't last long. A little over a year later, he was fired because he refused to go along with certain practices he believed were unscriptural.

The ministry was gone—and so was our income. By that time, we had two more mouths to feed, 3-year-old Frederick III and 3-month-old Angela. We tried not to despair.

"Everything will work out if we remain true to God," I told Fred. He was encouraged.

I decided to find a job and work until Fred could come up with a job of his own. With the help of another pastor's wife, I was hired at the Internal Revenue Service. The pay was minimal, but it gave us breathing room and helped put food on the table.

Soon, Fred found a secular job. But his heart was bent toward the ministry. When we joined the African Methodist Episcopal Church and Fred was offered a pastorate, he took it—even though the congregation had fewer than a dozen members and the salary was no more than $5 a week. For two years, from September 1957 to August 1959, he ministered to the tiny church, keeping his full-time secular job to pay the bills.

Then came the vote for a new bishop, an exercise the African Methodists go through every four years. The leadership of the denomination voted one way, Fred voted another. That September, he found himself without a pastorate.

Once again, I encouraged Fred to remain true to God. I was sure that was the key to get us through the rough times.

We joined the Presbyterian Church. Fred went back to school to get the education required to be a minister in our new denomination. This time, I was discouraged. I was tired of all the constant change, the moving from church-to-church and job-to- job. I never expressed this to Fred, however. I knew he was earnestly seeking to find the place in which God wanted him to serve. He needed my support. I determined to speak only positive words.

I wasn't always successful. Our financial struggle grated on me. We scraped to get our basic needs met and never had any money left over for "extras." I knew this was due in part to Fred's frequent job changes. He couldn't help that—he was following the Lord. But he also had a tendency to make unwise purchases—buying the right thing at the wrong time.

One day, I reached my limit. Fred told me, "I'm doing the best I can!" I shot back, "Your best just isn't good enough!"

He was shocked. Up to that day, I had never complained. That one statement caught his attention. Nothing more needed to be said. He became more sensitive to my needs and began to change some of his spending habits. Still, money was tight.

There were times when the pressure and finances wound me in such a knot that I did not feel like being intimate with Fred. Instead of being relaxed and open with him, I was overcome with worry. Where would we get the money to put food on the table and clothes on the children? How would we pay the bills? I fought against my preoccupation. I knew that sex was important to marriage and that by giving myself freely to my husband I could encourage and strengthen him. I asked God to help keep the pressures I was feeling from affecting our sexual relationship. He answered, and our sex life did not suffer.

It was during these difficult times that we were struck by tragedy. On his way home from school, our only son, Frederick, was hit by an automobile and killed. He was just eight years old. Suddenly, all the struggles we had gone through up to that point were insignificant. Our only son, dead. We were overwhelmed with grief and tried to comfort one another as best we could. Fred was devastated, but he refused to believe that *God* had taken his boy. Even though he did not fully understand about the ways of the enemy, he sensed that Frederick's accident was an attack. I agreed and encouraged him to go on.

I begged him to let me get a job so I could help with the bills. He was hesitant. His mother had worked when he was a child. So had his friends' mothers. With no supervision at home, the kids had all gotten into trouble. He didn't want that for his two daughters—Angela and Cheryl (Stephanie and "little Fred" would come along later).

Finally, I convinced him that our situation would be different—I would arrange for good child care while I was working. He consented, but only half-heartedly.

Employment was not the panacea I had expected it to be, however. The money pressures I had wanted to alleviate were quickly replaced by other, less tangible pressures even more difficult to deal with. I worked— at home or on the job— from 5 a.m. to 10 p.m. But I was no super-woman. After one year and nine months, I quit the job and vowed never to work again.

For over five years, while working a full-time job, Fred ministered on and off as a preacher, going by invitation from one church to another. He was discouraged that he was not able to function in full-time ministry or respond to the call he felt upon his life to be an evangelist.

In 1965, a friend called to say that he was leaving his pastorate to go into full-time ministry with the Billy Graham organization. He wanted Fred to take over for him as pastor. Fred hesitated at first. This was not the evangelist role he had been envisioning. He prayed fervently over his decision.

I encouraged him to take the job. In my heart I felt he was a pastor. He needed that kind of consistent ministry. Finally, he decided to give it a try.

"If it is of God, it will work. If it's not, it won't work," he said.

In June 1965, Fred became pastor of the West Washington Community Church, a congregation of the Christian and Missionary Alliance. There were nine members. Fred still had to work another full-time job—

his salary at the church was only $35 a week. Soon, though, the little group began to grow. By 1969, there were 125 members. Fred was offered a new salary which allowed him to pastor full-time.

I was excited. Now that Fred would no longer need to divide his time between secular employment and the ministry, I was sure we would begin to see the church really move. We had so many ideas. We couldn't wait to get out into the neighborhoods and knock on doors to invite everyone to church.

But something was wrong with Fred. For the first time in his ministry, he was a full-time pastor. He had both the time and the resources to serve God the way he had always wanted. Yet he was unhappy and disturbed.

That Christmas he had read Kathryn Kuhlman's book *God Can Do It Again*. It left him restless in spirit. He didn't fully understand why.

"There's something missing in our prayer meetings at the church. It's like a casserole dish with something left out," he said.

He attended a couple of Kathryn Kuhlman meetings. His restlessness and hunger grew more intense. In the past, Fred had had a strong interest in the supernatural. I had discouraged him, however. I was afraid he would stray from God into the occult. But this time I felt he was going in the right direction. Even though I understood nothing about the Spirit-filled life, I encouraged him.

At one of the Kuhlman meetings, Fred ran into a chaplain friend. The chaplain invited him to lunch and gave him a book about the Holy Spirit. Fred raced through the book and concluded that the Holy Spirit was the missing ingredient in his life and ministry.

He became more frustrated than ever. He knew he needed to be filled with the Holy Spirit, but he didn't know how to make that happen. He stood in the pulpit the next Sunday and cried.

''If I don't receive the Holy Spirit, I will stop preaching!'' he told the congregation.

That became his only thought: to receive the Holy Spirit. For two months, while he agonized and searched and prayed, I took over many of the things at home and in the church that were normally his duties. One night, several ministers came to dinner at our invitation. Fred was so preoccupied that he forgot to show up. I entertained as best I could until they decided to go home.

Finally, the breakthrough came. Fred was filled with the Holy Spirit and spoke in other tongues. He came home and laid his hands on me. Immediately, I, too, was filled with the Holy Spirit and began to speak in an unknown language.

I had never seen Fred so excited about anything. He shared his experience with the congregation. About 80 percent were filled with the Holy Spirit. Our church life, our home life, our entire life took on a new dimension. Most of Fred's friends—other denominational ministers—rejected his testimony and criticized him. But we stood together, and our church supported us.

Soon we were cramming 300 people into a church building designed to fit 158. Fred continued to increase in his knowledge of the Word and the power of the Spirit. The same chaplain who had given him his first book about the Holy Spirit gave him some books by Kenneth Hagin on faith, prayer and healing. These, too, became keys to ministry for Fred.

People of every race poured into our church. Calls

came from all across Southern California to invite Fred to minister. More people than we had ever realized were hungry for the Holy Spirit.

We decided to believe God for a bigger building. By faith we received it—a church with seating for 1,400. In 1973 we moved in with 300 people and changed our name to Crenshaw Christian Center. Our offerings for the first eight months were never big enough to make the payments on our loan, but we trusted God and somehow the money was always there.

By the end of 1975, we had filled the sanctuary. By 1977, the walls were bursting. Over 4,000 people were coming to two services. We used overflow facilities but still did not have enough room for everyone.

We found a 23-acre lot in Inglewood, the only vacant land in the Los Angeles area that was spacious enough to build our dream—a 10,000-seat auditorium. The church board voted to put $100,000 down on the property. But before the deal could be closed, the city passed a law prohibiting a church from building on more than three acres. The down payment was lost.

"I think I will ask the board members to stand with me, since they voted to make the down payment," Fred said, when it was time to tell the congregation the news.

"But, Fred, if you had a positive announcement to make, you would make it alone," I reasoned. "You should make this announcement alone, too." He agreed.

Soon we were thinking ahead to new property. We learned that the 32-acre Los Angeles campus of Pepperdine University was up for sale. It had been on the market for two years with no takers. When we approached the sellers, they agreed to give it to us for $14 million. They even offered to work with us on the financing. It was a gift from God.

We purchased the property in 1980 and moved onto the campus in September 1984. Today, over 5,000 people come to three Sunday services, and we have broken ground on our 10,000-seat sanctuary.

I still encourage Fred. He doesn't need me so much to remind him of God's Word or lift his faith. He has grown in these areas and has learned to depend on the Holy Spirit in difficult times. But he is so busy—he pours himself out to so many—that he becomes physically tired. Then I encourage him.

I pray constantly that God will help Fred discern between the good and the bad. Many people have wanted to attach themselves to our ministry, but not all have had the right spirit or motivation. Fred has not always been able to see this. I continue to ask God to protect him from any voice or spirit that is not right and to surround him with the good people he needs to help him fulfill his calling.

Always, I stand beside him and support him. As the ministry has grown, I've stepped out of my background role and have begun to assist Fred "up front"—by participating in decision-making and counseling, leading the women's fellowship, and answering personal letters and phone calls.

In all of these ways and more, I encourage Fred. This is my ministry. God has called me to it—just as He has called other pastors' wives. We may have other ministries, too. But to me, nothing is more important than encouraging my man of God.

Betty Price was born in 1934 in Gloster, Mississippi, one of 11 children. Although the family was poor, Betty's parents were Christians and raised their children in an atmosphere of love and faith.

Betty met her husband, Fred, in high school and married him in 1953. He is pastor of the Crenshaw Christian Center in Los Angeles, California. He is also a well-known TV preacher and convention speaker.

As the center's "pastoral assistant," Betty oversees the ministries for both married and single women who work in and out of the home. She also travels frequently with her husband.

The Prices have three daughters, ages 29, 26 and 18, and a son, age 7. Another son died as a young boy. All three daughters are employed with their parents' ministry.

There are two grandchildren.

Chapter Thirteen
Healing the Wounded Heart

by Jackie (Mrs. Jamie) Buckingham

It was a Sunday evening during the time of ministry at the altar in our church in Melbourne, Florida. Jamie had been preaching and at the close of his message had invited those who needed ministry to come forward. I saw a young woman come and kneel, and I slipped in beside her. She turned her head, looked in my eyes and said, "I have a broken heart. Would you pray for me?"

Even as I prayed for her, I breathed a sigh of thanksgiving to the Lord for what He has done in my life. My heart, too, had been broken once. But I have been healed, and now I am able to look back and praise God for what I have been through. The healing of my own broken heart has allowed me to understand and help others who have the same problem.

The young woman, sensing I did understand, began pouring out her heart. She had been hurt, deeply hurt. Even as I listened, I remembered.

All I ever wanted in life was to be Jamie's wife. We began dating when I was a sophomore in high school. Both of us had been born in the same little Florida town of Vero Beach. He was a year older, a high school athletic hero and class leader. We dated steadily through high school. On our third date, I knew he was the one I wanted to live with for the rest of my life.

Jamie's parents worked actively to keep us apart. They encouraged him to attend Mercer University, a Baptist college in Macon, Georgia, many miles from home. When he left for school he promised to write me every day. (He now jokes that that was the start of his writing career—complete with deadlines.) He also gave me an engagement ring. However, his father, fearing early marriage, convinced me to hold off wearing it until Jamie finished his freshman year.

I was finally able to follow him to Mercer. In time, his parents came to accept me but wisely encouraged us to hold off the wedding until Jamie graduated. We were married one week after the graduation ceremony. It was like a fairy tale for me as we drove off into the sunset to live happily ever after.

Those early years were tough—but wonderful. We moved to Ft. Worth so Jamie could enter Southwestern Baptist Seminary and I could finish my senior year in college at Texas Christian University. He had no specific goals. He knew he was called into "full-time" ministry but had no idea where that should be or in what capacity. I had already achieved my goal—to be Jamie's wife.

Jamie worked long hours—early morning and late night—driving a city bus. The rest of the time he was attending class or studying in the library. We had close friends who, like us, had virtually no money. George and Betty Deadwyler, Bob and Betty Baggott—former college classmates who lived on our block—were also in seminary. They were our "extended family." No one had a TV and usually someone's car was broken, so we shared automobiles and food and helped each other out when one of us would run out of money. We all had children the same age, so we also shared baby food and diapers.

Jamie's future as a Southern Baptist pastor and leader seemed bright. My infatuation and love were all tied together in one package. My heart was full, my dreams fulfilled. I had no idea of the heartbreak I was about to go through.

Jamie was success-oriented—determined to reach the top of the ecclesiastical ladder. Everything seemed to fall into place. We left the seminary and moved to Greenwood, South Carolina, where Jamie was called to pastor the South Main Street Baptist Church, one of the larger churches in the state. At 26 years of age, he was moving toward the top—rapidly.

Those were busy days. By then we had four children, and a fifth on the way. Jamie was deeply involved in church activities. We both know now that it is impossible to do God's work without God's power. Then, however, it was a matter of "leaning on our own understanding." The result was tragic. Although the church was thriving, Jamie gradually grew away from me. A vacuum was created—a perfect setting for an affair.

We've learned a lot of things since then. We know that ministers are no less susceptible to the surging drive of sex and passion than anyone else. If anything, they are more susceptible. They're exposed to every kind of emotional and spiritual sickness. Those who come for help are reaching out for love and empathy. Jamie has a strong mercy gift. He enjoys touching with compassion. But like any gift, this one can get you into big trouble. It did with him.

It started when my closest friend, the wife of one of our church leaders, told Jamie she was "in love" with him. He couldn't handle it. Instead of confiding in me, he relished their "relationship" and let it grow. In a matter of weeks, it was a full-blown affair.

The sordid relationship lasted for more than two years. I knew something was wrong but was not sure what it was. I began to pick up on the signals being passed between my husband and the other woman. I tried to back off—no more dinners together with this family, no more socializing, no more vacations with her along. Jamie insisted we keep them as friends. Her husband seemed oblivious to any wrongdoing and I had no positive proof, but my woman's intuition was working overtime.

I pleaded with Jamie to tell me the truth. "I can handle it," I wept. Instead of leveling with me, however, he lied. He knew that the truth would end the affair. It's something Jamie has taught on many times since—that all adulterers are also liars. They lie to their wives, to their partners, to the world, to themselves and to God.

It was too much for Jamie. No man can ride three wild horses at once and retain his balance when they are all going in different directions. Jamie was being torn apart as he tried to ride marriage, ministry and mistress. He broke off one illicit relationship only to find himself sucked into another. He was as addicted as a man on drugs or alcohol. Our home was a battlefield. My heart was broken.

In the end Jamie was discovered. He was exposed

because God wanted him exposed. The board of deacons, which was the controlling element in the church, demanded his resignation. We were given three months' salary and three months' use of the parsonage. We were not welcome back in the church. As painful as it was, however, I somehow believed God was in this surgery. It was his way of amputating the cancer.

Jamie has covered much of the detail of what followed in two of his books—*Risky Living* and *Where Eagles Soar*, so I will not do it here. We moved back to Florida, just a few miles from home, and started all over.

Things were tough. We had been on top. Now we were on the bottom. But healing had begun. Within a short period of time—on a trip to Washington, D.C., where he was researching his first book, *Run Baby, Run*—Jamie received the baptism in the Holy Spirit. The night before he came home, he called me, weeping. He told me he loved me. For the first time in many years, I sensed he was telling the truth.

The following night we sat up until dawn, talking. Jamie opened his life to everything he had done—and everything he had been planning to do. He told it all— the lies, the deception, the immorality. It hurt. It hurt deeply. But I had told him all along the lies were more hurtful than the action of his sin. All I wanted from him was the truth. I knew I could forgive—but not unless he confessed. When he did open up, the pain was intense for both of us. But it was the hurt of a lanced boil. It was the hurt of healing.

Jamie kept asking me if I wanted details. I didn't need them. Not any more. All I had wanted was my husband. It was as though Jamie had given me the firing pin of a grenade and said, ''You hold it. You can blow me up at any time if you want to, but you need to know everything about me. I know the risk I am running in telling you everything, but I will never again let anything come into our lives that I cannot share with you. Not anything.'' When he said it I didn't need to hear more. My husband had come home.

I knew Jamie was a changed man. I wanted what he had. After all, the problem had not been all his. My reaction to his sin had been as bad as his sin. I was filled with resentment, bitterness, fear and a sense of unworthiness. I asked Jamie to lay hands on me that I might also receive the Holy Spirit. He said he didn't know how—that I would have to receive as he did, by asking God.

Day after day I got in the car and went to people in the community I knew to be Spirit-filled. Many of them prayed for me but nothing happened. I read the copies of *Voice* magazine Jamie had brought home from the Full Gospel Business Men's Convention he attended in Washington, but I couldn't identify with any of the testimonies. I got on my knees and begged Jesus to baptize me in His Holy Spirit. Nothing. Yet as I read the Bible, it was alive as never before. I had never noticed all those stories of miracles, deliverance from demons and the marvelous power those early Christians must have had to perform "signs and wonders." I knew it was for me, too.

One night as I was sleeping, I dreamed I was baptized in the Holy Spirit. I woke up feeling as though electricity were running through my body. I woke Jamie, but he was too sleepy to comprehend. I got up and spent the rest of the night wandering through the house praising the Lord in the dark, so great was the experience.

I shared the dream with those friends who had been praying for me. They said I had been baptized in the Holy Spirit. Indeed, I had. I wanted to saturate myself in the Bible. Jesus became close and real. For the first time in my life I was not afraid to die because heaven seemed so glorious.

Several days later I made a special visit to see Woody (Mrs. Bob) Johnson, the wife of a local Southern Baptist pastor who had also been filled with the Holy Spirit. As we prayed, I received my prayer language, speaking in tongues for the first time in my life. That opened another door for healing to come in, allowing the Holy Spirit to pray through me, cleansing my mind and healing my broken heart.

There were several people who lived in our community who ministered to me during that time. None of them was a member of our little church (although all became part of it at a later date.) I am grateful, in particular, for Elbert and Mary Jones, Kent and Diana Busing, Glenda Corley and several others who knew what I had been through and how deeply my self-esteem had been shattered. These friends spent countless hours praying with me, helping me through my feelings of guilt and rejection. I went through intense deliverance as they took authority over the demonic spirits which had tormented me, setting me free from the fear that had consumed me. For years it had seemed as if a cloud of darkness and heaviness had filled my head. As my friends prayed for me, in private and in the small prayer meetings I attended where they were teaching, I felt the cloud lift.

For the first time in years I felt worthy to take my place beside my husband. God had opened the door to a future far more wonderful than Jamie or I could have ever imagined—a door which keeps swinging wider each day.

Of course, there were a lot of lessons to be learned. I discovered that healing doesn't happen overnight. But it starts with truthfulness, as painful as that can be. And it *does* get better. I still have scars—and I guess I will for the rest of my life. I take hope, however, in knowing that God does not remember us for our sins—He remembers us for our scars.

Now, though, I focus on the happy experiences of our recent years instead of on the bad memories of the dark past. When an echo of the past reappears, as it does ever so often—a memory triggered by a song, a smell or a chance encounter Jamie may have with some woman he used to know—we can face it together, with openness.

Because I believe marriage is forever, God enabled me to hang in there. Now He has blessed us beyond our imagination. I am convinced that a mystical union in marriage is a reality. Jamie and I have become one. Our five children, now grown, married and producing grandchildren at a rapid rate, are all moving in the Spirit. Four of the five have moved back home and are building their houses on our property so they can be near us and be part of our church. Our other son and his family want to be here, but his job as a rancher keeps him in Georgia rather than Florida. Our kids like us. It is the greatest of all honors.

Jamie and I are no longer two people living in the same house, two bodies sleeping in the same bed. Something has happened in our spirits which has made us one. This oneness of marriage necessitates that each partner have total access to everything going on in the mate. That does not mean constantly dredging up the past, and certainly not living in the fear it will repeat, but it does mean living in an "open now" relationship.

A lot of wounded pastors and their wives show up at our home—a place we call "Hebron," after one of the ancient cities of refuge. I counsel couples the way I wish someone had taught us when we started out. I tell them: Make a covenant together that no matter how much it hurts, you will share every feeling you have with your mate. Not facts alone, but feelings as well, because feelings are the things that always lead us into fact. We are not responsible for our feelings, but we are responsible for how we express and act them out.

Adultery alone will not destroy a marriage. It is the lie which destroys the spiritual union. Therefore, all things must be done in the light. To allow a feeling—or a fact—to grow in darkness always breeds deception.

There is one thing more. In those early years I not only loved Jamie, I trusted him. When he broke that trust I was devastated. Crushed. Now I understand we are not called to trust one another. Everyone, including my husband, is capable of letting me down. I, too, am capable of betraying other people who trust me. Instead, I am called to trust the One who will never betray me, never let me down. I am called to trust God—and love people. If my husband lets me down, I will continue to love him. Jamie treats me the same way. Our uncondemning love is the thing that covers a multitude of sin.

Some things I did wrong.

1. I used the children. I had no other weapons. I never confided in them (they were too small), but on occasion, when I felt I was being ripped to shreds, I would

say to them in Jamie's presence, "If you only knew what a hypocrite your daddy is...." Instead of convicting Jamie, however, my words would only infuriate him. Sometimes he would leave the house, slamming the door behind him. When that happened I knew I had driven him into the arms of another woman, but the pain was so deep I seemed unable to keep from lashing out.

2. I confused love with infatuation, in my life and in Jamie's. I assumed he was "in love" with another woman. I did not know that real love is monogamous. You can only love—agape love—one person at a time, else you will, as Jesus said, "love the one and hate the other." A man can no more love two women at the same time than he can love God and mammon. In Jamie's case, he loved me. That was evidenced in the fact he did not want a divorce. But he was infatuated with others. Had I recognized that difference, I would have been able to handle it better.

Also, I did not realize at the time that I had my earlier infatuation with Jamie confused with real love. I had set my husband on a pedestal. I never imagined he would treat me in any way other than the way I treated him. I thought he could do no wrong. I was really trusting him more than I was trusting God. When I discovered his flaws, I was devastated. Not only was I hurt, I was disappointed. Yet this forced me to turn to God in my pain. My relationship with Christ began to deepen. Since I had no one else, He became more real to me.

3. I did not understand the real battle was in the heavenlies, not on earth. I thought I had to fight the battle alone. I did not realize Jamie was under demon influence, and those same demons (or their cousins) were attacking me as well. The harder I battled, the more

I was bloodied. Now I know the power of intercessory prayer and the power of spiritual authority. I know I can literally take authority over the demons which try to bind my husband, my family, myself. In the name of Jesus I have the power to rebuke them—without having to rebuke my husband.

4. I had no pastor, no one to advise me, encourage me. My pastor had been my husband, and when he went bad—when he became the source of my problem rather than the answer to it—I was left uncovered. I literally had no one to turn to.

Because of the structure of our church, had I gone to one of the other leaders, a deacon, for instance, it would have put my husband's position in jeopardy. We didn't need to be dismissed from the church; we needed help. None was available for the senior pastor.

Now we are part of a small group—an "extended family"—which accepts us as we are. The members are dedicated to correcting us without rejecting us. I know I can go to any of the people in our group and receive the help I need, without being rejected. On several occasions, when Jamie and I have had major disagreements, one of us has brought these before the home group at our weekly meeting. The group has loved us, but spoken truth—and then has helped enforce that truth by holding us accountable until our lives have changed. The same is true among the leadership in our larger family at the Tabernacle Church where Jamie is the senior minister. Our elders, our senior pastor, our church staff—all are dedicated to this principle of correction without rejection.

5. Even though Jamie had broken off the relationship and we had moved to Florida and were in an ex-

citing, new church, I still felt the anger and pain of the old wounds. I knew he was capable of falling right back into another affair. Even after he received the baptism in the Holy Spirit and began to show evidence of radical change, I was afraid to believe God had changed his basic character. I lived with constant fear that Jamie would return to his old life. As a result, I remained fearful, suspicious and extremely jealous. As time went by, God began to reveal to me my self-righteous attitudes. I was still judging my husband critically and feeling sorry for myself, and I reached out to possess him, to control him. If I could just hold onto him, not let him out of my clutches, he couldn't go wrong anymore. That possessiveness also caused me to try to change him so we wouldn't have any more trouble.

I finally saw that if God had started this new work in Jamie, only God could complete it. So with all my will I relinquished him totally to God—I turned him loose. "He's yours...he really doesn't belong to me." That is when the real healing started.

Some things I did right.

1. Although I used every means available to fight, I never backed off on my physical affection to Jamie. I knew that to turn frigid sexually would drive him even deeper into his illicit relationship. I did not sleep with him out of duty; I slept with him out of love.

2. We never considered divorce. As the word got out and the rumors spread that Jamie was being unfaithful to me, some of my friends said I ought to divorce him. That never entered my mind, however. Nor did Jamie ever consider it. We might deeply hurt one another, but we were going to remain together—until death parted us.

I have discovered, by the way, that most Christians

who seek divorce on the grounds of their spouse's infidelity have been wanting out of the marriage for a long time—and simply use infidelity as a justifiable excuse. I do not believe Jesus justified divorce by His statements in Matthew 5. In that passage the Pharisees attempted to trap our Lord into some statement with which they could take issue, but He declined to interpret Moses' words, simply stating that if they were looking for a reason for divorce, the only one that would stand under the law of Moses was fornication. When I married Jamie I vowed to stick with him for better or for worse. This was the worse, and I was trusting God for the better. But even if "better" did not come, I was married to Jamie for life.

I do not condemn those who choose divorce. That is their decision, and I know God understands and restores and continues to use them in ministry. But in my case, I chose to stick it out. I have never regretted it, for I have seen God honor my decision in my husband, my children, my grandchildren, our wonderful church and our ministry around the world. I am so blessed.

3. I never went public, never went before the church or the board of deacons. Despite what my husband was doing to me, I was still his wife. When others accused him, I stood up for him. The night he was exposed in a deacons' meeting and told he had to resign as pastor, he called me from the church office, weeping. I rushed to him. His enemies—even though he had driven them to be his enemies by his foolishness—were my enemies also because he was my husband. He was in trouble and needed help. When he asked for it, I was there to give it. In fact, giving help was part of my own healing.

When you love someone, it is easy to forgive.

Failure is neither fatal nor final. God is a restoring God who picks us up where we are and gives us a new beginning. Jamie and I have walked through hell together. Our children accompanied us. That is part of the price we paid when we committed to love forever. But we stand as a testimony that regardless of how dark any marriage situation is right now, or how much of a cloud may hang over you because of past failure, God can forgive completely. When the locusts came they ate not only the grain, but the weeds as well. Now God has planted new seed, and our fields are wonderfully restored with beautiful crops.

There is a little chorus that someone wrote—but God has given to me as my life goal:

I want to spend my life healing broken people;
I want to spend my life removing pain;
So let my words
Heal a heart that hurts;
I want to spend my life healing broken people.

Born in Vero Beach, Florida, in 1933, **Jackie Buckingham** grew up in a four-room house, sharing a bedroom with her older sister and grandmother. While her father ran a drag-line and worked as a fireman, her mother owned and operated a small dress shop and took her three children on Sundays to the Primitive Baptist Church.

Jackie's husband, Jamie, grew up in the same town. They met and dated steadily throughout high school and married after Jamie graduated from Mercer University.

Since 1967, Jamie has been senior minister of the Tabernacle Church in Melbourne, Florida. He is also editor-at-large for *Charisma* and *Ministries Today* magazines and is an author and international speaker. Jackie has traveled widely with her husband and has appeared with him on numerous platforms.

The Buckinghams have five children, all married, and eight grandchildren.

Chapter Fourteen
Handling Grief: When Your Husband Dies

by Ingrid (Mrs. Walter) Trobisch

"Grief is the price we pay for loving," a young widow wrote after losing her husband unexpectedly after only 17 years of marriage. To grieve, which means literally, "to be burdened by sorrow," is only a part of the mourning process, but it is an essential part. Until "grief work" is done, we cannot go on.

Grief that is not dealt with can keep a person from being fully alive. I recall a conversation I had with a German pastor and his second wife who took part in one of the Family Life Seminars that my husband, Walter, and I conducted. The pastor's first wife had died unexpectedly after a marriage of 25 years. Despite his despair, he had appeared unmoved, even stoical at her funeral. Friends worried because he refused to grieve. When he remarried less than a year later, they breathed a sigh of relief. Perhaps now all would be well.

But all was not well. Three years later, at our seminar,

163

the pastor and his second wife were asked to share with each other their answers to the questions: "What unites us the most? What separates us the most?" The wife was very frank when she told her husband that she felt a barrier of separation between them because he had never been able to share with her his grief at losing his first wife.

I talked with the two, and as we shared, a miracle took place. With tears in his eyes, speaking hesitantly at first, the pastor began to tell us about the deep sadness that had enveloped him like a fog when his first wife died. The pain and grief he had kept hidden deep in his heart came bubbling to the surface. His body shook as he tried to describe his feelings. This strong man, this spiritual leader, cried—and so did we. Now a time of cleansing and binding would come. The long-delayed healing process had begun.

It is not enough to place a Band-Aid on a grieving heart and hope that all will be well. The pain has to be expressed. My aunt, who lost her husband after 50 years of marriage, told me her secret for handling grief. When the pain became too great, she simply went into her coat closet and screamed. She felt better after that and went on with living.

My heart was heavy one day because I was concerned about one of my children. I shared this sadness with my husband. He listened patiently. As I rested my head in his lap, he stroked my hair and said, "Ingrid, just let the deep pain hurt."

Two days later, on a clear October morning, Walter died of heart failure in our little home in the foothills of the Austrian Alps. My world stopped that day. In the more than seven years that have passed since, I've often remembered Walter's quiet wisdom: "Just let the deep pain hurt."

"Blessed are those who mourn, for they shall be comforted," the Bible says. In order to be comforted, we must let ourselves mourn.

I now recognize the stages of grief as similar to what Nobel prize-winning author John Steinbeck described when he wrote to the widow of his publisher: "After seeming cut off and alone, you will be able to pick up a thread and draw in a string and then a rope leading back to life again." I found in my early grief that it was important simply to pick up that thread, to put one foot in front of the other and keep walking, even though the way seemed dark and frightening. The Scandinavians put it this way: "When you're in a storm, pray, but don't forget to keep rowing."

Learning to walk alone, especially when it comes after a close partnership and marriage of many years, is no easy task. It seems simpler just to give up—even to run away—than to face the pain. As one couple who had been married 58 years wrote to me: "It is not death that we are afraid of, but the grief that one of us must face alone."

Luci and Harold Shaw, well-known Christian publishers, faced the reality of death together after Harold was diagnosed with lung cancer. According to the doctors, he had, at most, 18 months to live. The Shaws and their friends prayed for healing, and for a while the cancer went into remission. But in spite of their strong faith, Luci and Harold both sensed that they would be separated.

As Luci said, "It was a narrow line for me to walk—to have real faith that God could heal, without fantasizing or being presumptuous with God."

Still hoping and praying for healing, Harold decided to put his affairs in order. He and Luci bought a grave site together on a sunny bank, just in front of a row of shade trees. He began to teach his wife about those things she had never had anything to do with before—finances, business affairs, legal matters, car maintenance, household repairs. He had the house painted and the driveway paved.

"It gave him great satisfaction to do these things for me and the family," Luci said. "Each time something was finished, he'd breathe a sigh of relief and say, 'Well, that's done. That's cared for.' "

Despite their preparation, when Harold died in January 1986, Luci grieved deeply. Losing her partner was like "radical surgery, like being cut in half," she said. "But I'm learning to welcome the pain and not dodge it. Pain teaches us what is real and what is temporal, what is superficial and what is deep. I'm trying to let pain do its work in me."

"Let the deep pain hurt," as Walter would say.

Harold and Luci were fortunate. They had time to face death together and put things in order. For so many of us, the death of a spouse comes unexpectedly. After Walter's death, I could only take one step at a time. I depended on my family and friends to help me make the immediate decisions that were required. Once the shock and disbelief wore off, an intensity of grief set in. It was like an amputation where I still felt the lost limb.

For me, it was difficult to accept the refining work of pain without being tempted to wallow in self-pity. Feeling sorry for ourselves is not the same as genuine sadness over our loss. The former is self-centered. The latter is centered on the one we've lost. The line is sometimes a thin one.

Still, we must try to distinguish between the two emotions. A Swiss marriage counselor and friend, Dr. Theo Bovet, has said that self-pity is poison to a marriage relationship. I believe it is even more dangerous when learning to walk alone.

In those early months and years after Walter's death, when I was tempted to pity myself, it helped me to think of my own mother. When her husband died at his missionary post in Africa during World War II, she was separated from him by thousands of miles. She was in her early 40s when he died, 10 years younger than I was when Walter died. She had 10 children to care for, and the oldest had barely begun his university studies. I, on the other hand, had only five children, and my youngest was soon to begin his university education.

Even though she had no fixed income, my mother was hopeful. "The future does not look dark. God has helped us until now, and He will continue to help us," she would say.

In my grief, it has helped to think of others, like my mother, who have faced or are facing greater burdens. One of my friends lost her husband not through death, but divorce. I realized that her climb to find the thread leading back to life was in many ways steeper than mine.

The wound of divorce will heal, but scar tissue often remains. A residue of hurt, rejection or failure is left behind. Losing a spouse to death is different. As my friend Luci Shaw says, "Death is just the cap on the bottle of perfume." The fragrance of marriage can still be remembered as sweet.

Remorse is just as much of a dead end as self-pity. A nagging inner voice may repeat, "Why didn't I insist that he go to the doctor? Why didn't I give him that word of praise or encouragement? Now it's too late." But that's just like beating ourselves to make what has happened "unhappen." It's futile and destructive. Anne Lindbergh, my favorite author and wife of the late pilot-adventurer, calls it "fooling yourself, feeding on an illusion; just as living on memories, clinging to relics and photographs, is an illusion. Like the food offered in dreams, it will not nourish; no growth or rebirth will come from it."

Guilt will also block the "grief work" that must be done. It is not unusual to feel guilt after a spouse dies. But we must deal with it, then move on. For me, it was helpful to write down and confess to my pastor all that troubled my conscience around the time of Walter's death. Just as in our marriage Walter and I had needed those times of unburdening, of confessing that which the Holy Spirit had convicted us of, I still needed those times after his death. I knew if I were to make real progress and not just spin my wheels, I needed to place my accumulated guilt and pain at the foot of the cross and hear God's words of forgiveness.

The words of another friend, a woman doctor, also helped me in those early months and years after Walter's death. "You must stop the bleeding points, Ingrid, if you are to recover from your loss," she said.

I put her advice into practice. Often in those days a painful memory would cross my mind. Unable to handle it myself, I would call a close friend, another woman of prayer. She would listen patiently to my hurt and then, with words of comfort, help me turn my eyes to Jesus—

the Savior who walks through our past, our present and our future and makes all things new. Another bleeding point was sealed off and I could go on.

How thankful I am for the friends and family who supported me after Walter's death! Just as babies take their first steps into the arms of someone who loves them and cheers them on, so we who have survived a great loss need a circle of encouragers. We need those who will kindly call us forth from our self-pity, remorse and guilt, who will help us find our new identity and self-esteem. Now is the time for those of us who've been mothering for years to allow ourselves to be mothered by others.

On a practical level, how well we handle grief will depend, in larger measure than we may realize, on such things as maintaining an adequate, balanced diet and getting enough sleep and exercise. A significant weight gain or loss during a time of grieving is likely to set off both physiological and emotional problems. Mourners need to watch calories—sometimes making sure they get enough—and eat daily from each of the four basic food groups: dairy, meat, fruits and vegetables, and grains.

We also need to drink more fluids than we might think necessary. How grateful I was whenever a friend made me a simple cup of tea! During those first weeks after my loss, a tightness constricted my throat almost constantly. The tea helped.

Walking briskly for at least 20 minutes each day and swimming once or twice a week helped me control depression. I could walk or swim away from my troubles for a short time. When I was finished and had to face them again, I was able to do so with more happiness and alertness. Later, at night, my body was tired from the exercise and more ready for the sleep that often eluded me. I made a strong effort to maintain some pattern of rest, even though there were many restless nights.

Eventually, I found that living at peace with myself involved discovering anew the joy of my five senses.

Touch. How wonderful it was to have the wind rush across my face or the rain fall on bare skin. How comforting it felt as I swam, completely surrounded by water, carried by it, even caressed by it.

Sight. How awesome when God opened my eyes "to see again" the beauty of nature, the miracle of a new baby, even the loveliness of age and wrinkles, which are the shorthand of our lives.

Taste. How delicious were the meals prepared for me by others, and those I prepared to show my friends and family I loved them and appreciated them.

Hearing. What healing I received as I listened to the great requiems of the masters, realizing that after the suffering of the crucifixion comes the joy of resurrection.

Smell. What happy memories and innocent joy were released at the fragrance of peonies, baked apples, a breast-fed baby, clean linens, fresh coffee.

Mourning is never easy, and it lasts longer than most people think. A poll conducted just after the Vietnam War by a journalist for a major Midwestern newspaper asked this question: "How long is it normal to mourn the loss of a loved one?" The majority responded that mourning is complete within 48 hours to two weeks after a death. Those of us who've actually walked through that valley know that two weeks is only the beginning.

Mourning is that journey which takes us from where we were before our loss to where we'll be once we've struggled to adapt to the change in our lives. No one can quite measure when those days are over.

Yet only one who has learned to live alone after a great loss can move into a complete relationship with others. It is a trap for a person bereaved of a partner to think that a new partner will fulfill his or her deepest needs. "Don't make a major decision for at least 12 months after the death of your spouse" is wise advice. As Judith Fabisch said in her book, *Not Ready to Walk Alone*, "If a widow can't readjust to living with herself, she certainly can't be expected to readjust to living with another person....People wrapped up in the solving of their own problems cannot be effective in solving the problems of others....On the other hand, remarriage is the highest praise one can pay to a deceased mate, for it says, in effect, marriage is good and I want to be part of that good relationship again."

We never honor the dead by dying with them. Walter's work was finished, but God's work is not. I can honor Walter's memory best by being God's servant and steward—by living for Him and for others.

The great poet Liebman put it this way: "The melody that the loved one played upon the piano of your life will never be played quite that way again, but we must not close the keyboard and allow the instrument to gather dust. We must seek out other artists of the spirit, new friends who gradually will help us find the road of life again, who will walk that road with us."

It took me many years in my marriage to learn that no man on earth can satisfy the great longings of my heart. Only God can. God is also the only one who can help me live with the deep hole that was torn in my heart when Walter died.

I don't believe, as some have told me, "But, Ingrid,

Jesus is your husband." The hole is still there. God hasn't filled it up yet, but He has made a bridge over it. I can live with it now. And as I stand on the bridge, I can reach out to others.

Ingrid Trobisch was born in 1926 in Moshi, Tanzania, East Africa, the eldest of 10 children. Her father was a minister and pioneer missionary to Africa. After returning to the United States, the family settled on a small farm in the Ozark Mountains.

While a post-graduate student at Augustana College in Rock Island, Illinois, Ingrid's pastor introduced her to her future husband, Walter, an exchange student from Germany. The two were married four years later in Mannheim, Germany.

In 1968, the Trobisches founded the Family Life Mission in Lichtenberg, Austria, which sponsored Bible-based Family Life Seminars throughout the United States, Africa, Europe and Asia. They continued as a team until Walter's death in 1978.

Ingrid makes her home in Springfield, Missouri. She is the author of *The Joy of Being a Woman* and *On Our Way Rejoicing*. She has five children and eight grandchildren.

Chapter Fifteen
Getting a Late Start

by Becky (Mrs. Glenn) Anderson

Our God is a God of miracles! He heals the sick. He raises the dead. He makes the lame to walk and the blind to see.

But would you think it heretical if I said He also makes seeing eyes blind when it suits His purposes?

That's what He did—I'm convinced—when my husband and I decided to get married. Glenn was a 40-year-old bachelor. I was a widow only slightly younger and a mother of three. As I look back now, it's a wonder that we ever took the plunge. Oh, don't get me wrong—I love my husband and he loves me. We're glad we're married. But from a worldly point of view, our relationship had three strikes against it from the very start.

Glenn had reached that point in life when he felt he should marry if he was ever going to. Besides, he figured, having a wife would be an asset to his ministry. I, on the other hand, had been a widow for several years and

175

was lonely for the marriage relationship. My children, ages 6, 11 and 12, also needed a daddy.

My first husband, Grady, and I had enjoyed a good marriage. Having been raised in Christian homes, we both came to know Jesus at early ages and were always regular attenders and workers in the Southern Baptist church. We had no warning that our happy life together would be cut short. Grady was physically well and reasonably fit at the time when—for no apparent reason—he was struck down by a massive heart attack at age 37. Within an hour after the onset of the chest pains, I found myself watching the life drain out of the man with whom I had expected to spend the rest of my life. I was shocked beyond comprehension.

I lived under God's anesthesia for the next few days. Somehow I was able to make all the decisions necessary for the funeral arrangements and the handling of the estate. "Becky, you're a rock to all of us," Grady's brother told me.

But soon the rock crumbled. Grief washed in, deep and overwhelming. There were days I wanted just to stay in bed and cry—it took too much effort to live normally. Self-pity welled up inside me. I resented my friends who still had their husbands. I questioned God. "Why, Lord, why?" I asked.

It was not that I thought God had been unfaithful to me. Not at all. On the first night that I lay alone in our bed, just hours after Grady's death, God's peace so flooded me that I knew He was in control. A quiet voice in my heart said, "I've gone to great lengths to prepare you for this. Don't you think I will see you through?" As the Lord brought to mind many of the things He had done for me and the children, I realized that He *had* prepared me, and He was with me.

Ultimately, it was God's grace that helped me face the difficult days, weeks and months that followed. If I wasn't actually triumphant, at least I was surviving! The hymn "O Love That Wilt Not Let Me Go" was particularly meaningful; Grady's love was gone, but God's love was always with me. He was holding onto me even when I didn't have the strength or the will to hold onto Him.

It was during this season of emptiness and despair that I began to desire and seek a deeper walk with the Lord. I knew that I did not have the fullness of the experience of God that I read about in Hannah Whitall Smith's *The Christian's Secret of a Happy Life*. My sister, Nancy, who had been baptized in the Holy Spirit a few years before, sent me this book and several others. I read them with great interest.

Of course, when Nancy first told her Southern Baptist family about her experience with the Holy Spirit, we rejected her testimony. But now things were different. Nancy was moving in victory. My life was at rock bottom. I was wide open for anything God could give me. I continued to search.

As time passed and I found some release from the pain, I thought seriously about the direction my life should take. My family's future depended upon me. I had worked for several years early in my marriage but had not been employed since the children were born. At my mother's wise suggestion, I enrolled in college to complete the degree I had partially earned years before. A college education, I thought, would help me provide for my family more adequately. In retrospect, however, going back to school did something that was far more crucial for our future than mere job training: it gave me the new lease on life I so badly needed.

I made straight A's in my first semester at a branch of the state university near our small South Carolina town. I was invigorated by my success. But to continue my course of study, I would have to transfer to the main campus in Columbia, the state capitol. A move seemed like a good idea.

Grady had been dead for nearly nine months. Still, the pain was ever-present. I felt it as I continued to live in the home that he and I had built together. Every inch carried so many memories. I felt it as I ran errands and visited friends in our small town. There was no place Grady and I hadn't gone together. I couldn't help seeing him in my mind's eye—at the post office, our favorite restaurant, the drug store, the gas station. I didn't want to forget him, but this daily knife-through-the-heart experience was killing me.

One day I heard my 5-year-old son ask his grandmother, "When are we ever going to stop crying about Daddy?" I knew then that I had to pull myself together, for my children's mental health as well as for my own.

That winter, I made my first trip to Columbia to register for the spring semester at the university. I began immediately to look for a house for me, the three children and my mother, who was now living with us. "A four-bedroom house to rent? You'll never find one," everybody told me.

"God, help me to find the right house," I prayed. He answered. When I approached one large house—not as close to the college as I would have liked and a little more expensive than I had hoped— I knew it was the one God had in mind for us.

We moved in as soon as we could. In short order, the two older children were enrolled in the neighborhood elementary school and we were attending the Baptist Church across the street from the school, where many of the children's new friends attended.

The pastor of the church was a nice-looking man with a warm, friendly manner both at church and when he visited in our home. Mother and I were impressed with his leadership ability and with the spiritual caliber of his Sunday messages.

One night, my oldest son, Brian, returned home from a church meeting with a strange announcement. "Mom, I don't think Mr. Anderson is married."

"Oh, surely he is," I answered. "I've never met his wife—only his mother—but I'm sure that's just because she's been at home with a sick child or helping in the nursery. Preachers' wives are usually busy with something!"

But as it turned out, Brian was right. Glenn Anderson was *not* married. It was a mystery to me how he had escaped! He was really very handsome, with a cute "Glenn Ford-ish" nose.

"Remember, I'm not looking for a husband," I reminded myself. I had told God early on that since He had taken Grady away from me, I trusted Him to give me the ability and strength to raise the children alone. I had informed Him firmly that if I was ever to marry again, He was going to have to make His will very clear—nothing less than handwriting on the wall or a voice from heaven.

"Coincidence" began to throw Glenn and me together, however. The church pianist suddenly quit and I was called upon to fill in, having served in that capacity in my former church. Before long, Glenn (we were on a first-name basis by then) and I were together frequently in groups. Though I tried to look at him as "just another church member," I began to realize how vulnerable I was and how much I missed having a man to talk to.

So this is why widows are so often called 'man-chasers,' I thought. Once a woman gets accustomed to male companionship, she's lonely without it.

I admitted to myself that I was very interested in Glenn, even though I had no indication that he was attracted to me. He seemed quite satisfied with bachelorhood and his current arrangements— his mother lived with him. Mutual friends tried to push him beyond the "friend-ship" stage, but he didn't seem to catch on until well over a year later (40-year-old bachelors are obviously not Don Juans, I decided).

In the meantime, my search for a deeper relationship with God led me to ask for and receive the baptism in the Holy Spirit. Spiritually, I was soaring. Sitting at the piano at church waiting for the next hymn, I would be almost raptured as I read the words of the next song— so familiar and yet brand new! I would begin to pray inaudibly in my prayer language and then nearly burst out laughing with the thought: What would all those good Baptists and my dear Baptist preacher say if they only knew that their pianist was speaking in tongues!

At other times I would be so full of joy that I would run into the restroom, lock myself in a cubicle and whisper, "Praise the Lord!" I laughed at the absurdity of it—having to hide exuberant praise to God because I was in church!

The Bible became a brand new book to me, even though I had read it all my life and knew many passages from memory. Prayer, too, was exciting, as were my personal worship experiences. I remember looking out of my bedroom window at the rocky field behind our house and suddenly thinking, "Now I know why God says the very stones will worship Him if we don't!" My understanding of God's glory and the reality of Jesus was reaching new dimensions.

I prayed about my attraction to Glenn but got no definite answer. No door was suddenly opened. Instead, God gave me a "rhema"—a personal word to hold onto. That word came, oddly enough, through the lyrics of a popular song that I was hearing on the radio: "There's a time for us. . . ." Somehow, I knew God was saying there would be a time for Glenn and me.

We grew closer. God worked in Glenn's heart as well as in mine. We talked openly about our feelings, and one day Glenn admitted that his attraction for me had turned to love—the kind that longs for a commitment. The time had come.

On August 17, 1970, Glenn and I exchanged vows in a beautiful Baptist wedding. Glenn also exchanged vows with my three children—a very meaningful act which made me appreciate my new husband all the more.

After a brief honeymoon, the children and I settled into the large home Glenn had built years ago for himself and his mother. We expected our lives to fall into place rapidly because we were confident that God had willed our marriage to take place. We had both sought God's will above our own and felt certain that our union was ordained by Him.

It was not that we didn't expect adjustments. Glenn knew that becoming an instant father to three children (then aged 7, 12 and 13) wouldn't be easy, but he felt he would be equal to the challenge with God's help. After all, he (like most childless adults) thought he knew exactly how children should behave and how he, as a parent, would evoke the required behavior. For my part, I knew it would not be easy to move in with Glenn's mother—into *her* home. There would be awkward times, I was sure, but I got along so well with my mother-in-law—she was such a lovely person—that I didn't think it would be too hard.

How blind we were!

Glenn discovered in a hurry that my children were not the perfect angels he had expected—and that they didn't respond to his discipline in acceptable ways. He found that four additional people in the house resulted in additional clutter and that everything was not always in its proper place when he went to look for it. He also realized that his new wife had a strong stubborn streak where her children's rights—or her own—were concerned.

My honeymoon bubble also quickly burst. I soon saw that Glenn and I had different expectations for our life together. I was disappointed that he did not automatically love the children as much as I did. I was upset that his ideas about discipline were not the same as my own. But by far the most difficult conflict I faced was not with Glenn—it was with the omnipresence of his mother. I felt threatened by the obvious fact that she knew far better than I how to please him in the little things of daily life. The more this truth was underscored, the more insecure I became.

I had agreed with Glenn before our marriage that Mrs. Anderson should continue to live with him—with us— even though Glenn's sister had strongly objected. I suppose I should have listened to her, but I figured that Glenn had been willing to accept my children as part of me; it was only fair that I accept his mother as part of him.

Mrs. Anderson was a very dynamic and capable woman, extremely active for her 70 years. She had worked hard all of her life. In her younger years, she had run a grocery store while raising her family. In the years just before our marriage, she served as hostess and female counterpart in Glenn's pastoral ministry. She was a woman to admire, someone who deserved happiness and security in her old age.

Soon, however, I became abundantly aware that her very assets were liabilities to me as I tried to find my place in Glenn's life. She and Glenn had already established a lifestyle. Even when she seemed weary of the requirements of assisting in his ministry, she would feel threatened whenever I tried to step into any role she considered her domain.

Conflicts also arose in the house itself. The furniture, lamps or knick-knacks I brought into the home had to replace something that was already there—something my mother-in-law preferred there. Resentment rose in both of us. Consciously and unconsciously, we vied for the status in Glenn's life, home and ministry that we both felt was ours, she by prior possession and I by being his wife.

Glenn, of course, was caught in the middle. He loved us both and wanted our happiness. He could not see that our needs and desires were mutually exclusive. At first, he tried to moderate and mediate. Later, he simply withdrew, telling us we had to work out the problem ourselves.

In frustration, I gave up. I determined that I would take no authority and expect no concessions. In essence,

I laid down my position as wife. I told myself I would only help around the house, be a mother to my children and share a bedroom with my husband.

In short order, however, the Holy Spirit corrected me sternly with these words: "You took a vow in the marriage ceremony to 'let no man put your marriage asunder.' You are doing just that by abdicating your responsibilities as a wife."

I knew the Lord was right. As difficult as it would be, I had to keep trying to take my rightful position in Glenn's life as best I could. I admitted to God that I had held false and unrealistic expectations about our marriage. Glenn had some wrong concepts, too. And I would have to be the key to his seeing our relationship in proper perspective.

At the same time, my most difficult battle was not with Glenn or my mother-in-law, but with the ugliness in my own heart. I had experienced loneliness and self-pity in widowhood, but I had not had to deal with the un-Christlike things in myself that could only be revealed through close relationships, as soul rubbed against soul. My present circumstances seemed to bring out the worst in me, a "worst" that I never even knew existed. I was often horrified at myself during those difficult days and weeks that soon stretched into months and years. Although I felt I was becoming worse and worse by the day, in reality I was only having to deal with the true "me" that had been buried and was now rearing her ugly head.

Resentment, bitterness, hatred, envy, jealousy and a host of other emotions warred within me. Many times I felt utterly defeated, but somehow the Holy Spirit would lift me up and set me back on the right path again. God told me more than once that I would not have been able to overcome, or even to endure, if I had not received His power through the baptism of the Holy Spirit. I wasn't moving in power to perform mighty miracles or deliverances—I was moving in power just to survive!

In those early years, God did move to provide some relief and a sense of direction and hope. Glenn had his own encounter with the Holy Spirit. His preaching changed, and his ministry took on a special anointing. But his open support of the baptism in the Holy Spirit upset many of the church leaders. He was pressured to resign.

For a while, he turned to a traveling ministry. Since I was employed as a school librarian at the time, I usually stayed at home while he was on the road.

But Glenn was meant to be a pastor, and he picked up that mantle again when the pastor of the Southern Baptist church we had joined resigned. At first I opposed his accepting the position, remembering how left out I had felt in the other church. But finally, I, too, was convinced that this was God's will—for Glenn and for me. At least most of the congregation never knew us before we were married. Maybe—just maybe—Glenn and I could be a "we."

Almost from the beginning, we were not a typical denominational church with predictable patterns of ministry. To our great delight, this new congregation was open to the move of the Holy Spirit. Glenn led them into the fullness of the experience. For the first time, I felt I had a place—in this wonderful new church and in Glenn's life.

But despite my new-found hope, the old problems, insecurities and resentments continued to crop up. I battled between feelings of victory and feelings of utter

185

defeat.

One Monday morning, just as I awoke, a clear word from the Lord came to me: "Go on a total fast for three days, Monday through Wednesday." I dared not disobey. I began to fast confidently, certain that God had something special in store. But instead of being a period of great triumph, those three days were among the hardest of my life—physically, mentally and spiritually. My body became extremely weak, my mental processes were hazy and I felt bombarded spiritually by forces I couldn't recognize.

On the fourth day, I slowly took nourishment again. I was thoroughly confused. All that torment and nothing was different. Had I just imagined the call to fast? Thursday passed uneventfully. On Friday I went back to my regular routine and cleaned house.

Suddenly, as I was scrubbing the bathroom in a very spiritual position—on my knees—something broke inside me. I felt as if chains were falling away in my innermost being. In an instant, I was free, unburdened. I was free!

My first impulse was to go to my mother-in-law and apologize for all the grief I had caused her. I knew the prompting was from the Lord. Before Satan could talk me out of it, I hurried into the room where she was, knelt at her side and asked her forgiveness. She gave it graciously. We embraced. I left her, lighthearted, with a song coursing through me: "Set my spirit free that I might worship Thee. . . ."

I wish I could tell you that everything was wonderful from that point on. It wasn't. The situation never really changed. Resentment rose up within me again and again when I felt my rights were being abridged, but thankfully the bondage of these feelings never again ensnared me as it once had. There was never a real "meeting of the minds" between Mrs. Anderson and me. Still, through God's power, I developed compassion for her. The Holy Spirit showed me that she was operating out of her own hurts and, quite naturally, was trying to hold onto the only true happiness, fulfillment and security she had ever known.

Satan often succeeded in bringing me under condemnation when I continued to experience negative feelings. He convinced me that Mrs. Anderson would always "be there" between Glenn and me until I was able to gain full victory over the situation.

That was not to be the case. Seven years after our wedding, my mother-in-law was diagnosed as having cancer. The disease moved quickly through her body. Over a six-week period, she was in and out of consciousness, lingering between life and death. I prayed fervently for her. I even prayed that God not take her away until I had mastered what He had for me to learn.

During that time, God did a sovereign work of reconciliation in her heart—and in mine. Mrs. Anderson did not survive long enough for us to work out that reconciliation in a viable relationship, but I had peace that even this was God's will and timing. While I had never really gained victory in the nitty-gritty of daily life, God showed me that I *had* been victorious in the attitude of my heart. That was what was important.

After Mrs. Anderson's death, a bit to my surprise, my marriage did not immediately improve. Suddenly, I was face to face with a horrible fact: while I had resented my mother-in-law and saw her as the center of my problems, I harbored even greater resentment toward Glenn, who had never upheld my role as wife or given my position priority in our household. Though I knew he had defended me to his mother on many occasions, my own self-pity caused me to dwell only on the times when I felt he let me down.

The communication barriers raised by all our unresolved conflicts were tall and wide. We never considered separation or divorce, but we were far from being "one flesh" in the highest sense. We were trapped behind the hurts we had inflicted consciously and unconsciously upon each other.

I often envied wives of pastors who had grown into the ministry with their husbands. Living through years of seminary, earning a "Putting Hubby Through" degree, starting out as a couple in a small church—I could see how these things could create a strong bond between husband and wife. Certainly, there might be financial struggles or other problems, but at least these couples went into the ministry as a team. Glenn had had a ministry team, too—he and his mother. I never really learned to be a pastor's wife. Nobody ever needed one.

Glenn knew my feelings and made conscious efforts to share his life and ministry with me. But somehow his trying so hard only demoralized me. I wanted it to come more naturally.

And over time it has. There've been no instant changes, no overnight breakthroughs. But as weeks have turned to months and months to years, God has healed—and He continues to heal.

What has been God's purpose in my life? It always seemed to me that I was a "Mary" person thrust into a "Martha" role. "God, if You wanted a round hole filled, why did You choose a square peg?" It was a quarrel I often had with the Lord. Of course, I never won.

But all along, God has been working to transform me into His image. I admit He's often had to use the "two-by-four between the eyes" approach to break through my stubborn shell. Sometimes He's had to drag me along, kicking and screaming. Still, He *has* known that it's my will to do His will, and He's been faithful.

Only God knows what He is seeking to accomplish in me, in Glenn, and in our life and ministry together. But we are sticking together, loving each other as best we can and as the Lord directs us, trusting Him to bring His will—not our own—to pass.

It was tough getting a late start. But that's better than no start at all. And there are some advantages—for one, it's not as far to the finish line.

God is working in our lives. He has been all along. That's all I need to know to give me strength to stick it out—with joy—to the end.

Becky Anderson was born in 1931 in High Point, North Carolina. One of three daughters, she was raised in the Southern Baptist Church where her father was a deacon.

Becky met her first husband, Grady, while a student at Furman University. They married and had three children before Grady died of a heart attack at age 37. Several years later, Becky married again—this time to Glenn Anderson, who was the pastor of the church she attended. Glenn is now senior pastor of the Forest Drive Baptist Church in Columbia, South Carolina.

Becky has a bachelor's degree in library education and a master's degree in media arts. In addition to being a pastor's wife and mother, she has had a career as an elementary school librarian. She has also been active in Women's Aglow and the International Christian Embassy Jerusalem. With Glenn, she has co-hosted five tours to the Holy Land.

Chapter Sixteen
My Husband's Seldom Home

by Anna (Mrs. Jack) Hayford

As a child growing up, I was never alone. I was born seventh of nine children—I couldn't be alone if I tried! There were always brothers and sisters around the house, running, jumping, laughing, crying, studying, working. I always had someone to talk to, to play with. Loneliness was one emotion I never experienced.

What a rude awakening I received when I became a pastor's wife! Before Jack and I were married, I was sure we would always be together—a team at home as well as in the ministry. Where he would go, I would go. If someone needed him, they would need me, too. But soon God showed me that His idea of "teamwork" was different from mine. No team can stay huddled together and expect to win the game. Each player has to take his own position. My position, it seemed, was at home—and alone far more than I ever expected or wanted.

191

In the beginning, my idea of "together" teamwork prevailed. As our first ministry assignment after our marriage, Jack and I were asked to itinerate for a three-month period. During that time we ministered in 72 different churches across six states—together. We sang together, drove together, packed and unpacked together.

Afterwards, we pioneered a church in Fort Wayne, Indiana. Together, we did everything: cleaned the church building, erected bookshelves in Jack's office (which was also the furnace room), called on parishioners and led the worship services.

When our first child, Becki, was born, suddenly I could no longer do all the things I had been doing at my husband's side. I tried to continue to minister with him, but my baby had to nap and eat, get bathed and changed. Those were difficult chores to perform on the run.

Jack was then offered the job of youth leader for the Foursquare Churches in Michigan and Indiana. He accepted and traveled from church to church to participate in rallies, camps and planning sessions and to promote the youth program. It was impractical for me to join him on many of these trips. Our car was not in the best shape, and the cold Michigan winters were not friendly to little babies.

Staying at home alone when Jack was traveling made me uneasy—especially at night. So before he'd leave, we'd always make arrangements to have a teenager, a college student or some other single adult stay with me. That helped, but I still had trouble going to sleep and staying asleep. I never felt rested after those nights.

I began to search the Scriptures for God's promises of peace, comfort and protection. Of course, the Bible was full of them. Some verses, such as Psalm 3:5 and

Psalm 4:8, even spoke specifically about God watching over me as I slept.

I read and re-read these and many other verses. As it became clear that my fears were merely the harassment of the enemy, Jack and I prayed regularly for the Lord's protection and covering. My heart was much more at ease as I began to appropriate the promises I found in God's Word.

But the Lord did watch over us—and not just in sleep. One day, Jack went out with the young boys of our congregation to help them sell candy. The money they'd earn would help pay for enrollment at summer camp. I stayed home with the baby.

After putting Becki down for her nap, I went into the kitchen to sew. An hour later, I heard unusual noises coming from the crib. I ran into the nursery and found Becki lying face down, breathing out in short, groaning puffs. I picked her up. She was completely stiff.

I panicked. Where was Jack? I had no idea how to get in touch with him or when he'd be home.

Suddenly, the Lord brought to mind a discussion I had heard a few days before at a women's meeting. It was about what to do if your baby has a convulsion. That had not been the subject that had been planned for the meeting, but it was just the one I needed to remember now!

I ran to the bathroom with Becki in my arms and started running cold water then warm water over her, clothes and all, to see if I could get her to catch her breath. When she didn't respond, I laid her on her stomach and began patting her on the back with one hand. I dialed for an ambulance with the other.

By the time the emergency team arrived, I had wrapped Becki in a heavy blanket, pulled together a complete change of clothes for her, written a note to Jack and put on my coat.

When the ambulance driver asked me whether we should take Becki to our doctor's office or the hospital, I answered, "The hospital," without thinking. It must have been God's Spirit that did the prompting. The doctor, it turned out, was out of his office and in the hospital that day! In short order Becki was breathing normally, and my heart had stopped its wild pounding.

Another time Jack was at the church, studying. I was at home with Becki, boiling an egg for breakfast. I decided to go up into the attic to look for something—I no longer remember what—that we had packed away in a box. Since Becki was playing quietly and the egg had a little more time, I ran quickly into the attic through the opening in the closet in the master bedroom.

In a moment, Becki came up behind me and, without blinking, shut the closet door. I went to the door but found it would not open from the inside. There I was— locked in the attic, an egg about to explode on the stove, my baby wandering aimlessly around the house.

I did everything I could think to do. I called through the louvers in the attic to a neighbor who was putting out her garbage. She couldn't hear me. I looked for another exit and found an opening down into the house that was filled with electrical wires. I decided not to risk it. I talked to Becki through the door, trying to keep her away from the stove.

Finally, I called out to God. He heard. Within a few minutes, Jack—who normally would have stayed at the church another three hours—walked into the house. When he opened the closet door, I hugged him, then

Becki, and thanked God. Then I went downstairs and cleaned the egg off the ceiling.

While we were still in Indiana, our second child, Jack III, was born. He was far too active a baby to take with me on ministry calls. More than ever, I stayed home when Jack went out.

Soon, our growing family moved to Los Angeles, where the Foursquare headquarters are located. For the first five years, Jack served as national youth director. For the next five, he was dean of students at the training center. Since he was not in a typical pastoral role, my responsibilities in the ministry were few. My life was filled with my children—Becki, Jack III and later, Mark and Christy. Jack Senior was seldom home. His hours were erratic, and he never took a day off.

I started to become concerned about how hard Jack was working. I pleaded with him to take a vacation, but he never found the time. Finally, I prayed: "Lord, You know Your son Jack needs some rest. I've tried to talk to him about taking time off, but he won't listen to me. Maybe he'll listen to You. You do something."

The Lord responded by reminding me of the principle of the sabbath. Even God took one day to rest after creating the universe! I knew God was saying that's where Jack should start.

I discussed with Jack my thoughts about everyone's need for a sabbath. It struck a chord with him. Soon he was taking at least one day off each week. The lesson of the sabbath became a regular part of his teaching.

As national youth director, Jack continued to travel a lot. To keep loneliness from setting in during the two or three weeks he would be gone, I planned major projects for myself—furniture refinishing, wallpapering, painting, heavy cleaning. On one of his longer trips, I re-did an entire room. Time passed more quickly if I kept myself busy.

It was on Jack's longest trip—seven weeks—that I found out God's people could be relied on to help me when my husband was away. Our oldest son, Jack III, caught the measles. For days, his fever ran much higher than normal. I couldn't get it to break.

I wanted Jack to come home right away but knew that he couldn't. I called his immediate supervisor—someone who has been a kind of "daddy" to us in the Lord. He came right over and we prayed for Jack III. Within hours, the fever subsided. Meanwhile, our doctor called, asking me to bring my youngest son, Mark, to his office to get a shot that would protect him from his brother's illness. What was I going to do? I didn't want to leave my sick son—and I didn't drive! I called a close friend, who agreed in an instant to drive Mark to the doctor's office. I breathed a sigh of relief and thanked God once again for watching over us. It was a lesson I've used many times. God's people are eager to help the pastor's wife. All she has to do is ask.

Sometimes, when Jack's schedule, my schedule and the children's schedules allowed, we did travel together as a family. These were work trips for Jack, and not always vacations for the rest of us! I learned to cope with restless, overactive children in a number of different situations and accommodations. I learned to keep everyone's clothes in order and to use the car window for a clothes line (no disposable diapers then!). I even potty-trained one tyke within 10 weeks—or 9,000 miles.

On those trips, I had to be ready and willing to handle anything. I juggled the kids, greeted people at our services, taught some classes and kept the suitcases packed and ready to go. It was hard work, but it was the price I was willing to pay to keep the children—and me—near Jack.

Toward the end of Jack's years as dean of students, we accepted a pastorate at a small church in nearby Van Nuys, California. Even though the church had only 18 members, we took on the new position with joy. For a while, I felt that "togetherness" I had experienced at the beginning of Jack's career. On Sunday mornings, Jack and I and the children would pile into the car, drive the 25 miles to the church, and arrive in time to clean the building before the other people came in. We were working together as a family, and it made me glad.

But as the church grew, Jack took on a heavy counseling load in addition to his regular administrative duties, study time and visitations. He was also still serving as dean of students at the training center in Los Angeles. Eventually, he cut back his responsibilities at the school to only that of a teacher. But as his pastoral responsibilities increased, his time at home became less and less.

Resentment rose up in me against all those people who "needed him." His family needed him, too, but our needs seemed to be low on the totem pole. I started to nag. "I can't take this anymore," I'd cry. Or "Why aren't you ever home?" Or "Don't you know the children need you?"

Quickly, the Lord pulled me up short, especially on that last statement. He made me realize that I was using the children to express my own needs. As far as they were concerned, everyone's father worked as much as Jack did. All they had known was a life of Daddy being busy at the office or off on a trip. The time he spent with them was special and good. I got the message and stopped badgering.

Jack did make an effort to be home for dinner. The dinner hour became an important family time. We played games (Hayford originals), discussed our days, prayed together for special needs and just enjoyed each other. Jack participated fully. Dinnertime always made up for the hours he was away from the house.

As the children grew up and started going to school, I had more time of my own. I looked for activities to get involved in—not just for my sake, I figured, but for Jack's and the children's, too. The last thing they needed was a frustrated wife and mommy with too much time on her hands. I joined craft classes, learned needlework and gardening, collected recipes—and tried them. I learned to drive. I got involved in several ministries at the church.

I soon recognized another benefit to my involvements, one that I hadn't expected. The times when I would "blow up" about Jack's schedule were getting farther and farther apart.

Maybe we were all growing up.

Now those "explosions" don't happen at all. Today, with 30 years of marriage behind me, I can honestly say I have no problem with the amount of time Jack spends at church or in travel to his many speaking engagements across the country. I am free to travel with him now, but I am also more independent at home. He is more sensitive and more faithful about taking a sabbath each week. We both are more flexible with our own schedules, as well as with each other's.

The Lord has taught us many things in 30 years. Jack and I are closer today than ever before because we have worked through the rough times and have learned to give and take as the need has arisen.

Ministry and family *are* partnerships, team efforts. Each spouse must work to bring harmony to the partnership. Each must contribute his or her own special talents to make a winning team. For a time, my major contribution was in the home. That meant spending a lot of time alone. But through prayer, my husband's support and the kindness of God's people, I learned to survive—and ultimately, to enjoy.

Born in 1933 in North Platte, Nebraska, **Anna Hayford** was seventh in a family of nine children. A heart condition kept her father from working outside the home, limiting the family's income. Still, the children were raised in an atmosphere of faith and prayer and always seemed to have "enough."

Anna met her husband, Jack, while both were attending Life Bible College in Los Angeles, California. They married in 1954 but continued their schooling until graduation in 1956. They have been involved in ministry ever since. Jack has been senior pastor of the Church on the Way in Van Nuys, California, since 1969.

The Hayfords have four children and five grandchildren. Their oldest daughter and her husband are on the pastoral staff at the Church on the Way. Another son is pastor of the Foursquare Church in Camarillo, California.

Mother

Chapter Seventeen
Raising a Family on a Pastor's Salary

by Joyce (Mrs. Karl) Strader

One sunny Florida day, I took one of the young ladies from our church out to lunch. Ramona had recently married a minister. Our conversation was lively and interesting as she shared about her new experience with me. I recognized myself in her. After all, I've been married to a minister for over 30 years.

As we returned to my home, I pulled the car into our garage. Our little family dog bounded out the door. Suddenly, Ramona turned to me.

"Joyce, you have arrived! You live in a nice home, you drive a Cadillac and you have a poodle!"

I was caught off guard. (I wasn't sure what the poodle had to do with it!) But in a moment, I responded, "Yes, I guess I have. God has been so good to Karl and me. But let me tell you what He's brought us through to get us here."

My mind raced back to Karl's and my humble beginnings in the ministry. We had not had material blessings showered upon us the moment we decided to serve God. Rather, we had many hard, lean years, years when Karl's salary was hardly enough to keep a roof over our heads. Years when I had to learn the lessons of stretching a dollar. Years when God showed us again and again that if we trusted Him, He would provide for all our needs.

Over time, the Lord has blessed us abundantly, far above all we ever imagined. He has more than given us our heart's desire. But it has been a progression, a learning experience, a training ground in trust.

After our marriage, Karl and I started a home missions work in Farmersburg, Indiana. The district organization gave us a tent for our services and their blessing—nothing more. My brother, Lloyd Wead, was a pastor in the area. He and his wife, Millie, allowed us to stay in their upstairs apartment. We had little money, but we did, at least, have a home and the security of being part of a loving family.

Our first son, Steve, was born in the county hospital. Somehow, the Lord arranged for the best obstetrician in the area to take care of me—and he refused to bill us for his services! Our only cost was $48 charged by the hospital.

Ten days after Steve's birth, our little family moved out of my brother's apartment and into a small house that consisted of three rooms and a *path*—to the outhouse. There was no indoor plumbing. Karl rigged up a shower by putting a hose over the rafters in the garage. It wasn't much, but it was affordable.

Every day, Karl and a group of men from the town worked on erecting a new church building. They hammered, sawed, nailed and sweated in the hot sun. My role was to feed the whole hungry crew on $10 a week. One sympathetic woman sensed my predicament and taught me to cook hamburger gravy and biscuits. I served it every afternoon, along with fresh cabbage and tomatoes that were cheap—sometimes free—and readily available during the Indiana summer. Not one man complained.

Toward the end of that summer, as Karl was literally nailing the last shingles on the roof of the new building, he received a call from Cy Homer, the president of Southeastern Bible College. Would Karl come to Lakeland, Florida, to serve as the school's dean of men? he asked.

Despite the closeness we felt to the people and the work in Farmersburg, Karl and I believed the move was in the Lord's plan. We loaded up our few belongings, most of which were the baby's, and headed for Florida. Our new home, like our old one, had three rooms, but there was a bath! Karl's salary was an unbelievable $75 a week. I was overwhelmed by God's goodness.

Several more moves were in store for us before we actually settled in Lakeland, however. After serving as dean of men at the Bible college for several years, Karl accepted a position as assistant pastor for a church in South Bend, Indiana. Later, he became a full pastor for a church in Gary. We were excited about having a pastorate, but financially, we fell into deep waters. Our house in South Bend had not sold, so our money was being eaten up by payments on a home no one was living in.

For a while, Karl considered getting a secular job to supplement his pastor's salary. But when the church deacons heard about our dilemma, they came to our rescue and helped us with our expenses until the house sold.

In time, Karl was called to pastor the First Assembly of God in Lakeland. Now called the Carpenter's Home Church, we have remained here for the last 20 years. And here we have experienced our greatest blessings—both spiritual and material.

Looking back, it is easy to see God's hand in providing for us. Each move was a step up financially. We never sought the positions—we were always too busy working where we were. And Karl never questioned what he received as remuneration. Somehow it was always enough.

Along the way, we found good family, kind friends, generous doctors, sensitive churches—each special gifts of God to us, the people through whom God worked His blessings. We also learned practical ways to help ourselves live happily on a pastor's salary.

The gravy and biscuits I learned to cook for the workmen in Indiana became only one of a large number of menus I developed around hamburger. Meals weren't always fancy in our house, but they were as nutritious as I could make them. We ate by candlelight and dined in style. The children were expected to use proper table etiquette, even when we were eating hamburger hash.

I furnished our homes creatively; that is, with pieces bought from second-hand stores and freight sales. I learned to re-finish furniture with an expert's touch. The pride I felt in each of our early homes nearly matched the fulfillment I received from having created something out of virtually nothing.

Three more children came after Steve. As they grew,

I faced the difficult task of outfitting them on a limited budget. Since I had no talent as a seamstress, I asked God for wisdom. He taught me to become the best bargain-hunter ever, buying most of the family's clothing off-season. These were not special purchase articles, but good quality brand names that the children could wear proudly and with style.

For myself, I refused to become a follower of fads, but did try to dress with a sense of fashion. Each season I would take inventory of what I had hanging in my closet. Most of the time, by adding an inexpensive belt or scarf, it was easy to update my "look."

Karl supported my efforts to make myself, my family and my home as attractive as possible. While we worked hard to stay within our budget and to keep from getting caught up in material things, we had seen too many pastors' wives and families beaten down in their souls because their homes were dull and lifeless and their clothing drab. We believed God was a God of creativity and beauty, even physical beauty. We trusted the Holy Spirit to teach us the resourcefulness we needed to bring that beauty into our lives.

Never once did we borrow money for pleasure trips. Vacations were important, but we found ways to keep from spending all our money on them. During the years when the children were small, we went to Christian campmeetings in or around the state. These were always working holidays for Karl, but he loves to preach and never minded. Meanwhile, I didn't have to cook, and the children were able to make new friends and see new places. We still remember those times as fondly as some of the more expensive vacations we've taken in recent years.

Even when we had barely enough money for groceries, we tithed. I was taught the value of the tithe as a little girl growing up in the Dakotas. If I earned a dollar or was given a dollar for my birthday, 10 cents went into a little jar I kept in my room. I remember one day when a fire swept over the prairie near our farm. I stood outside with my father, watching the fire approach our fields, praying.

"Lord, You know everything I have belongs to You," Dad spoke out loud. "I've been faithful to tithe, give offerings and feed the poor. Do You really want all our grain to go up in smoke?"

Apparently, He did not. The fire burned right up to our fence and went out.

From the beginning of our marriage, Karl and I were set on this one thing: we would not rob God. We believed the lesson of Malachi 3 that if we gave freely to the Lord, we would be blessed beyond measure.

We were also determined to be good stewards of the money God gave us. Karl has always kept the household books meticulously. It was his job from the beginning, not because he is a man, but simply because he's better at it than I am. Now our oldest daughter, Karla, who is excellent with figures, helps her father. Oftentimes, the woman is the better bookkeeper. In those families, she should have the job. That's just good stewardship.

The most important lesson we learned, however, was how to receive from others. Someone once asked why mothers love their babies so much, when the babies give so little to them. The answer: because they give so much to their babies! Everywhere we went, our church people wanted to give to us and do things for us. With gratefulness, we let them. We accepted their gifts of time, effort and material things as gifts from the Lord. As a result, we were always very much loved in every church we pastored. We were blessed, but so were they. As Jesus taught, "It is more blessed to give than to receive." We never wanted to deny our people a blessing by turning them away.

Raising a family on a pastor's salary has not always been easy. But God has been faithful. He has provided and He has prospered, not all at once, but in His timing.

"Beloved, I wish above all things that you prosper...even as your soul prospers," the Bible says in 3 John 2. We can expect God to bless us—physically, spiritually, materially—if we trust Him and follow Him.

Born in 1929 in Selfridge, North Dakota, **Joyce Strader** was the youngest of six children in a Christian family. Her father, a merchant in North and South Dakota, was the frequent host of traveling ministers and missionaries.

Joyce met her husband, Karl, at Bob Jones University in South Carolina. She worked as recreational director for the Shriners' Hospital for Crippled Children, and the two were married in the garden on the hospital grounds. They started immediately into full-time ministry as part of a home missions work in Farmersburg, Indiana.

The Straders first moved to Florida when Karl was asked to serve as dean of men at Southeastern Bible College in Lakeland. They left the state to pastor churches in Indiana for a time but eventually returned to Lakeland, where Karl pastors the Carpenter's Home Church.

Three of the Straders' four children are involved in their ministry. There are two grandchildren.

Chapter Eighteen
When Death Takes a Child

─────────

by Anne (Mrs. James) Beall

I watched from the living room window as my eldest
son, Jimmie, made his way down the steps of the city
bus and up the street to our driveway. Something was
wrong. Why was he swinging his foot out and around
in that peculiar manner? What was wrong with him?

This was the fall of 1969. Jimmie, 22 years old, had
been employed for several months at the Eisenhower
Post Office in downtown Detroit. The government job
was a real answer to prayer. Finally, our young man
was on his way to becoming self-sufficient.

For many years, my husband, Jim, and I weren't sure
we'd see that day. Most of Jimmie's schooling had taken
place in special education classes because of a learning
disability. He could read and communicate, but he drew
a mental blank when confronted with a math problem
or a situation demanding deductive thinking. But because
of his unique memory he could, in a limited way, sur-

vive in the working world.

Still we worried. Who would watch out for our boy if anything ever happened to us?

When Jimmie came in through the back door, I began my "20 Questions."

"How do you feel, Jimmie? Is your leg all right? Did you hurt yourself?"

"My foot feels as if it has gone to sleep," he said. "It feels numb. I'm not sure I have my foot on the ground when I walk. I swing my foot so I will know it is out there ahead of me."

Oh, no, I thought to myself.

"Why didn't you say something? How long has this been going on?" I asked my son, looking into his eyes. I knew I would not learn much from his answer. Jimmie was not a complainer and rarely, if ever, talked about the way he felt.

Well, whatever is happening, we'll get to the bottom of it, I told myself. After all, that's what doctors are for.

In November, Jimmie was admitted to Harper Hospital. The neurologists ran a battery of tests over a two-week period but found nothing conclusive.

At the time, our church, Bethesda Missionary Temple, was celebrating its annual fall festival, and Jimmie became the focus of our prayers. Minister friends from all over the country came to share in the spiritual festivities. Many went with us to Harper Hospital. Prayers were prayed and prophets prophesied our son's immediate healing. We believed for Jimmie's healing without a doubt or question. We rejoiced in our expectation.

The Broyles family (mine) and the Beall family (Jim's) were and are believers in Christ—committed believers.

We believed the Lord could and would heal all our diseases. Brothers, sisters, aunts and uncles could all testify to miracles of healing. The Lord had been good to us. We were a healthy bunch and were spiritually indignant that any in our number should catch a common virus, let alone experience numbness in a foot or limb. But James Broyles Beall never worked again. During the next year and a half, he went back to Harper Hospital three times. Finally, on Good Friday, 1971, the doctors reached their conclusion. Jim and I sat stunned in the office of Dr. Raymond Bauer as he told us Jimmie had a rare disease called Olivo-ponto-cerebellum deterioration.

"A rare disease? How could Jimmie get a rare disease in this day and age? How does one get such a disease? What do you do about it?" We fired our questions like gunshots.

Calmly, Dr. Bauer explained there was little known about Jimmie's problem. The medical journals only devoted one paragraph to it. Since the cause was unknown, there was no known treatment or cure. He did know, however, that as our son's cerebellum deteriorated, his control over body functions would also deteriorate. The prognosis: two years at most to live.

We returned home, sat down, turned our chairs toward the front window and stared at the world in disbelief. This simply could not be happening to us. We were shaken to the very core.

After a few days, however, we pulled ourselves together. Our fighting spirits took over. Would we accept the verdict of death? No! We had our God, and He would see us through. Bethesda Missionary Temple rallied around us. We prayed. We stormed heaven.

Intercession went up from the prayer tower at Oral Roberts University. Kathryn Kuhlman and other minister friends in the United States and around the world joined us in prayer.

But our son's condition worsened.

In the beginning of his paralysis, Jimmie was able to maneuver with a cane. In a short time, however, a walker became necessary. By the end of the first year, he was confined to a wheelchair. One muscle after another—and one motor ability after another—fell asleep. We began to feed Jimmie all his meals.

In June 1973, Jim and I drove Jimmie and our other two children, Analee and John, to New Orleans for the annual convention of the Word of Faith Temple. Pastor Charles Green, his wife, Barbara, and their two children, Mike and Cindy, were special people in Jimmie's world. He wanted to see them again. It was Word of Faith's 20th anniversary and Jimmie's 26th birthday. After the two rollicking celebrations, we left Louisiana and headed to Florida for a summer vacation.

As the excitement of our days in New Orleans subsided and we settled in to rest, Jim and I were able to take a closer look at our ailing son. We were frightened by what we saw. It was obvious that Jimmie had become too weak to bear a long automobile trip back to Michigan. Jim, Jimmie and Analee flew back to Detroit. Somehow, John and I made the long drive. But what had we come home to?

Jim put Jimmie to bed as soon as they got in from the airport. That was where he was when John and I finally arrived. And that was where he was to remain for the next 10 years.

Bethesda's annual youth conference began the next

week. The day before the festivities got under way, Jimmie fell out of bed. Jim and I did our best to get his 6'1'' frame back under the covers, but in the process, Jim sprained his back. My husband, the fellow who always prided himself on being able to win in any sport over men half his age, suddenly didn't fit the image of youth he once had. He was being worn down, and so was I.

Something had to be done. Our world had to change, I thought. How can we continue to care for our family, the church and our terminally ill son? We must get someone to help with Jimmie. But who? And for how long? Oh, God, help us. We need answers!

Our answer came in the form of a young man, Larry Ruehlen, and his wife, Nancy. They were gifts from God. Larry was studying to be a registered male nurse, and for the next five years he came to our house every day between classes to help with Jimmie. In later years, Nancy took up the task and ministered to our son every day until the day he died. My sister, Sallye, also came every Sunday morning so I could attend church. Many others helped in other ways.

Had Dr. Bauer told us we would be taking care of a bedridden son for 10 years, I don't know if we could've handled it. As it was, we learned to live one day at a time. Early on, Jim and I settled the fact that Jimmie was *our* son, not mine alone. The bulk of Jimmie's care from day to day was my responsibility, but Jim had a responsibility, too. Emotionally and spiritually, I needed my husband. Jimmie needed his dad. So Jim limited his travel (he's in great demand as a conference, convention and church speaker) to Thursday and Friday nights, except for special occasions. Besides being good for Jimmie and me, this light schedule was good for Jim, too. He had time for writing, for radio and television broadcasts, for weddings and dedications of babies and funerals—for pastoring. The church grew.

Our relationship grew, too. Marriage, as I understand it, involves two people sharing both the good and bad of life. Trouble will either bring you closer together or drive you farther apart. Jim and I chose to be together through it all.

Caring for our dying son brought me face-to-face with my faith. I realized how much I knew about God, and how little I knew. I had honestly thought I had a lot of answers to life's questions. In reality, I had very few.

When people like us believe in healing, and healing is either delayed or does not come at all, we are faced with why. Jim and I asked ourselves this question. Other people asked us, too. "Where is your faith?" "Are you sure you're right with God?" "You don't really expect God to heal, do you?"

During Jimmie's illness, Jim and I exercised all the faith we knew how to muster. We prayed every prayer we knew and endeavored to learn new ones. We demanded. We pleaded. We cried. We fasted. We quoted the positive promises of God. We bargained for Jimmie's health.

Finally, we laid the matter in the hands of God, believing that gains and losses in life are always mysteriously intertwined. We felt inner peace at last.

Jim decided to share our lessons by writing an article that he titled "Learning How to Cope." Upon its publication in a national magazine, however, we were lambasted with indignant letters. Good Christians wrote to tell us that if we had as much real faith as we had "coping faith," our son would be healed. A few had choice words to say about our "hidden sins." Some were downright cruel.

Other good-intentioned people decided they could "help." One woman reasoned that what Jimmie needed was physical therapy. While I was away one afternoon, she came into the house and put our dying son through a rigorous exercise program. Jimmie was out of touch with reality for several days following her visit.

Some were sure that our son would be healed if they could lay their hands on him. We allowed this for a few months. Then we noticed that Jimmie's emotions were being torn apart. He believed with all his heart, yet no healing came. It was more than he could bear. Finally we said, "No more." We welcomed prayer on Jimmie's behalf, but we believed God could heal even if the prayer was offered some distance from the house.

One day—I have no recollection of the actual date—Jim and I settled in our hearts that Jimmie was going to die. We determined that we would make things as comfortable for him as we could. We would go on living our lives. We decided, with God's help, not to feel sorry for ourselves, not to cast a cloud of gloom around us, not to get angry with God, not to quit the church or stop preaching, not to stop planning for the future.

The Lord gave and the Lord was taking away. By His grace we were going to say, "Blessed be the name of the Lord."

I picked myself up and turned to serve my family with renewed vigor. We celebrated the weddings of Annalee and John. We welcomed into the world a granddaughter from each union. The two little girls learned to sit on Jimmie's bed and pat his cheek before they could walk or talk. He loved them.

I served in the church. I kept the books, prepared the payroll, wrote monthly letters to our missionaries, taught a teachers' training class. I was once again the pastor's wife.

Jimmie's funeral was held on November 1, 1983. He was 36 years old. Jim and I and the rest of the family sat quietly on the front row of the sanctuary as the minister conducted the service.

This is not the way we expect life to treat us, I thought. Fathers and mothers are not supposed to bury their firstborn sons. Children are supposed to mourn at their parents' graves, not the other way around.

But for us, that order of life was not to be.

We listened intently as the minister read from Romans 8:38-39: "For I am persuaded that neither death, nor life, nor angels, nor principalities, nor powers, nor things present, nor things to come, nor height, nor depth, nor any other creature, shall be able to separate us from the love of God, which is in Christ Jesus our Lord."

Yes, that's right! The words of Scripture comforted us. Jimmie's death must not, would not, be allowed to separate us from the love of God.

Several years have passed now since that day. Christ's love is still ours—the most real thing in our lives. Jim and I are as busy as ever. Our families and our church are thriving.

We've not let go of Jesus. And praise God, He's not let go of us.

Anne Beall, born in 1925 in Tulare, California, was one of four children raised on a farm in Tennessee. Her mother was a Methodist preacher. Together, Anne's parents started two churches, both of which are still in existence today.

During the second World War, Anne's family moved to Michigan and began attending Bethesda Missionary Temple in Detroit. There she met the pastor's son, Jim—her future husband— who had come home from the Navy. They were married the next year.

Jim has pastored Bethesda for the last 40 of the congregation's 52 years. The church is currently building a new complex on 92 acres in nearby Sterling Heights.

The Bealls have two married children and four grandchildren. Their eldest son, Jimmy, died after many years of illness and disability.

Chapter Nineteen
So Your Kid's on Drugs?

by Marilyn (Mrs. Wallace) Hickey

If there's anything a pastor's wife hates, it's to be put in an embarrassing situation in front of her congregation. I think it's easier to be embarrassed in front of your children, your husband, your parents, your co-workers, even the audience at a crusade meeting in another city, than to be ashamed or embarrassed in your own church.

I don't know why pastors' wives want to appear "perfect" before their congregations, but they do. As a pastor's wife, I always wanted to look well, act well, speak well and do everything I could to make my congregation think I was "turned-on" spiritually. I never wanted to be an embarrassment either to the poorest member of our church or to the banker's wife. I always wanted them to say with pride, "And this is my pastor's wife, Marilyn Hickey." Maybe that wasn't a very spiritual goal, but it was a goal, nevertheless.

That was before I found out that my son had a problem with drugs. At age 16, Mike openly declared that he was smoking marijuana. He said he enjoyed it, and he was going to continue smoking it whether Wally and I liked it or not.

When Mike made this announcement at home in Denver, I was in Des Moines, Iowa, conducting an evangelistic meeting. My initial reaction was to want to hide myself. Unfortunately, I was scheduled to speak in less than an hour!

How can I go before that congregation as a victorious Christian and present anything of value? I asked myself, despairing. I felt that I was the poorest mother—the poorest pastor's wife—in the world. How could I hold my head up? I was sure I had failed my child, my son— the most precious, vulnerable thing in my whole life!

I realized later that a lot of pastors' wives have had the same experience and the same feelings. They were not really "allowed" to be absent from a church service. So, like me, they pasted on a smile, checked their appearance, prayed and asked God to give them the strength to walk out and do whatever it was they were supposed to do. And somehow, they made it through to the end.

That night in Des Moines I spoke with a suffering heart. I had to depend on God for every word. But as a result of my dependency, an unusually heavy anointing fell on the meeting. The response to the altar call was tremendous.

When I got home to Denver, Wally and I sat down and talked with Mike. We could see plainly that he was very, very rebellious in spirit. Oh, he said all the right things—"I won't smoke pot anymore," "I'll straighten up, I promise''—but his father and I both had the sinking feeling these were outward, not inward, responses.

We decided to trust Mike. Soon, however, we realized he had been lying. Again and again we found evidence of marijuana—in his room, in his backpack, even in his clothes before I threw them in the washing machine.

I read books on how to handle a child on drugs. I prayed. Nothing changed. Finally, when Mike was 19, Wally told him he could not live at home and continue to be involved with the drug scene. Mike had to make a decision. If he wanted to live at home, he could not take drugs. But if he wanted to take drugs, he would have to go out and get a job to support his habit. Wally made it clear to Mike that we loved him too dearly to support anything that would damage or hurt him.

Mike chose to leave home, and our hearts broke. Soon afterwards, I heard he was sleeping in one of the city parks. I was horrified! News reports had been circulating about murders being committed in the parks. Night after night, the devil would wake me to taunt me about how poorly we had handled Mike's situation, filling me with fear for my son's safety.

Fortunately, I knew that the Bible said in Psalm 34:7: ''The angel of the Lord encampeth round about them that fear Him....'' So I claimed that those same angels would encamp around my son. Whether Mike feared the Lord or not, I certainly did. I also claimed Proverbs 11:21: ''...the seed of the righteous shall be delivered.''

The Scriptures gave me great hope and encouragement. It's an experience many can testify of: in times of crisis and despair, God's Word gives very special promises. These are promises each of us can stand on all the way to victory! I keep a notebook full of Scripture verses that have been God's nourishment and support for me in difficult times. They are like familiar friends to me; I lean upon them, and they bring me through.

Wally and I knew we couldn't hide our son's drug problem from the congregation. Mike had even approached some of the other teenagers in the church to sell drugs to them! What do you do? Do you smile and act as if everything is all right? Or do you "spill your guts" to the whole assembly? After much prayer, we decided to "spill our guts."

Wally and I stood before the church and, with sadness and humility, told the people we had been battling Mike's drug problem off and on for three years.

"We know we haven't been perfect parents, but we have sought the Lord, and we believe we've done many of the right things," we said. "We love Mike. We're desperate, and we need your prayers."

The response to our disclosure was overwhelming. Never in my life had I felt such warmth and love from a congregation. Whenever I walked into the church, someone was right there to minister a word of encouragement. One person would give me a Scripture verse. Another would tell me how God had brought his son or daughter through a crisis. A few came to me very openly and said, "I was embarrassed to tell you before, but I have the same problem in my home. Would you please pray for my child?" Many assured us they were praying.

The presentation of our need opened their hearts. Suddenly, I realized that *I* was the one who had expected me to be "perfect"; the people had not. Of course, we did receive some criticism, but that was only natural.

The most important thing I could do was to please the Lord. I will never totally please the congregation. But if I please the Lord, the people will be blessed.

For six years there was no change in Mike's lifestyle. We saw no light, not even a glimmer of response to the gospel on his part. When would the clouds break? I cried.

Then one morning as I was praying in church, the Holy Spirit spoke very sweetly to my heart. I had just been telling the Lord that Mike's circumstances were worse than they'd ever been. He responded, "That is what I use—circumstances." And it was at that very moment that the circumstances of Mike's life were beginning to turn around.

Mike was 25. The girl he was living with, Barbara, was pregnant. She already had a four-year-old child, and the three of them had just been thrown out of their apartment. It was a cold, wintery night in Denver, and they had no place to go. Finally, a friend agreed to take them in for a few weeks.

At the friend's home, Mike told Barbara they needed to pray. She agreed, and in a very simple way, they spoke to the Lord. Less than seven days later, they came to a church service.

Mike had come to church occasionally during those years, but it was usually just to con us for money or to con someone else in the congregation. This time we knew he was sincere. It wasn't long before he sought Christian counseling. He made little, tiny steps at first, but they were steps! Then, one night, a woman from the church went to pray with Mike and Barbara. Together, they recommitted their lives to Christ.

Their wedding followed. We were glad Mike asked

his father to perform the ceremony. Still, Wally and I had mixed feelings. As happy as we were about their new commitment to Christ, we knew, and the congregation knew, that Mike had spent years rebelling against all the things we stood for. Now he and his seven-months-pregnant bride looked the very picture of rebellion. Nevertheless, our congregation stood with us, not against us.

There are still problems. Sometimes Mike came to our services so dirty and smelly that I wanted to look the other way and say, "This is not my son." But everyone knew he was. And instead of hating me or criticizing me, they loved me and showed greater compassion and faith for the need in our family.

Today, Mike and Barbara have a sweet baby girl named Melia. Five-year-old Tabby attends the Christian school in our church. Mike and Barbara still have their ups and downs, but now there are more "ups" than "downs"—praise the Lord!

Do you face problems with your children? Are you afraid to let your congregation know? Then you need, first of all, to be honest with God. Tell Him you are hurting. There is nothing more painful to a mother than when her children hurt her. God knows this.

Next, be honest with your congregation. Don't run *from* them—run *to* them. You need their prayers, their love and their faith too much to hide behind embarrassment or pride.

I've been a pastor's wife for 25 years. Sometimes I think I've been through everything—although I'm sure there've been a few things I've missed. But let me encourage you: if you ever have a problem, now or in the future, remember that God is faithful. And your congregation is, too!

Marilyn Hickey is the wife of Wallace Hickey, pastor of the Happy Church in Denver, Colorado. Married in 1954, the couple has two children, Michael and Sarah.

Marilyn has a bachelor's degree from the University of Northern Colorado and has spent over 19 years in intensive Bible study. Initially, she felt that her main ministry was to assist her husband in the pastorate. However, while meditating on the Bible one day, she heard God call her to "cover the earth with His Word."

In response, Marilyn founded the Marilyn Hickey Ministries, which has grown into an international organization ministering around the world through publications, radio and television programs, conferences and crusades, charity funds, a Bible training institute and counseling services. She considers the practical application of the Scriptures to everyday life her ministry specialty.

Chapter Twenty
Vacations Are Special

by Gail (Mrs. Stephen) Whyte

Somehow it doesn't seem spiritual for a pastor and his family to take a vacation. It is the proud—and overtired—minister who boasts, "I haven't had a holiday in five years." Most people apply to a boss for time off, and an impersonal system gives the OK. But the pastor has to announce his plans to hundreds of people. Some of them don't have enough money to take a vacation of their own. Others are hurting and will most likely have a crisis while he's gone. What kind of pastor would choose a frivolous thing like a holiday over ministering to his flock?

If he does plan a vacation, then certainly he must go to a Christian retreat center or make plans to minister en route to his destination. It is better for him to say he is going preaching and bringing the family along than simply to say he is taking a holiday.

Right? Wrong! A pastor *needs* vacations. It is the wise

congregation that encourages him to take them. They know he'll come back rested, refreshed and all the more effective in service.

Vacation means just that: to vacate. To leave all work behind. Like a vacant house, to empty it of all ministerial furniture so it can be refurnished with things that are really important—God and family.

Pastors' families need vacations, too. Fortunately, my husband, Stephen, recognizes this. If he won't face the church to ask time off for his own sake, then he'll do it for mine and the kids'. He'll do it for the family.

Like every untitled, unsalaried pastor's wife, I share in the pastoral ministry. I worry, pray, cry over erring ones and devote my energies to helping Stephen bring God's purposes to pass in our local assembly. I open my home and my heart to dozens of "angels unaware" who pass through. I also run a strategic discipleship program for four trainees—my children, Anne, 13, Lisa, 11, Timothy, 8, and Katherine, 6. Sometimes I need a vacation.

The children are brought up with a corporate mentality that says we minister as a family. When we have guests, they help with the extra cleaning, cooking and preparations. They entertain along with us. When Stephen and I minister out of town, they minister by praying for us and being trustworthy in our absence. Then, of course, they have their daily work routines, their school lessons, their extra-curricular activities. Sometimes they need a holiday, too.

Vacations are family times. When we go away as a family, we see only each other. We give back to each other in lump sum the moments that were gobbled away by pressures, stress and a million separate activities throughout the year. Our family holidays have not been memorable because of the places we've gone or the money we've spent. Rather they've been great because of the time and attention we've given to each other.

One of our favorite vacations was a trip to Florida—a mystical, tropical haven to those of us living north of the 49th parallel. We stayed rent-free (a gift from friends) in a furnished condominium with all the comforts of home, overlooking a quiet, deserted beach.

Disney World and Epcot Center were within easy driving distance, so we spent a day at each park. But all their man-made wonder and excitement didn't compare with that of the beach. We passed most of our days building sandcastles, collecting shells, burying Stephen ("Daddy") in the sand, ducking under waves, poking at little sea and sand creatures formerly unknown to us, and soaking up the sun. We watched with wonder the tides and the constant shaping and reshaping of the beach. We mused at God's power and authority in decreeing the bounds of the tossing surf.

At night we sat together in the living room, the children all washed and scrubbed and ready for bed, and held family devotions. It was near Easter, so we reviewed the events that led to Jesus' crucifixion. Stephen and I were amazed at the questions the children asked, the sudden insights they had and the prayers they spoke out loud. Their conversations with God went on and on—in large part, we knew, because they wanted to put off bedtime for as long as possible. We didn't mind. We'd left clock-watching at home.

There was a sweet sense of the Holy Spirit that lingered after the children were asleep. Stephen and I sat and read long into the night. We were as one, together with God. The only sound was the rhythmic pounding of the waves. It was a moment in heaven.

Other vacations have taken us thousands of miles from home in the trusty family station wagon. We travel packed-down, our space limited, often covering a few hundred miles at a stretch. One time we actually motored 1,500 miles in less than three driving days with four children, all under seven years of age—and enjoyed it!

We go prepared. First, we pray. Then, from Stephen on down to Katherine, we commit ourselves to happiness. It's our holiday, and each one of us must submit ourselves to the higher goal of an enjoyable time for all. Songs, stories, tapes and simple handiwork, not to mention a tin of Traverner's Fruit Drops, help occupy six busy minds and keep the peace. We follow the biblical principle found in Proverbs 17:14: "It's hard to stop a quarrel once it starts, so don't let it begin."

To help release stored-up energy, we plan our stops. Even a simple refueling at the gas station is an opportunity to run laps around the car. We stay in motels with pools and playgrounds. And rather than go into restaurants, we choose roadside stops, parks and picnic areas to eat the bran muffins, deli-style foods, dried and fresh fruits and other goodies that I've prepared and packed. After riding in the car for four hours, the last thing any of us, Stephen and I included, wants to do is sit around a table in confined quarters and behave.

Luxury is not necessary for a great vacation, we've found. Several summers ago we rented a cottage in northeastern Ontario at a friend's recommendation. Although we had only seen a few snapshots of the place, we were intrigued by our friend's description of a tranquil, idyllic spot far away from the city. Our anticipation grew as we learned that the cottage was waterlocked and came with a 14-foot motorboat to make the two-mile trip from the local marina to the cottage.

We weren't prepared for what we saw when we tied up at the small, decaying dock and helped the children out of the boat. The cottage was indeed isolated. It was bounded at the rear by the tapering end of a high escarpment, in front by the lake. Dwellings on either side, which we were told were usually vacant, were hidden by trees.

The steep steps that led up to the house were dilapidated and had no handrail. Stephen and I looked at each other a little nervously. Silently, we went in to inspect.

The cottage had no ceiling, only rafters and a roof. The walls separating the rooms were single sheets of paneling. Curtains served as interior doors. There were few conveniences—only cold running water, electric heat and an outhouse. Television, radio and phones were all missing. We groaned.

We felt as alone and cut off from the world as we could be. We had expected quiet, but now we panicked. City life, four children and a busy pastorate were no preparation for a place like this.

We had reserved the cottage for two weeks. How could we last that long in the wilderness? Stephen and I wracked our brains to think of someone to call—from the phone back at the marina—to take the cottage for the second week of our commitment.

No one came to mind, so we sat down and tried to regain our composure. Slowly, a peace came over us. Stephen spoke.

"Gail, now that I think about it, isn't this the kind of place we both want and need? No telephones, no doorbells, no distractions?''

I mulled over his statement. ''Well, yes, maybe a little quiet and simplicity will do us good,'' I said. ''And isn't it good, too, that the children have no one to play with but each other? I've always said I wanted them to grow up being one another's best friends.''

We decided to stay. Much to our surprise, the cottage turned out to be the very haven our weary souls needed, so much so that we went back every summer for the next six years.

Those two weeks were filled with canoe rides, water sports, Scrabble games, quiet chats and jogs in the woods. Time was measured by the rumbling of the stomach or the length of exposure to the sun's rays. Little things became the stuff of life. Even the lowly hot dog was elevated to gastronomic delight after a full day of fishing, catching frogs and collecting wildflowers.

We made many new discoveries, not only about nature, but about ourselves. Early in the first week, Stephen and I found ourselves at odds over the children. I thought he was watching them. He thought I was. Meanwhile, they were running about with no one in charge.

''How come I don't have any trouble looking after the children when you're not here?'' I asked Stephen accusingly.

''Well, I don't have any trouble when you're not here, either!'' he shot back.

We sat down and discussed the problem. Little by little, we traced the source of our confusion to one of authority—not of usurping it or trying to hold onto it, but of both of us surrendering it at the same time.

For most of the year, I was at home with the children

while Stephen was at work. I was the day-to-day manager of the household, and the children were my responsibility. But now that Stephen was with us during the day, I assumed he would take over the children's direction. After all, he was the head of the household.

For his part, Stephen assumed I would continue in my management role. He didn't feel that my leadership in the area of child-rearing, even on holiday, undermined his own position.

We spent many hours over the next several days hammering out the specifics of what each of us expected from the other. It was good to have the uninterrupted time to explore each other's feelings, needs and concerns. Stephen didn't have a meeting to run off to and I didn't have to answer the telephone. Instead of pushing us apart, the conflict drew us closer, oiling our relationship like fine machinery.

Much of our conversation took place on the lake. While the children cleared away the supper dishes in the early evenings, Stephen would paddle me across the water in the canoe. I'd sit in the bow, luxuriating over a cup of steaming coffee. We'd talk about our immediate concerns and about our future. We'd imagine for ourselves lives we knew would never be ours, as well as lives that could be. These were precious times of oneness for us.

Often during our nightly devotions, we'd lose track of time, just as in the day. One evening, God visited us in a special way. As we began to pray, one of the children started to cry. We sensed the Holy Spirit moving upon us. For the next hour and a half, we all cried, laughed and danced spontaneously. The children sang in the spirit and prophesied. We confessed sins and praised God. Our souls were thoroughly refreshed.

Later, Stephen and I mused about the deep encounter we had with the Lord. Such encounters take time, time we often didn't have in the city. But in that simple little cottage on the lake, time was on our side.

Vacations are special. When all is said and done, the greatest gift Stephen and I can give our children—and each other—is our time, our energy and our God. Throughout the year, we are able to snatch a few moments here and a few moments there. But it is only on holiday that our time is uninterrupted, our focus undisturbed and our hearts truly free.

Ecclesiastes says there's a time for every purpose under heaven. I believe there's a time for vacations, yes, even for a busy pastor and his family. *Especially* for a busy pastor and his family. Plan one now.

Born in 1943 in Toronto, Canada, to a Scottish Anglican mother and English Presbyterian father, **Gail Whyte** was raised in a Canadian farm community, the youngest of four children. She came to know the Lord as a child.

Gail met her husband, Stephen, at church. Their courtship lasted five years, and they were married while both were attending different universities.

Stephen taught school before accepting a position as assistant pastor under his father, A.A. Maxwell Whyte. Since 1976, he has been senior pastor at Dayspring Christian Fellowship in Toronto, Canada.

Gail graduated from the University of Toronto and has taught in elementary and secondary schools. The Whytes have four children, ages 13, 11, 8 and 6.

Chapter Twenty-One
Teaching Your Kids to Pray

by Jeanne (Mrs. Jack) Barron

When the pastor's family consists of three active kids—in my case, two teenagers and an adolescent—the pastor's wife does a lot of praying. She has to. Prayer, coupled with family devotions, is our survival kit in this generation. Not only do parents have to pray, they must teach their children the value of prayer.

Often as I am drifting off to sleep, one of my teens will crash into the room with "Mom! Can you pray with me?" I love it. I love having my children come to me with their questions, frustrations and problems, requesting that I pray with them! But this confidence in the power of prayer did not just *happen* in my children's lives. It was developed from the cradle.

In fact, there was a time when I was not at all sure I would survive parenthood, much less have three children who would grow up loving Jesus.

Jack and I had been married several years before our

first child came along. Neither of us had given up hope, even though our doctor said there was very little possibility I could conceive. We prayed earnestly, and constantly, for a miracle. Then it happened. A baby was on the way!

In the midst of the excitement I began to see there was more to this than just having a baby. The word "responsibility" kept piercing my thoughts as I prayed. And it involved far more than the natural things I was looking forward to: nurturing, loving and caring for the baby's physical needs. It had to do with spiritual matters.

Once I realized that, I would lay my hands on my tummy and pray for God's blessing and perfect will for the life of my child. Then one very warm August day, the Holy Spirit spoke to me about preparing my child to receive these blessings.

On a note pad, I wrote down Scripture verses that pertained to child rearing. Both the Old and New Testaments offered a gold mine of instruction. I searched these verses for the key.

I found it in 1 Samuel, chapter one. Hannah, Samuel's mother, conveyed a quality of life to her young son, well before he was presented at the temple. Hannah was a woman of prayer. She knew the Lord. And she communicated her belief in prayer to her son, for he was to grow up a praying man.

Eli, the priest, was a carnal man, certainly not the inspiration of Samuel's great spiritual development. Samuel was God's man in Israel largely because of his praying mother. With my hands on my expanding stomach, I dreamed that I, too, might inspire spiritual greatness in my child by following Hannah's example.

On a pastor's salary, I would probably never leave

a legacy of great material wealth, but I could provide something of eternal value. I could lead our son or daughter to know and love God. I could teach him—or her—to pray.

In the minutes after our baby was born I experienced what mothers for all ages have felt—inexpressible joy as she was placed in my arms for the first time. Touching her red, wrinkled face, I whispered, "Thank You, Jesus, for such a beautiful little girl."

During those early days, long before Adina could perceive the full joy and power of prayer, I began teaching her to love to pray. After Jack left for work, I would hold her close to my breast while I read the Bible out loud. Then I would gently rock her as I prayed, talking out loud to God and singing little songs of praise. I could sense that she, too, was praying and praising.

Then, fourteen months after the birth of Adina, we had another miracle. The calm order of our lives was interrupted forever as Lance arrived seven weeks ahead of schedule.

I was not prepared for the new life-style this bundle of joy brought into our home. Lance was full of energy. My quiet times with the Lord were sabotaged by this toothless wonder. I felt helpless and frayed. Scenes of the serenity Adina and I had enjoyed haunted me. Was I never to feel the gentle breath of quietness again?

Within weeks my spiritual strength faded without those daily times of refreshing. I became irritable and frustrated with even insignificant tasks. I was convinced I had failed as a wife, mother and pastor's wife.

Finally, my fighter spirit surfaced. I *would* be victorious. I *would* soar above it all, with my heavenly Father. I *would* renew my daily quiet time. Whatever the cost, I would overcome!

I planned to rise an hour earlier in the mornings—a true sacrifice since I am a nocturnal creature. But I hadn't bargained for the alarm waking me *and* Lance! And when Lance woke, the entire world got up. He would not be pacified with a warm bottle and demanded my undivided attention.

Many mornings my tears mingled with his as I tried to re-establish my hour with the Lord. By the time Jack and Adina were ready to start the day, I was drained. Jack gently suggested that my body needed that extra hour of sleep, my morning devotionals were too impractical. They were too hard on all of us!

I cried out to God to restore order, His order, in my life. In answer, the Holy Spirit prompted me to talk openly with Jack about my longing for a quiet time, and to ask for his recommendation.

To my great relief, Jack helped me structure our days to include a time when I could slip away from the children, from him and from the phone for an hour or so. During this hour he watched Adina and Lance while I drove in the country, walked down a shaded lane or hid in an obscure room in the church. Wherever my solitude, my soul was being restored.

During the recovery process I again became acutely aware that Adina and Lance needed a devotional pattern. I designed a plan I believed would give our children a solid spiritual foundation. Some days, the devotions were joyous and beautiful; other days, they were a total disaster. But Jack and I determined to pray daily for and with our children.

Shortly after we made this resolution I faced the most crucial change of Jack's ministry.

The day was icy. We had not seen the sun clearly for almost a week. The children were asleep and the house was quiet. Standing at the kitchen window, I drank in the beauty of the winter wonderland on the trees and shrubs. Snowflakes danced gracefully to the shimmering earth. Humming softly, I praised Jesus for the peace He had given me. What more could a woman desire? I was blessed with a loving husband, two beautiful, healthy children and a flourishing church.

Jack had been in the sanctuary most of the day, in fellowship with the Father. Often, after such times, he would tell me what the Holy Spirit had revealed to him. My heart stirred as I heard him come in the front door.

He slipped his arms around me, assuring me of his love and commitment to me and the children. For the brief moment that he held me, I wished everyone could know the same kind of love and security.

Jack's next words shattered my peaceful little world. The Holy Spirit had indeed spoken to him. Jack was certain He had commissioned him to resign the pastorate and travel as an evangelist.

He planned to sell all our belongings, purchase a small mobile home and evangelize. I had never seen him so stirred. My eyes stung as I quoted Ruth's words to Naomi, "Whither thou goest, I will go."

The decision made, we moved rapidly. Within weeks we had sold most of our furniture and were living in our very own mobile home, traveling from town to town. It was an exciting two-and-a-half years. The little house on wheels became our temple of prayer.

Adina was not yet two and Lance was only a few months old when we began our adventure on the road. I soon learned that, in a micro-home, there is no place to retreat into a closet of prayer. I became quite adept at shutting myself in with God as the children played at my feet.

But this opened another dimension of training in the art of prayer for Adina and Lance. The exposure they had to my personal relationship with the Father was opening their hearts to talking with Jesus.

I did not teach my children standard, memorized prayers. I wanted them to talk directly to their loving heavenly Father—not to say prayers, but to pray.

Before Lance could form sentences, he was kneeling beside me and talking with the Lord in his baby prayers. "T'ank 'ou, 'esus," was one of the first phrases he spoke. Together we prayed for the simple things of life: food, clothing and shelter. Then we would praise Jesus for providing these basic needs.

Because of this introduction to prayer, it was natural later to talk to the Lord about more "difficult" needs. Hurt fingers, fevers and sore throats were all brought to the Father. And we praised Him before and after the answer came.

When Lance was 4 years old, he put prayer and praise to work. He believed God for a bicycle. He had not shared his request with us—I overheard him praying in bed late one night. His faith never waivered. Jack and I could have been the "answer" to his prayer, but we decided to trust God with him. How wonderful it was when his answer finally came and we received a child's bike through an unexpected source!

When our third "miracle" arrived, I was nearly 30 years of age. By this time we had settled again. We had sold our mobile home and moved back into a parsonage. The church where Jack was pastor was involved in a major building project. Parsonage life, ministry demands and motherhood once again took its toll on my mental and spiritual well-being.

I was sending Adina off into the big world, via the school system. Lance was still, literally, a bouncing boy. And now there was Chad, another little package of boundless energy.

Many mornings, Jack was gone before I got the children up. And more often than not, they were tucked into bed before he returned at night. Jack just could not always be home for regular family devotionals. Even though I led the children in a daily devotional time, I felt guilty that this arrangement was not sufficient for their proper spiritual growth.

Again, the Holy Spirit instructed us on how to maintain a spiritual education program for the children. So Jack and I set about to provide this ministry for our family.

We decided that at least two times a week (or more if possible) Jack would make it a priority to be with the family, leading us in a time of prayer. We planned for these times as carefully as we planned any area of our lives. We were wonderfully rewarded, too, as we watched our children grow into their own meaningful relationships with the Lord. Their prayers became more complex, and their expressions of praise delighted us.

It would be less than honest to say we always held interesting, beneficial devotions. Frankly, there were times when they were neither! As our children grew older, we sometimes wondered if the devotions were doing any good.

But time proved we were right. Family devotionals are a necessity in any Christian home. In the parsonage family, they are a lifeline.

A pastor's family often experiences un-Christian treatment at the hands of church leadership or revered members of the local body, not to mention those outside the church. As parsonage parents, we must keep a divine balance in the home. Through exalting Christ and developing their own relationships with the Lord, our precious cargo, our children, can rise above the storms that often rage in full view of the pastor's family.

Adina was five years old when Chad was born. She took it upon herself to bring him to spiritual maturity. She would stand beside his crib and pray earnestly for him or tell him some of her favorite Bible stories. By the time he was talking, Adina had him praying.

One day, I suddenly realized the children were too quiet. Upon investigation, I found the three of them kneeling beside Lance's bed. Lance was scolding Chad because he had not prayed in Jesus' name. He admonished his brother that if he expected God to answer his prayers, he must say "in Jesus' name." He then proceeded to make Chad pray again. "This time," he said, "do it right."

As the children grew older, our methods of presenting family devotions had to be adjusted to meet their growing needs and concerns. We kept our times special and brief. We found it profitable to use their weekly Sunday school lessons as guides for our reading and discussion. During the years they had workbooks in Sunday school, we did the workbook exercises. As they improved in their reading skills, we asked them to read the Scriptures for the family.

When Adina entered the seventh grade in public school, we were suddenly operating in a new arena. The peer pressure she had experienced up until then was nothing compared to what she faced in junior high school. We took advantage of family devotions to reinforce moral standards and to emphasize the need for personal private times with the Father. During this period Adina established her own personal devotionals.

In the teen years, self-esteem can be pulverized. Family support, acceptance and love through family devotions can be a mainstay for our teens. Being open to discuss the subjects they raise can give valuable insight into their world. Jack and I had to learn not to panic when our children questioned our faith and doctrine. Today, the Holy Spirit continues to give us wisdom and patience as we try to help them make decisions and find solutions to their personal problems.

Our family has found that prayer is an ever-learning process. Together, we learn new concepts in the reality and power of prayer. Our faith is tested to the limit, but He is faithful who has promised. We strive to instill this truth in our children so they can withstand the onslaught of the enemy of their souls.

Lance's room is directly above ours. Just last evening after all was quiet and most of the family asleep, I heard Lance praying. Many nights I've thought the family was asleep, but not everyone was. On those nights, Lance bounds down the stairs, and with the precision of a guided missile, he lands on our bed. "Hey, Mom, you asleep?"

Usually those late night chats lead to a very special prayer time. The problem may be a personal problem, concern for a friend, or a relationship in which he needs direction. It is always exciting to share the lives of our children and pray with them. If we as parents establish family prayer even before our children fully understand, we will see great rewards. Prayer should be a natural process—their way of handling whatever life deals them. It is vital in their spiritual development.

I take a few moments each day to pray with each of our children, usually as they are leaving for school. But it can also happen on a special lunch break, before a big date or game, or in a few quiet moments before bed. These short yet personal prayers help bond our hearts together.

Recalling answers to specific prayer requests builds faith in us and in our children. Some of the testimonies are quite humorous, and we marvel that the Father is so loving and attentive. By reviewing past blessings, we are more able to trust God for whatever our present need might be.

As a mother, I rejoice when Adina, Lance or Chad shares with me how they faced some personal battle or decision with prayer. How refreshing to see God move in my children and their friends!

At times, each of the children has rebelled against family devotions. Each one has found excuses to be absent. As parents, we have to be especially open to the Holy Spirit for wisdom and understanding. He may prompt us to insist that they attend. Another time, we may go ahead with those members of the family who are present, making it a point to pray for the absent one.

After such episodes, Jack or I will spend some quality time with the rebelling child. By loving them, we can pinpoint the root of the rebellion and deal with it. Restoring the child's spirit is vitally important to spiritual maturation.

We have to be alert to those times when a child is

present physically, but not mentally or spiritually. In those times, the child yearns for love and understanding. Scolding or chiding does not settle his inner turmoil.

On occasion, our children's prayers are sobering. One night as I was making my rounds, briefly touching the life of each child, I heard Adina crying softly. She was lying on the floor, her face buried in her open Bible and tears streaming from her eyes.

She wanted to know God's perfect will concerning her relationship with the young man she was dating. She wasn't sure he was part of God's plan for her. We searched the Scriptures for guidance and prayed.

The answer to Adina's searching and prayers was heartbreaking. The relationship with the boy was wrong. She had to break it off. But it was her decision, not mine. Had she not built a firm foundation of trust and prayer since the cradle, I am certain she could not have withstood the pain. But she did withstand, and she continues to search and pray for the Father's perfect plan for her life.

Teaching our kids the art of prayer is the most precious gift we can bestow upon them. I have no guarantee that my three children will follow the Lord all of their days. But I have given them the key to success in this life and the hope of eternity.

My family faces the same battles as any family with three children in or near the teen years. Peer pressure, fashion, hair styles and music preferences are discussed—not always calmly. Yet we have a tremendous force that draws us together. Family prayer is our mighty fortress.

The devotional time we have woven into our parsonage life has been a great tool in keeping our family bound together in love. It has kept the wolves of destruction and disharmony at bay. It has opened our children's hearts to us and unified us. Now with the older children working, and all three involved in school and related activities such as music, sports and clubs, we are constantly re-evaluating our priorities and working to keep our family devotionals a ministry to our children.

Effective family devotionals do not just happen. They are planned, prayed over and executed in love and power. The rewards are endless, and God's grace abounds.

Excuse me, I hear my children praying.

Jeanne Barron was born in McAlister, Oklahoma, in 1944. Her father was a lay minister until her early teens, when he entered the full-time ministry. Struck by a potentially fatal illness at age 6, Jeanne experienced a complete, miraculous healing and never suffered another side-effect from the disease.

Jeanne met her husband, Jack, at a joint Sunday afternoon service held by two churches for the residents of a local rest home. The couple was married 11 weeks later.

The Barrons entered the full-time ministry in 1965, on their second wedding anniversary. Jack is pastor of the First Assembly of God in Clinton, Oklahoma.

In addition to teaching Sunday school, Jeanne has conducted seminars on child evangelism and has written material for "Kids' Krusades." She and Jack have a special ministry to young people who have been called into God's service.

The Barrons have three children, ages 17, 16 and 12.

Chapter Twenty-Two
Just a Mother

───────

by Jackie (Mrs. Jamie) Buckingham

I was on my way through the Atlanta airport one morning, rushing to catch a connecting flight from my home in Melbourne, Florida, to wherever it was that my husband, Jamie, had called for me to meet him. As I rounded a corner, I came face-to-face with a woman about my own age.

"Oh," she gasped, a look of recognition spreading across her face. "I know you. You're Bob Mumford's wife."

I laughed. "No, I'm Jamie Buckingham's wife."

She threw her hands up. "Well, hallelujah! I knew you were somebody's wife."

She was right. But I am more than somebody's wife: I am somebody. I am called to the highest calling in the world. I'm a mother.

At church one Sunday night, my husband called on several women to testify. One of those was our grown daughter, Robin, who is married to Jon Moore. Robin and Jon met at Oral Roberts University where he was studying health and recreation and she was getting a degree in special education. After they married, they moved back to our town and built their house next door to our house in the country. Robin had planned to teach school, using her degree from ORU. Instead, she started raising her own students—three beautiful daughters now ages 6, 4 and 1.

That night when her daddy called her to come to the platform, she turned to me and whispered, "But I don't have a testimony. I'm just a mother."

"Go on, honey," I coaxed. "You've got something important to say."

I watched Robin proudly as she shared with the congregation. In her face, I saw myself. I have five years of undergraduate study in the field of education but have never stood before a classroom to teach. Instead, I started having babies—five of them.

My own mother had raised her family while working long hours in a full-time job to help supplement my father's meager salary. It had been extremely difficult for her, as well as for my brother, sister and me. I knew that wasn't what I wanted for my children if I could help it. Jamie and I agreed I would stay home.

That night, when Robin finished speaking, Jamie said something absolutely profound.

"What's wrong with spending four or five years in college to get a degree in education, or home economics, or nutrition, and using it to raise your own children?" he asked. "Who says everyone with a college degree has to go to work in the secular world? If the highest of all callings is to be a mother and a wife, why not go to college to prepare for your calling?''

Robin came back to her seat and squeezed my hand. ''I guess I'm just following in your footsteps, Mom,'' she said.

If she does, it will be the most exciting life imaginable.

Like Robin, we had our children early. Jamie was a student at Southwestern Baptist Theological Seminary in Ft. Worth. I was trying to finish my senior year at Texas Christian University when our first son, Bruce, arrived in 1955. Robin was born a year and a half later, before we left the seminary. Bonnie came along shortly after we arrived in Greenwood, South Carolina, where Jamie had accepted a call to pastor a Baptist church. Tim arrived two years later and our last daughter, Sandy, was born in 1962.

It doesn't take a college degree to have five children in eight years, but I defy anyone who says being a mother isn't a full-time job.

All five of the children gave their hearts to Christ at an early age. All were baptized by their father. All were later married by their father as well. Our three oldest children graduated from Oral Roberts University and our two oldest daughters met and married ORU students. Bruce worked in Washington for several years as special assistant to our congressman before meeting his wife-to-be, Michele, who was also a congressional assistant. All three of our oldest children are now living on our property in the country.

Our number four son, Tim, married his childhood sweetheart, has finished agricultural school and is managing a ranch in Georgia. Our youngest daughter, Sandy, after a year at ORU, returned home, married and finished her college work locally. She and her husband are also living in a cottage on our property.

None of the children has ever had a major crisis. None has ever been seriously ill. Growing up on the east coast of Florida has exposed them to a heavy emphasis on free sex and illicit drugs, but all five have chosen to stick with kingdom principles.

The family, as you can see, is close. Although we have not encouraged it, we are pleased they are migrating back home and are raising their children in a close family setting. Without planning it, we have taken on much of the flavor of the ancient tribes. Jamie is our patriarch. The children have pitched their tents next to ours. My job has been that of a shepherd girl to a small flock. I have checked the water for poison, chased away a few wolves, smacked the unruly ones who wanted to stray and led them to the Green Pasture. The Chief Shepherd has done the rest.

In short: mother is a full-time job.

A friend stopped by one day and asked what my hobbies are. Hobbies are for those who have spare time. Maybe, when I am older and the grandchildren are grown, I will have time for a hobby. When you are cooking dinner for as many as 12 of your own family at night, cleaning five toilets each day, riding the tractor, answering the phone, dealing with anxious editors who want to know where your husband is, trying to find out why the well is pumping salt water—you don't have much time to needlepoint.

Our son Tim, the rancher, grew up with animals. He was constantly bringing home stray creatures—not just dogs and cats, but horses, hogs and cows. One of his pets was a 2,000-pound Brahman cow a local rancher gave him when it was a day old and its mother had died.

Tim brought it home—but I was the one who went out five times a day to feed it with a bottle. It grew to the size of our Volkswagen with horns longer than my arms. The back half of our 20 acres is fenced as pasture, but when something weighs 2,000 pounds it can eat wherever it pleases—fence or no fence. I was constantly out in the yard, beating on the cow to get her out of my flowerbeds and back into the pasture.

One afternoon, as I was pounding on her with a broom, she turned and looked at me. I knew I was in trouble when she lowered her head and muttered something like, "I've had enough."

I started backing up but she kept coming. Fortunately, I had lost 30 pounds the year before so that when she backed me up against a fence post, I fit right in between her horns. She pinned me against the post with her huge head, then started moving up and down. I was holding on to her horns with both hands, my feet off the ground, my back against the fence post which was wrapped with barbed wire, screaming at the top of my lungs. Two sons-in-law, Jon and Marion, heard me hollering and rushed to my rescue, pounding on the cow until she dropped me in the sandspurs and ambled back into the pasture.

Hobbies? Over the last five years my life has been occupied with two cats (one of them pregnant), two big dogs, eight puppies, two horses, four pigs (which seemed to leave their pen whenever they wanted to in order to eat my potted plants), two cows (both of which got pregnant and delivered calves within a week of each other), five children, five children-in-law, seven grandchildren (and a pregnant daughter-in-law living in our upstairs bedroom), constant guests from all over the world, and one compost pile.

I don't have time for hobbies. I'm too busy chasing pigs off the patio, pulling puppies out of the swimming pool and going after a four-year old grandson who has learned how to start up the tractor and is on his way down the driveway dragging the bushhog.

Someone once told me that John Wesley's mother, Susanna, had 12 children and a wood stove. The only way she could find quiet time was to reach down, grab the hem of her dress and pull her long skirt up over her head. There, in her little cloth closet, she would pray.

Actually, it is prayer which has enabled me to function in my multi-faceted role of pastor's wife, receptionist, editor, travel agent, farmer, plumber, hotel manager, cook—in other words, mother. Jamie has never wanted or expected anything of me other than what I wanted to do. From the beginning of the church we founded, Jamie has taught that each person should find his own gifted area and operate inside his gifts. I am not a public speaker, worship leader, Sunday school teacher or co-host of a church television program. My gift is that of mother—and now, grandmother.

When I was a child, growing up in the small community of Vero Beach, Florida, we always heard stories of preachers' kids who "went bad." Later, as a college student at Mercer University, I met a number of "PKs" in my dormitory who were really wild. When Jamie and I moved into our first parsonage I lived with the constant, nagging fear that our children might turn out that way—rebellious and reactionary.

It has not happened, perhaps because we have given our children the same liberty Jamie has given our church—to find their gifts and operate in them. Besides this, we have been a loving, touching, laughing family. Jamie and I both believe in physical touch as a part of love. Even today it is not unusual to come in and find one of our grown daughters sitting in her daddy's lap, or to have one of our married sons pick me up and carry me in his arms.

We talk as freely about sexual activity as we do about prayer. Jamie has written two children's books on sex. In them, he freely quoted from our own children and gave graphic examples of various situations they fell into. Instead of being embarrassed to see their escapades in print, they thrived on it. We try to practice personal modesty, but with this many people living this close together, there's always someone walking in on someone else who's in some stage of undress. It makes for a good dinner story when it happens.

Primarily, though, we have learned the secret of Jesus' parable in Matthew 13 of the tares and the wheat. There He said to let the weeds grow up alongside the wheat and not trample through the tender growth trying to extract each tiny sin. The angels, he said, would do the harvesting. My job as mother is to make sure the soil is prepared, plant good seed, do lots of watering and fertilizing, and trust God to reap the harvest.

Perhaps the biggest test of this principle came when our youngest daughter, Sandy, announced she wanted to marry a young man we didn't approve of. We had given each of our older children the freedom to make their own choices, but we severely questioned Sandy's judgment when it came to Jerry Smith, whom she had dated all the way through high school. In fact, we had done everything we could to break up their relationship.

Although Jerry was a Christian and a member of our

church, he had not been raised in a Christian home. His Catholic parents had accepted Christ about the time Jerry entered his teens. Spirit-baptized, they were dedicated to the Lord, but those earlier, violent years had scarred their son. Jerry was an outstanding athlete, but was impulsive, short-tempered and often violent. At times he and Sandy had physically battered each other, sometimes in public. This was entirely foreign to our gentle way of life, and Jamie and I were deeply concerned that Sandy might become an abused wife if she married Jerry.

We met with Jerry's parents. They were equally concerned. We recommended counseling for the kids and both submitted themselves to a friend who has a deliverance ministry. Things got better, but evidences of the old life were still there. The Smiths cooperated with us by insisting Sandy and Jerry break off their relationship for a year. Sandy went off to ORU and Jerry attended Evangel College in Springfield, Missouri. At the end of the year, Sandy was back home. The phone bills were staggering and the relationship, even from afar, was just as strong.

There was another year of separation when Jerry joined the U.S. Coast Guard. Jamie and I kept praying, hoping Sandy would meet another boy, or Jerry another girl.

"Mom," Sandy kept saying, "why can't you see the good in Jerry that I see? Underneath that rough exterior, he is a real man of God. He's just frightened of you and dad. That's the reason he seems unfriendly when he's around you."

Then one day Sandy made her announcement. "Jerry and I are going to get married. We'll not do it until you and Dad bless us, but we are going to get married."

I talked with Jamie. "We've done everything we can to break them up," he said. "Maybe God wants us to start blessing them rather than cursing them."

We looked at Matthew 18:18 together: "I tell you the truth, whatever you bind on earth will be bound in heaven, and whatever you loose on earth will be loosed in heaven."

"Let's loose them," Jamie suggested.

"OK," I agreed, warily.

Jerry was to be home the next week on leave from the Coast Guard in New Orleans. We took the young couple out to dinner and Jamie laid it out for them to understand. "All these years we've 'bound' you," he said. "We've done all we can to separate you. Now God has told us to 'loose' you. We are going to bless you. If you want to get married, we are going to bless that, too."

They looked at each other in amazement. Slowly Jerry's ever-present scowl turned into a grin. "You really mean it?"

"We mean it," I said. "Jamie's parents did everything they could to keep us apart because they didn't approve of me. But when they loosed us, when they started blessing our relationship rather than cursing it, everything changed."

It was a tough decision, for in the flesh we didn't see any hope for the marriage to work out. But over the next eight months before the wedding, we watched Jerry become who Sandy had said he was all along—a man of God. His violence, which we now realize was his only defense against our disapproval, disappeared. In its place emerged a kind, polite, Christian gentleman who has made a wonderful husband for our daughter—

just as she had faith to believe.

One of the special privileges of motherhood is watching your children grow up and step out in faith. Sandy's faith for Jerry was far more powerful than the facts we were using for evaluation. Because of it, I have grown in faith also and now give thanks. Like the mother in Proverbs, I am able to "laugh at the days to come" (Prov. 31:25).

Pastors' wives serve in many ministries. Me? I'm just a mother.

Minister

Chapter Twenty-Three
Hospitality, Houseguests and Horror Stories

───────

by Frances (Mrs. Quentin) Edwards

Trudging along the dusty roadside of Interstate 4 on a sweltering Florida morning, it seemed as if the day would never end. I wished it had never started! Walking beside me were Charles and Betty Blair, Christians whom my husband, Quentin, and I had admired for many years. We had invited them to speak at our pastors' school in Winter Haven. This was their first trip out of Denver since their difficulties, which were told later in the book *The Man Who Could Do No Wrong*.

The Blairs stayed with us an extra day but, despite our entreaties, were firm about their need to get back to Denver that night. Charles was performing a wedding. Since Quentin had a meeting at the church, I agreed to drive our friends to the Tampa Airport. I used Quentin's car—there was more room for all the suitcases.

What I did not notice was there was very little gas.

265

Between Winter Haven and Tampa, the car glided to a dead stop. Horrified, I looked at the gas gauge: empty. I should have known. Quentin habitually lets his tank get down near empty before he stops for a refill. I always keep my car near full.

Calmly, Charles suggested that he hitchhike to a gas station we had passed a few miles back. "I'm so sorry," I repeated over and over. Betty was empathetic.

"My busy minister-husband is a lot like yours," she said as we watched Charles walk down the highway, his thumb out. "Others often help him keep his car filled with gas."

In an hour, Charles returned. We were all thirsty and drained from the heat. We poured the can of gasoline into the tank and set off again for Tampa.

I drove fast to make up for the lost time. Suddenly, the car swerved. Hearing a familiar "thump," I groaned. A tire had just gone flat.

Hundreds of cars whizzed past, but no one stopped to help. Once again, Charles got out to see what he could do. He looked into the trunk. A half-dozen bags and suitcases were sitting on top of the spare. My heart ached as I watched him lay aside his beautiful tan suitcoat, roll up his white, starched shirtsleeves and remove all the luggage. His Countess Mara tie flapped in the breeze as he changed the dirty tire.

With a few strokes of the jack, he lowered the car onto the spare. It sank. The spare was flat, too.

This is the bad side of hospitality, I thought, as the three of us walked together to find another gas station.

We found one about two miles away. Hot, tired and discouraged, I asked the manager if he would drive the Blairs to the airport.

"No, ma'am. Don't have anyone to stay here and pump the gas," he said.

"Do you have a tire in the size that we need?"

"Nope. Sold out. Sorry."

I called Quentin. He could not come to help us. He was 50 miles away, headed for another meeting. With a few telephone calls, however, he arranged for a tire company to bring the tire we needed to the service station.

We got the tire, put it on and finally arrived at the Tampa Airport. As we said our good-byes, Charles took my hand and kissed it.

"I will never forget today," he said.

And he didn't. A year or two later, we flew to Denver at the Blairs' invitation to preach at Calvary Temple. Charles met us at the airport. As we got into the car, he chuckled.

"Look at the gas gauge," he said to me, his eyes twinkling.

Empty!

I have such wonderful memories of keeping some of God's chosen servants in our home! Even the worst "horror" stories have become soft around the edges as I think back on them.

When Quentin was an evangelist, I was on the receiving end of hospitality. So many people in so many places and in so many ways made me feel at home with them! Now that my husband is a pastor, it's my turn. I cherish the opportunities I have to be hospitable. And as I seek to serve those God sends to Winter Haven, I believe Quentin's ministry is affirmed in a practical, personal way. Jesus' ministry is also affirmed, because we receive these friends (and sometimes strangers) in His name.

Quentin is usually a private person, but with God's servants, his home becomes theirs. What an influence missionaries, evangelists, pastors, teachers and others have had on our lives as we have opened our home to them! And what a heritage our sons, Darrell and Victor, have enjoyed because Quentin and I have chosen to be hospitable! I've even teased about selling tickets to folks who want to see the beds where so many people of God have slept.

Hospitality is definitely a ministry. It requires love, discipline and self-sacrifice. For some, it comes easy— but that is rarely the case. Most of us have to learn to be hospitable through experience.

When you want to fly high, your attitude determines your altitude, I've discovered.

I was looking forward to getting home to Quentin after a trip to Israel with Karl and Joyce Strader, our pastor friends from a neighboring Florida town, and W.L. and Fern Rodgers, our friends from Kentucky. When we arrived in Bangor to go through U.S. Customs, a movable stairway slipped as it was being towed, damaging our plane. We were forced to stay overnight in the crowded airport.

I stood in line for 40 minutes before a telephone was available for me to call home to tell Quentin about our delay.

A woman whose voice I did not recognize answered the phone.

"Hello? Edwardses' residence."

"Would you accept a collect call from Frances Edwards?" the operator said.

"Just a moment, please," the woman responded.

"Let me wake up the Edwardses' son and ask him if his mother's name is Frances."

What is going on in my house? I thought.

When I finally arrived home, a day late and with very little sleep, I found the house filled with people. Quentin was entertaining Bob and Kathy Larson and a missionary couple from India. Coming home to company was not the kind of greeting I had had in mind.

Fortunately, the situation did not become a disaster, although it required more than a moment of attitude readjustment on my part. I determined then and there to turn my negative thoughts into positive thoughts. With God's help, it worked, and the visit ended up being a pleasant time for all of us.

During that visit, and at other times too, I've been unsure of my ability to do what I've needed to do at the moment. I can't handle this! I've thought. But God is so good. He has always comforted me and directed me in my anxious moments, as I've turned to Him.

Sometimes my ideas about entertaining are different from Quentin's. For the most part, though, this has not been a serious problem for us. We simply flex with one another, and as we do, we find that the situation almost always works out.

Besides, "what I am is more important than what I have," as Quentin always says. True friends want us to be real with them. Preachers and other leaders see a lot of pretense and falseness; there are so many people who are trying to impress them. Our guests want naturalness and love. They've seen all the other things.

When Quentin and I were living in Dallas, Jimmy and Frances Swaggart came to visit. They were friends of Quentin's from his single days as an evangelist. I had never met them.

Just before they arrived, I came home from the store and found that our carpet was soaking wet. The French doors in the family room had been left open during a rainstorm. I was already discouraged because the money we had saved for furniture and a new carpet had been sent to India to meet a crisis in a church project. My house was a wreck. What would the Swaggarts think of me?

I'm sure you know the answer to that. They accepted me fully, in spite of my home's disarray. We've been close friends ever since.

You'd think that incident would have prepared me for a time, several years later, when Florida governor Bob Graham was scheduled to speak at our church, the Cypress Cathedral. Two days before his arrival, I was at an Assemblies of God campmeeting in Illinois, where Quentin was a guest speaker. My husband chose that time to tell me the governor would be coming not only to our church that Sunday, but also to our home for lunch!

My head swam. I was 1,500 miles away from home—a new home that didn't even have the light fixtures installed. At best, I'd be there half a day before the governor arrived.

We couldn't get home fast enough. Quentin and I quickly put up the light fixtures, but only in those rooms we knew Governor Graham would see. Was I nervous? More than I care to remember!

I prepared several kinds of beverages for the lunch. As I listed them to the governor the next day, he stopped me and asked if I had any orange juice. I didn't! Being from Texas and having lived only a few years in Florida,

I hadn't yet made it a practice to serve orange juice at social functions, as Floridians do. My embarrassment increased as I suddenly recalled the commercials I had seen on TV—Governor Graham urging everyone to drink Florida orange juice.

Believe me, you can find fresh orange juice at my house now—anytime of the day or night!

As I've mentioned, Quentin and I have always been influenced by our guests. Each one carries a special part of God's message and we seek to learn from them while they are with us. When Juan Carlos Ortiz spoke at our church, he challenged us about winning our neighbors to Christ. We were convicted. Cypress Cathedral is the largest church in town, but our neighbors had never visited. I decided that I would try to reach our neighbors for Jesus by giving a Christmas party for them.

Quentin thought this was a good idea and believed with me for a large turnout. I knocked on each door on our street, told the neighbors about the party and followed up with an invitation by mail.

The big night finally arrived. With great anticipation I watched the clock as the starting time, 7 p.m., approached. It came—and went. No one was there. With the table loaded with painstakingly prepared hors d'oeuvres and my discomfort not easily concealed, we waited. Forty minutes later, despairing, I turned to Quentin.

"I still believe they'll come," he said.

Suddenly, the doorbell rang. I looked through the peephole but saw no one. Confused, I opened the door. There, filling the front yard, were my neighbors.

The barrier was broken. Since then, most of the people in our neighborhood have visited Cypress Cathedral, and several have called on us in times of need. Some have even been saved.

Sometimes, of course, hospitality has to have limits—for the family's sake if not for your own. For example, I enjoy working with some of the troubled girls staying in a government-funded Transition House in town. However, I've never brought any of the girls home with me. Instead, I meet them at the house or at the shopping center. I've also worked with abused wives who are escaping violent husbands, and have been in danger for my own life because of it. I do not bring these women home, either.

My husband and sons keep very busy schedules. It would be too disruptive to their lives to bring home people who may make demands on my life, but who needn't make demands on theirs.

Also, I juggle my time a lot to be ready to go with Quentin when he travels. I don't stay home because someone else has asked for my time. Other people may have to wait, but I will not make Quentin wait. It's a matter of priorities. I believe the number one responsibility God has given me (outside of my relationship to Him) is my husband and family. I stick to this.

Still, more often than not, our house is open. Guests are treated like family. We try to make them comfortable, without pressure. We don't plan every minute of their time for them. We offer them a key and a car, and we sit down with them at mealtime and at meeting time. This way they are free to do as they please, we can get some work done, and our time of fellowship is special.

One of our guests reportedly saw an angel in our home. I don't doubt it, knowing the way she and her husband live.

One couple who stayed with us had a great time preparing their own breakfast and cleaning up afterwards. Amazing, but even in the kitchen, as in their ministry, they work together!

One gentleman kept his private pilot waiting while he tried with all his might to beat Quentin at ping-pong. According to his wife, it was the best "letting his hair down" time he had had in years. Another guest played ping-pong with Quentin until 2:00 in the morning, and this after a long church gathering that evening. The two of them still made it to the prayer meeting early the next day. (Hospitality tip: invest in a ping-pong table!)

Right now, our co-pastors at Cypress Cathedral, Quentin's brother Dwight and his wife, Mary, are living in our home. They've been with us for several months while they've been looking for their own place. What a joy it has been—loving one another, living with one another and working together to see lives changed for Christ!

Now if you will excuse me, I must hurry to the airport. I am meeting a Christian singer who is coming to stay with us for a few days. I sure hope she likes the guest room—and the orange juice!

Frances Edwards was born in Dallas, Texas, in 1941, the daughter of Christian parents. She learned early about the power of faith and prayer when she witnessed the miraculous healing of her brother, who had been paralyzed from polio.

Frances met her husband, Quentin, a traveling evangelist who came to her church, when she was still in high school. They were married shortly after her graduation. For 11 years, the couple traveled extensively with their ministry.

From 1971 to 1986, Quentin served as senior pastor of Cypress Cathedral in Winter Haven, Florida. Since the writing of this chapter, the Edwardses have moved to Toronto, Canada, where he is senior pastor of the Christian Centre.

They have two sons, the younger of which is the youth pastor of Cypress Cathedral.

Chapter Twenty-Four
I'm on the Church Staff

by Barbara (Mrs. Charles) Green

I could hardly believe what I was hearing. Charles and I were holding our annual convention at our church, the Word of Faith Christian Fellowship in New Orleans, and I had called together a meeting of the pastors' wives. I had barely finished welcoming them when one of the women raised her hand.

"How are you accepted by your church?" she asked. "Do you have any role in your husband's ministry?"

"Well, yes, I do have a role," I answered. "I'm a significant member of the church staff. The congregation fully accepts me."

A nervous titter crossed the room. Many more women raised their hands. Their questions reflected their frustrations.

"How did you manage it?"

"My husband would never allow me to work in the church office. Bad for the image."

"Do the church secretaries laugh behind your back?"

"When I make suggestions to the staff, they ignore me."

What hurt, frustration and discouragement were expressed that day! I went to bed that night thankful that my experience as a pastor's wife had been so happy and fruitful in comparison. I determined to offer a message of hope and encouragement to my counterparts in the ministry.

Marriage in and of itself can be a wonderful and exciting adventure. Mine has been. But my joy and excitement has been doubled, even tripled by the fact that my husband is a pastor, and I am involved—not only in his ministry, but in the ministry of the church. It's not just his ministry. It's our ministry.

Every pastor's wife may not be called to stand in the pulpit. But every pastor's wife *is* called to stand with her husband. She has a key role to play, and God needs her there.

When I was nine years old, the pastor of a Baptist church in Kansas City, Missouri, invited all those who wanted to dedicate their lives to the Lord to come to the altar. I went forward. Even at that early age, I knew I would marry a minister. I was as certain as any preacher, evangelist or missionary that I had a special call of God on my life.

That call was fulfilled when I married Charles Green in 1950. As a young pastor's wife, I was apprehensive about the role God had chosen for me. But because I knew I was where I was supposed to be, I tackled the job with energy.

One day, the telephone rang.

"Hello, is the pastor there?" a woman asked.

"No, I'm sorry. He's not at home," I answered. "If there's a message, I'll relay it to him and have him call when he gets back."

"Oh, no. I could never tell *you*. He's the only one I will speak to."

I was instantly angry and defensive. "Well, that's all right," I shot back, without thinking. "You can tell *him*, and then *he* will tell *me*."

After I hung up, I panicked. Why had I said that? What would she think of me? What would Charles think?

I didn't have to wait long to find out. A few minutes later, Charles walked in the door. Apologetically, I related the incident to him.

He was quiet for a moment. Then he fell on the bed and burst out laughing.

"It isn't funny!" I cried.

"I think it's hilarious!" he said, catching his breath. "I'm proud of you. You're a part of this ministry, and I don't want you to be pushed around by anyone."

From that moment on, I knew I had my husband's full support. The telephone call had been one of those small but critical incidents that can shape entire lives. If Charles' reaction had been negative or critical, I might have withdrawn. I might have decided not to "interfere" in the ministry. Instead, I was affirmed and encouraged in my role.

Charles talked later with the woman who had called.

"Barbara is going to be fully involved in my ministry and in the ministry of the church," he explained in a matter-of-fact tone.

She understood. (We eventually became great friends!) Others have understood as well.

From the very beginning, I was on the church staff. In fact, when Charles and I first started the Word of Faith fellowship in 1953, we were the only staff. If there was anything to be done, we did it. Our first services were in a rented hall. Early every Sunday morning, we'd arrive with brooms, Lysol spray and dust pans and clean the auditorium before the people came. As a team, we'd share their concerns and needs, pray with them and do everything we could to bless them.

When God began to increase our numbers, it was only natural that I was accepted as Charles' right hand. That's the role the people saw me in from the first day. As our need for a staff grew and we hired others to work with us, I was already there, in the middle of things.

Our staff became our friends, our family. We never felt that they worked *for* us. Rather they worked *with* us.

This attitude helped make it easy to be the pastor's wife and a key staff person as well. Today, more than 30 years later, our attitude is the same, and our church office runs happily and smoothly. The staff looks out for me and I look out for them. I am our secretaries' greatest supporter—I know how hard they work! In turn, my word is respected, and when I speak, I am not ignored.

My strongest supporter is Charles. He has constantly encouraged me, "Be yourself, Barbara. Don't be bound by other people's expectations of you." He wants me on the staff because he believes my instincts are good. He says I have an ability to listen to the difficulties that come before a busy church on a daily basis and cut through to the heart of the problem. He needs that input.

I admit that I am a good listener. People seek me out and want to talk with me. I have often been able to help various members of our staff, the office personnel, and many people in the congregation by simply listening to them and offering simple solutions to their problems. Sometimes I counsel with them alone. Other times Charles and I counsel together. I am usually able to discern whether the person is in sincere need of help, or whether he or she needs to be challenged to make a change in attitude or conduct.

I am free to confer with Charles if I think something is wrong in the church. We discuss the problem and pray about it. Sometimes I will be the one to follow up with a solution. Other times he will, or we'll work together.

If the problem is a person, I often call him or her up and make an appointment to talk. Or I catch the person in church and discuss the situation on an impromptu basis. The congregation not only accepts this, they seem to love it.

Mine is not a pulpit ministry, although I have preached in the church on a few occasions. Primarily, I see myself as a teacher, an administrator and a minister. Charles has often invited me to sit on the platform with him on Sundays, but I'm more comfortable sitting with the congregation. I'm also more useful there, because that's where the needs are. I've trained myself to keep my eyes open to all that is going on around me. Many times I am able to help nip problems in the bud while my husband is busy with other phases of the ministry.

We work as a team among the congregation and in the office, too. When Charles is away at a convention or speaking engagement, I often take over many of his chores and duties. Since I've been beside him from the beginning, I usually know how to handle almost anything that comes up. His load is that much lighter when he returns. Many husbands would feel threatened knowing their wives have taken over in their absence. Mine is relieved!

People have tried to use me to get to Charles. Others have tried—consciously or unconsciously—to divide us in our beliefs or our methods. But whenever Charles and I have disagreed, we've discussed it privately. We never allow a problem to become a point of contention between us in front of the staff or the congregation. We also try to deal swiftly with problems. We don't allow small things to grow into the large things that can cause division.

Charles and I are together constantly—at home, in church and at the office. We never seem to grow tired of being with each other. Working together has only served to draw us closer. It's given us a common concern and a common goal.

In fact, working together has drawn the whole family closer. Since our children always saw Charles and me ministering as a team, it was only natural for them to want to join in. From a very early age, both our son, Michael, and our daughter, Cynthia, wanted to be in the church building and around church people as much as possible. Following our example, they learned to serve. When they were old enough, they came on staff.

Today, Michael, 31, is our co-pastor. His wife, Linda, is the church pianist and the editor of our newsletter. Cynthia, 29, is Charles' administrative assistant. Her husband, Matthew, is a pastor and teacher and is in charge of the television ministry. We are, in the literal sense, a family church. Our family—Charles, me, our two children and their spouses—lead the family that has grown up around us.

Being on the church staff has been an exciting, fulfilling experience for me. It still is. But I'll admit there's a down side: the pay is poor. For most of our church's early history, I simply came with the territory. I worked long hours cleaning floors, playing the organ, helping in the nursery, acting as financial secretary, counseling and going on ministry calls with Charles. For all of this, I received no pay at all.

In the last few years, we've corrected this. Charles and I concluded that any pastor's wife who accepts a responsible, full-time position on the church staff should be on the payroll, just like everyone else.

I don't have fixed hours or an official title. But I'm filling a lot of roles—corporate secretary, counselor, bridal consultant and director, financial administrator, "trainer-upper" of our younger staff members and organizer of our women's ministries. I work hard, and the rest of the staff knows it. They don't begrudge me a salary!

Are you thinking about becoming a part of your church staff? If so, you need to ask your husband and yourself a few questions.

First of all, what will your duties be? What will your husband—and the other staff members—expect of you? Can you do the job? "Well, I'm the pastor's wife" is no excuse to drop the ball. Other staffers will resent having to bail you out.

Second, you need to be secure in your relationship with your husband. Is everything OK on the homefront? Does he believe in you and your ability to do the job? Will he publicly stand beside you and make it clear to all naysayers that you are not only his partner at home but his partner in ministry as well? Your husband's attitude on all these counts is the decisive factor in whether your job will be a heartache or a joy. If your answer to any of these questions is no, perhaps you need to work on mending your marriage before coming on staff.

Finally, be sure you are secure in yourself and in your relationship with God. What is truly motivating you to become a staff member? Do you feel a call of God on your life? Do you love the Lord enough to suffer the possibility of misfortune, heartache, misunderstandings, slights and all the other things that can happen when you make yourself available for service?

If you love God, your husband supports you and the call burns in your heart, then go ahead. Tackle it! I did. The excitement, happiness and fulfillment I've found have been beyond all my expectations. The same will happen for you.

Barbara Green was born in Kansas City, Missouri. Her mother and father became Christians when Barbara was 8.

While the family was living in Baton Rouge, Louisiana, Barbara met her husband, Charles, who had been called to be the youth leader and music minister of the church they were attending. After their marriage in 1950, Barbara and Charles traveled in an evangelistic ministry.

In 1953, Charles founded the Word of Faith Christian Fellowship in New Orleans, Louisiana. From the beginning, Barbara has been an integral member of the church staff. Their two children, along with their spouses, are also employed full-time with Word of Faith. Their son is a co-pastor and their daughter is Charles' administrative assistant.

Chapter Twenty-Five
We Are the Pastor

by Jean (Mrs. Jack) Coleman

I was not a stranger to exclusion and rejection. For many years before entering the ministry, my husband had worked behind closed doors in a government agency dealing with matters of national security. He would work each day behind a high fence handling secret data, hidden away from the eyes of the world. When we first married, I quickly learned not to ask questions about his job. He had a life from nine to five that was completely separate from our home life. I had no part in it.

It took a lot of adjustment to learn to cope with this facet of my husband's life that was so completely closed to me. A simple question like "Did anything exciting happen at work today?," asked in total innocence, could bring stony silence and a feeling that I had intruded into an area where I had no right to be.

I was an American citizen in good standing, but since I lacked the treasured "security clearance," I often felt like a second-class citizen. I was the one who stood on the outside of the fence looking in, wondering what was going on inside the place where my husband was privileged to work.

Through all this I learned to cope with exclusion and rejection. I also learned, however, that exclusion and rejection can easily lead to bitterness and resentment if left to grow unchecked. Although I learned to cope, I was, at the same time, an unhappy and discontented housewife, begrudging my husband his "secret life." As the years went on, his job became a rival—a glamorous "other woman."

Then Jesus came! Suddenly, we were two new creatures walking hand in hand with the Savior. Our marriage was filled with love, forgiveness, compassion, understanding and the joy of serving the Lord together.

Jack still went to work every day and I stayed home with house and children, but our attitudes changed—and our priorities. We knelt together and prayed, "Use us, Lord," and quickly learned that the Lord answers prayer. We opened the doors of our home on Thursday evenings, and before we knew it, nearly a hundred people were coming weekly to praise the Lord. Invitations came to us from meetings and churches, and soon we were traveling up and down the East Coast every weekend, preaching and teaching. Jack's job remained secret, but I no longer saw it as his mistress for we were a team in ministry together. We were truly one. Our names were linked together in a growing ministry—Jack and Jean Coleman. I had a vision of evangelizing the world, spreading the gospel to the four corners of the earth.

But the Lord had other ideas. He was calling us to establish a church right where we lived—in Laurel,

Maryland. My husband was excited about the idea, but I had many reservations. When he left his job and stepped out in faith as a pastor, I found the old pangs of exclusion and rejection, bitterness and resentment welling up within me again.

Jack rented office space and purchased furniture for his study. I stood back, wondering where I fit into this new ministry. Once again, I felt on the outside looking in. Once again, Jack was behind closed doors—only this time doing "kingdom business." I was left behind, feeling like a second-class citizen. A simple question like "How did the counseling session go with Mary Jane today?" would bring that familiar silence that insinuated I was probing into privileged information.

I struggled to find out where I fit into the church. Jack and I were no longer a team in ministry. I had been cast into the role of pastor's wife—allowed into the bed chamber, but not into the inner sanctum of the church.

I found that I had some very definite pre-conceived ideas of the role of a pastor's wife—and I wasn't sure I could fit the mold. I pictured her as a person blended into the background, nearly invisible. She was someone pointed out to visitors to be scrutinized and judged. From my stereotyped viewpoint, she was virtually non-existent as a functioning part of the church, taking little or no active leadership role in church activities. You could almost forget that she existed, for although she was important to her husband, she played no important role in the church. In most cases, she didn't even stand at her husband's side by the door following Sunday services. The pastor's wife was a non-functioning, nonentity in the life of the church as far as I was concerned.

And now I was one!

Had my ministry to the body of Christ come to an end? I loved my husband, and stood beside him as helpmate and wife. But did God mean for me to be passive and inactive in the church? Was the team that had carried the ministry together no longer to be yoked? Was I to lay aside the call of God on my life in response to a tradition that dictated that a pastor's wife has no active role in the ministry of the church?

I wondered how God perceived the role of a pastor's wife. Is her sole ministry to her husband, or does it extend to her husband's church? I was willing to lay down my ministry if that was the sacrifice the Lord required of me, but I was uncertain that it was. I was confused as to who I was and what God wanted me to be.

It was not an easy time in my Christian walk. I struggled to find my identity. I knew who I was in Christ, but in the church I was an enigma. We had elders, deacons—and Jack's wife. Even the church was confused about how I fit in the overall picture, what authority I had (if any), and my role in the day-by-day functioning of the Tabernacle—the name of our church.

I sought the Lord for guidance. "Lord, even as I am content to be hid in Christ, let me be content to be hid in Jack." I asked myself if pride was raising its ugly head, causing me to desire identity and status, or whether it was the Holy Spirit leading me to share my talents and gifts on a broader scale. I desperately needed to know God's will.

My identity crisis came to a head when my husband had new calling cards made. In the past, our cards had always read, "Jack and Jean Coleman." This time they read, "Jack Coleman, Pastor."

I looked at the card, and I suppose the expression on

my face gave me away.

"Do you want me to have some cards made for you, too, honey?" Jack asked. "What do you want them to say?"

"I don't know. What is my position in the church?"

And even my husband didn't have the answer for me.

A week later he arrived home with a small package. "For you," he said, placing it in my hand.

It was a box of calling cards. I glanced at the top line. "Jack and Jean Coleman, Pastor."

He smiled. "God told me that *we* are the pastor."

"*We* are the pastor?" I queried.

"Yes," he responded. "It's so simple really that I don't know how we missed it. The Bible says that a man shall leave father and mother and cleave to his wife, and the two shall become one. No longer two, but one. God has joined us together and made us one, and *we* are the pastor," he concluded.

The revelation began to unfold before our eyes. We began to see God's plan for our lives—to be a man and woman serving Him together as one. A man and woman of one heart, one mind, walking together in the Spirit as one, fulfilling one office: pastor.

We read several times in the Scriptures about a husband and wife team, Aquila and Priscilla. Or Priscilla and Aquila. We find it both ways in the Bible. The order didn't seem terribly important to the Holy Spirit as He recorded their names in the Word. These two disciples worked together as tentmakers, and then moved together into a traveling ministry as they went with Paul to Ephesus. We are told that together they expounded the way of God to a learned man from Alexandria, and that they even had a church in their home. Two moving together as one in the Spirit.

Over and over reference is made to the church as a family—the family of God. The Great Shepherd entrusts His children into the care of pastors—parents—who will train them up in the way they should go.

In the First Epistle of John, the family of God is described as fathers, young men and little children. We are shown a picture of the family in various stages of development. And what is a pastor really but a father in the Lord?

But where are all the mothers? A child needs both father and mother. It's true in the natural, and it's also true in the spiritual.

Jack and I began to see that churches need both a father and a mother. A husband and wife ministering to the children together—hand in hand responsible for their growth and development. We began to see that our pastoral ministry was simply an extension of our role as parents, and as husband and wife. We complement each other, and in our togetherness is seen the completeness of the pastoral office.

God is trinity: Father, Son, Holy Spirit. The three are one. Why shouldn't this apply to a husband and wife called into ministry? The two are one: two people, but one pastor.

Does that make me any less a pastor's wife? Not at all. A pastor's wife's role is to function as the church mother. She and her husband are the parents of the church. Together they pastor their spiritual family.

As we began to understand what God was showing us, everything became so simple. At home, we carry out different tasks. Jack takes care of house repairs, tends the yard and takes out the garbage. I do the shopping, the cooking, the dishes and the laundry. We each have our separate areas of responsibility. There is no competition, no striving. Everything is done decently and in order.

Our roles in the church are very distinct also. Our individual functions are vital and important to the well-being of our church family. We are one, with different administrations.

My husband is the senior pastor. Just as in our home he makes the final decisions, in the church he also makes the final decisions. We are open and honest with each other. I give him my input. If I am not in agreement with him, I make it known. But ultimately, he has the last word. This is the only way a joint ministry will ever work. It's scriptural, and it's effective. A husband and wife who have a good, solid marriage will also have a good, solid ministry if they apply the same principles they use in their home.

All over the United States, I've seen couples being raised up by God to pastor churches. These churches are thriving. A family with a father and mother who love each other and their children is going to be a healthy, happy family.

But if this is God's will, why haven't we seen it before? Is a pastor's wife to be a bench warmer or an active part of the team? Has the devil so blinded the eyes of our understanding and hardened our hearts with prejudice that pastors' wives are sidelined and out of the action? What do we do with these women who are filled with the Spirit and obviously set apart for ministry and leadership in the church? Do we just close our eyes and pretend they don't exist? Or do we recognize God as sovereign and acknowledge that if He wants to raise up a woman as a co-pastor, He has that privilege?

I have not been immune from criticism for being the wrong sex. (Is their really a wrong sex?) Often I am excluded from pastors' breakfasts. I have been to gatherings where my husband was invited to sit on the platform and I was placed on the front row of the congregation. We have had people stop attending the Tabernacle because it has a woman pastor. One young man used to roam the halls during Bible study because he refused to sit under a woman's teaching. Another time, a visitor was found sitting in the lobby reading her Bible for the same reason. They would rather not hear the Word than hear it from the lips of a woman.

My husband, who is a very wise man, once said, "People get so upset when they see the wrapping a gift comes in that they don't stick around to enjoy the gift." A ministry wrapped in female flesh is often cast aside.

On our Sunday afternoon drives, I usually sit on the front seat of the car right next to my husband. Jack does the driving, but I am still at his right hand on the front seat—not in back. But how many potential co-pastors take a back seat as a "pastor's wife" because the congregation or denomination will not accept them in any other role? Can a woman move as a true helpmate if she is excluded from her husband's ministry? Hundreds of pastors' wives are yearning to be at their husbands' sides—not only at home, but also in the church.

Several years ago I attended the National Women's Leadership Conference where Iverna Tompkins was teaching a seminar on "The Pastor's Wife." During that seminar I witnessed firsthand the frustration, the loneliness, the futility and the despair experienced by many of these women who have been hindered by tradition from working alongside their husbands in the harvest field. I sensed the bitterness and resentment they harbored within, as they openly shared their fears of being left behind and the exclusion they battled day after day. I saw them weep before the Lord, and I wept with them. Wasted lives along the roadside—victims of religious prejudice.

Is every pastor's wife called to co-pastor with her husband? Probably not. Yet I do believe the potential is there—but often hindered by doubt, fear, rejection, tradition and prejudice. If you tell a person often enough that they cannot achieve something, eventually they will believe it.

However, if a woman believes she and her husband are called together to pastor a church, God can bring gifts and talents to the light to be used for His glory in the kingdom. If the Lord knows that she is willing to step out in faith into ministry at the side of her husband, miracles happen to prepare her to function effectively in the body.

I had never sung a note publicly—now I lead worship with a 14-piece orchestra backing me up. My amateurish piano playing has now been developed to the point that I play at conferences; I have composed worship choruses that are being sung throughout the United States. Writing that used to be confined to personal correspondence is now channeled into articles for Christian magazines. Over 50,000 copies of my book have been sold. The woman who once trembled with stage fright is now a recognized convention speaker. Organizational skills long confined to running a household are now used in the household of faith.

I do not say these things to boast or to build myself

up, rather to clarify what Jesus can do with a yielded vessel. We tend to forget that Peter and John were unlearned and ignorant men until they began to minister in the power of God.

I had no college degrees, no particular skills or talents. My only claim to fame was a blue ribbon I won for swimming at camp when I was 12 years old. Our children used to talk about building a trophy case in the family room where they could display all the trophies, plaques, certificates and awards they had accumulated. Then they would always say, "What about poor Mom? She doesn't have anything to put in it."

The trophy case was never built.

That was the story of my life. Poor Mom. I was an underachiever.

But Jesus made a difference. I found that I really could do all things through Christ who strengthened me. If I believed God wanted me to do something, and in faith I attempted it, I found I could do it!

Pastors' wives have been put down so much that it is hard for them to see themselves through God's eyes. If a woman is willing to move into the role of co-pastor, God is faithful to equip her.

The majority of women have many doubts about their ability to function in the role of a mother when they are expecting their first child. Yet, when they bring the new baby home from the hospital, they find they can handle the youngster without difficulty. In fact, they are often amazed at how comfortable they are in the new role, and how competent. Raising spiritual children is no different.

Would God call a man to pastor—to be a father in the Lord—and not also call his wife to be a mother?

How can two walk together except they be agreed? If the two are truly one, does the Lord split them down the middle? Remember, children need two parents, a father *and* a mother.

Every child needs the authority and strength of a father, and also the compassion and gentleness of a mother. A son needs a father to tie his swing to the branch of a maple tree, and a mother to fill the cookie jar with warm cookies straight from the oven. A daughter needs a father to set the curfew on her first big date, and a mother to hem up her skirt to just the right length.

Spiritual children have the same needs. Can a male pastor reach out and take a young woman into his arms so she can weep on his shoulder? A woman pastor can. Can a woman pastor move with authority as she is called to the county jail to deal with a prodigal son arrested for pushing drugs? A male pastor can.

Can we really expect one man to supply all the pastoral needs of a church? Is the single parent God's design for raising children? Or has He provided male and female, father and mother, to meet a child's total physical, emotional and spiritual needs? Of course a single parent can raise a child. Many do; but is it really God's perfect will?

Male or female, pastoring is a full-time job. The complexities of a growing congregation are manifold. I have asked myself how I would manage if something were to happen to my husband. I believe that I could carry on—bring the flock to maturity—but it would be a tremendous burden without a partner at my side. A single woman pastoring a church would have a hard road before her.

Our congregation likes having a father and a mother. In the beginning, there were reservations on the part of some. Now, however, the church respects me as "Pastor Jean" and lovingly refers to me as a "pastorette."

Nearly seven years have passed since I moved into the role of co-pastor of the Tabernacle. I have my own office at the church and receive a salary. When I first began to function in ministry at the Tabernacle, I only went to the building for scheduled appointments and meetings or when I had specific tasks to accomplish. But as the congregation and my responsibilities expanded, I came onto the staff full-time. With our children now grown, Jack and I often spend more time at the church than at home. But we both want it that way. The church is our family, and it is such a blessing.

I feel good about myself. I am fulfilled. My husband is fulfilled. I believe our church family is fulfilled, also. I am a true helpmate at last, helping to carry the tremendous load involved in pastoring some 700 children.

The Lord said, "It is not good that man should be alone. I will make a helpmate for him." A helpmate—someone to share a man's life in the church as well as in the home. Jack and I are together nearly 24 hours a day. We think the same thoughts. I have his mind on most matters in the church. Our areas of responsibility are very clearly defined. He preaches, administrates, works with the men and the leadership, and oversees the church in general. I teach, lead worship, minister to the women, coordinate the children's programs, do writing and promotion, and most important, encourage and support my husband. We move as one and share one vision.

Isn't this the picture of Christ and the church? The heavenly Bridegroom and His bride work together in unity to build the kingdom of God. "For we are laborers *together* with God" (1 Corin. 3:9). The church is not relegated to stay at home and watch Jesus work but is sent forth to preach everywhere, *the Lord working with her* and confirming the Word with signs following.

What about that verse from Paul's letter to Timothy? some ask. "I suffer not a woman to teach, nor to usurp authority over the man, but to be in silence" (1 Tim. 2:12).

On my knees I sought God for the proper interpretation of Paul's words. Isn't he actually saying, "I do not allow a woman to dominate her husband, nor to override his authority"? Isn't he counseling a woman to have a quiet and gentle spirit, not seeking to control her husband and her household, but showing a submissive attitude?

That's how my husband and I interpret it. When Jack is questioned about my teaching ministry or my role as co-pastor, his comment is: "She's not usurping my authority. I have delegated it to her. She's anointed to teach, and I have asked her to feed the Tabernacle flock."

No authority has been usurped—only authority delegated. I am not telling my husband how to run the church, rather submitting myself to him and working at his side in ministry.

We are the parents in this particular household of faith. I am still a wife submitted to her husband in divine order, not only in the home but in the church as well. Yet we function as one. We are the pastor.

Jean Coleman was born in 1935 in Tulsa, Oklahoma, the granddaughter of a Baptist minister. While attending Greenbrier College in West Virginia, she met her husband, Jack, a "town boy." They were married in 1953.

Jack entered the ministry after 26 years as a government employee in the Washington, D.C., area. Active for many years with the Full Gospel Business Men's Fellowship International, both he and Jean have spoken extensively at FGBMFI and Women's Aglow meetings. Together, they co-pastor the church they founded, The Tabernacle in Laurel, Maryland.

Jean is a widely published free-lance writer. Her book, *Chapter 29*, has been printed in three languages. She is also a composer, worship leader, and conference speaker and teacher.

The Colemans have three children. Their son is youth pastor at The Tabernacle.

Chapter Twenty-Six
I'm a Minister, Too

by Anne (Mrs. John) Gimenez

The ride to the airport was routine. It was Monday morning. I had just finished one set of meetings and was on my way to the next revival where I was scheduled to speak. The pastor who was driving me made the usual small talk. I smiled, made a few comments and watched the scenery roll past the car window. Suddenly, his tone changed.

"Sister Anne, you have such a strong preaching ministry that few men could handle being married to you," he said, his eyes never leaving the road. "In fact, the men I know who could deal with it are already married. I believe I must counsel you to plan on staying single for the sake of the ministry."

I was jolted to attention. Never marry? I had often prayed that God would send me a partner with whom I could share my life. I believed in my heart the right man would come at the right time. I never pictured

299

myself an "old maid."

But now this pastor was telling me to give up on marriage. Maybe he was right. I was 33 years old. At the rate I was going, maybe time was running out. Most of my friends were married. That hadn't bothered me much—until the babies started coming. As I watched their happy, growing families, I sometimes ached from loneliness. Would I never have the husband, the home, the family I had always dreamed of?

As we continued the trip in silence, my mind wandered back to a morning several months before in Indianapolis. Kneeling in prayer, I had heard the voice of God as surely as if it had been audible. It came suddenly and unexpectedly.

"A change is coming in your ministry," the Lord said. "You have walked alone and been faithful, but you will not walk alone any longer. I'm going to give you someone to walk by your side and share the joy and the sorrow of the ministry with you."

I smiled as I remembered those special words. I knew the pastor sitting beside me was concerned about me. He wanted me to "face facts." But the fact was that God had spoken. I relaxed once again in my seat. I was not going to be alone.

In the weeks and months that followed, I received more than just that one pastor's counsel against marrying. In fact, most of my friends and family seconded his advice. Still, I held on to God's promise.

I didn't realize at the time that I had already met my future husband. It had happened not long after that morning of prayer in Indianapolis, while I was at a speaking engagement. John Gimenez was also there. He was a member of "The Addicts," a group of ex-drug users who were giving their testimonies all across the country.

I knew little about drug addicts except that I didn't want to have anything to do with them—reformed or not. It never occurred to me that this was the man God had chosen to "walk by my side."

My path and John's path continued to cross as we both ministered. Despite our differences in background and experience, a relationship developed. We were attracted to each other and our feelings grew stronger at each meeting. No one was more surprised than John and I to find the subject of marriage crossing our minds. Me marry an ex-drug addict? John marry a woman preacher? His friends told him I would end up leading him around by the nose. That idea raised his Latin blood pressure. My friends told me he would probably never let me minister once I was his wife. Yet ministry was my life.

I prayed and searched my soul to be sure marriage was indeed God's will for me, not just my own will. The answer was a resounding yes. With great joy and anticipation, John and I were married two-and-a-half years after we first met.

Merging our lives and ministries was a big adjustment. But it was easier than most of our family and friends had predicted. John has always been my biggest fan when I minister. I am his greatest supporter. In the early days of our marriage, we had no problem with our dual roles. Sometimes I would step aside for him. At other times he would be the one to step aside. John is a unique man. So, I have observed, are the husbands of other women called to the ministry. God chooses special men for this walk—men of strong character and courage, with strength enough not to be overshadowed and courage enough to support their wives' calling. Of all the prominent women ministers I know, not one is married to a weak man. None of the husbands is the kind to be "led around by the nose." Rather, each man seems genuinely to enjoy and encourage his wife's role in the ministry.

Unfortunately, other Christians have not always adjusted as well. John and I had been married only one year when Pat Robertson invited us to come to Virginia Beach to be his guests on "The 700 Club." While we were in Virginia, we visited a number of churches. In that very traditional Southern state, we ran into a great deal of prejudice against women in ministry. On one occasion John wanted to "take a baseball bat"—as he put it —and go visit one of my critics.

I calmed him down. "If God is with us, He'll fight those battles for us," I told him. That was not the last time we've needed that reminder.

Nor was that our last contact with the state of Virginia. In fact, God led us to establish a new church—Rock Church—in Virginia Beach.

A lot of heartache went with those early years of Rock Church. But the greatest heartache had nothing to do with our new work—it had to do with our desire to start a family. John and I both wanted a baby very badly. We weren't getting any younger. I went from doctor to doctor trying to find out why I had not yet conceived. Their preliminary examinations turned up nothing.

"Wait until the first of the year, Anne," one doctor said. "If nothing happens by then, we'll start running some tests."

We waited, and we continued to pray. One day John

came in with an announcement.

"I've put out a 'fleece' to God," he said. "If we're supposed to stay in Virginia, you'll get pregnant. If you don't, we'll know God has a different plan for us."

I was surprised to hear John's words. Little did he know that I had prayed exactly the same prayer.

It wasn't long before I had an announcement of my own. I was pregnant! I made an appointment with the doctor to confirm the obvious signs.

John and I waited anxiously for the day. It finally came—but then something went wrong. I never made it to the doctor's office. Instead, I found myself in the hospital, having a miscarriage.

John and I wept together and comforted each other as best we could. We had wanted that baby so badly! Our sense of loss was overwhelming. Finally, we pulled ourselves together and dried our tears. I had gotten pregnant and I could again. We stayed in Virginia Beach and threw ourselves into the business of building the church.

At that time, we also began a youth ministry. It was the late 1970s—the years when the drug culture was pervasive and the Jesus Movement was in full swing. John had a great rapport with young people and the authority of experience with older groups. He spoke constantly in high schools, civic clubs and businessmen's meetings. I, in turn, watched over the church.

When Sundays came around, however, I always insisted that John take his place behind the pulpit as pastor, even though he would have easily given the position to me.

"Nothing doing," I told him. "I'll end up with a church full of women."

So John pastored. Men as well as women flocked to Rock Church. Soon the walls could not be pushed back far enough to accommodate all who were coming.

Where failure had been predicted by naysayers and opponents of women in ministry, we saw only the favor and blessings of the Lord. And soon those blessings included the desire of our hearts. I became pregnant again and gave birth to a beautiful baby girl, Robin Anne. John and I have been married and in ministry together for over 20 years now. Rock Church draws more than 4,000 worshippers each Sunday, and that number is increasing. Our ministry at home and throughout the country continues to grow.

As John and I have ministered together, we've discovered that our differences are a large part of our strength. While John is a real soul winner and leader of men, I am a teacher and preacher. He wins people to the Lord, and I teach them the basics of God's Word. That combination has proved to be a success—for us and for our congregation.

Of course, the enemy has often tried to destroy the unity in our marriage and ministry. His attacks, more often than not, are not full-scale torpedoes to the bridge, but smaller darts simply aimed at putting John and me at odds with each other.

One Sunday evening John and I had a disagreement just before going to church. We were silent as we drove to the meeting, and cool toward each other as we entered the sanctuary. I was scheduled to lead the worship service, but I knew in my heart I could not lead the people while I was angry with my husband. What could I do? We were within seconds of going out onto the platform.

"John, we have to talk and get ourselves right," I

said quickly.

"I'm all right," he replied calmly. I looked into his eyes and saw that he was.

"Well, I'm not. I'm sorry I got so angry. Please forgive me."

He smiled and gave me a quick peck on the cheek. In an instant, my heart was light. Together, we went out to worship the Lord.

Unity is critical to our ministry. Not only does God see my heart, but when I'm in the pulpit, I believe the congregation sees my heart, too.

Once I was counseling a mother about a problem with her teenage daughter. As she was leaving, she turned suddenly and said, "May I ask you a personal question?"

I was taken aback. "Well, I'll answer if I can."

She looked me straight in the eyes. "Is your relationship with your husband at home as good as when you're on the platform together, or is that just a show for the people?"

I answered slowly. "What you see is what you get," I told her. "We've never thought of putting on a show."

Of course, sometimes pressures do build up. We're human. John and I have found that our best recourse is simply to get in the car and drive somewhere—anywhere. If we can be alone for a few days, away from outside worries and distractions, we can easily smooth any rough edges in our relationship. All we need is time together.

A few years ago, John and I realized we were spending too much time going separate ways, traveling to separate speaking engagements and involving ourselves in separate projects. We were becoming adjusted to living apart. After talking it over, we decided to cancel all meetings except those where we could go together. For over a year, we didn't go out of town unless it was with each other.

Eventually, we began attending separate engagements again—but only if they were very important. We still try to keep them at a bare minimum. We've seen too many marriages—even good ones—begin to disintegrate as husband goes one way and wife goes another. John and I refuse to cultivate separate ministries and thus separate lives.

John is not in my shadow, nor is he walking ahead without me. We're partners. After all, God didn't simply promise me a husband. He promised me someone who would "share the joy and the sorrow of the ministry with me."

Born in 1932 in Houston, Texas, **Anne Gimenez** was raised in a non-religious home. Her family attended church only on special occasions. As a high school senior, however, Anne visited a tent revival meeting held by T.L. Osborne and was baptized in the Holy Spirit. She began attending a full gospel church and eventually followed a call to become an evangelist.

While traveling as a preacher, Anne met her husband, John, who was also involved in a traveling ministry with a group called the Addicts. The two were married two-and-a-half years later.

Together, Anne and John established Rock Church in Virginia Beach, Virginia, and later the Rock Christian Television Network.

Anne is the founder of Women in Leadership National and author of the book, *The Emerging Christian Woman* (Strang Communications Co., 1986).

The Gimenezes have one daughter, age 16.

Chapter Twenty-Seven
Have Ministry, Will Travel

by Minnie (Mrs. Dick) Coleman

The ceiling of the enormous Pittsburgh arena rolled back slowly. Stars twinkled in the night sky overhead. I looked over at my husband, Dick, whose face was upturned. What are we doing here? I wondered.

How did two small-town people like us end up sharing this magnificent platform with leaders from some of the most powerful ministries in the world?

Oh, the Lord works in mysterious ways!

Dick and I were raised in the same county in Florida, in neighboring small towns. Our mothers were childhood friends. To their delight, we began courting in 1947 and were married in 1948. Dick was a student at the University of Florida and I was fresh out of high school.

We survived the usual struggles of a young, newly married student couple with a weekly grocery budget of $10. After graduation, Dick was offered a job as pro-

gram director for a radio station in Leesburg, Florida.
We were thrilled! I remember thinking, Life has finally
begun for us.

But several years and two babies later, I wasn't so
sure. Dick and I were unsettled, unfulfilled, dissatisfied.
What was missing? We had a good car, a comfortable
home. Dick's salary was adequate, and we had joined
all the right clubs. We even went to church on Sundays.
So where did this deep emptiness come from?

As we sought answers, we moved instinctively toward
the Bible. God began to reveal to us through His Word
our need to know Jesus Christ personally. Slowly, we
realized that while we were church members, we were
not "born again." This was what had been missing all
along! Together, Dick and I accepted Jesus as our
Savior. We joined a local Baptist church and were
baptized.

In the excitement of those first weeks as Christians,
we prayed, "Let us serve You, Lord." Apparently, God
was ready and willing to answer that prayer: in 1956,
Dick left his job to become a minister.

We sold our home in Leesburg and, with two small
children in tow, moved to Wake Forest, North Carolina,
so that Dick could attend Southeastern Baptist Theological Seminary. For the second time in our married life,
Dick was a student. At the same time, he became a
pastor when a local church called him to be their full-
time minister.

I knew how to be the wife of a student, but suddenly
I assumed a new and somewhat overwhelming role: pastor's wife. I had no prior experience, no training. There
wasn't even a book to read on the subject! Fortunately,
the Mt. Harmony Baptist Church had called other "stu-

dent pastors'' before us, so they were gracious about our failures and shortcomings.

I remember well that first day as pastor's wife. One church lady showed me around the kitchen of the parsonage as several others filled the pantry with luscious, home-canned vegetables and jams. My guide pulled out several large storage bins capable of holding 20 to 30 pounds of flour or meal each.

"These are for the cornbread and biscuits you'll be baking," she said.

I was terrified! The last biscuit I had baked looked and tasted like a golf ball.

With great conscientiousness, I set about learning what was expected of me in my new role. (I eventually learned to cook a real lip-smacking country meal—with biscuits and gravy—after months of observing the church's accomplished homemakers.) My biggest and most devastating mistake, however, was that I set goals for myself—or allowed others to set them for me—that the Lord had not intended. I tried to be a role model for every woman in the congregation. I thought I had to keep an immaculate house, present my two little boys (soon to be three) with eternally washed faces, work dedicatedly in the church and still find time to be an attentive and loving wife.

As hard as I tried, this lifestyle of perfection eluded me for the four years we were at Mt. Harmony. Still, our life was good. Dick and I rejoiced with our people, visited their sick, stood by as their babies were born, mourned as we buried their dead. I learned to celebrate, love, share and cry. I learned in some measure to fight exhaustion, fear, loneliness, financial problems and rejection. I learned the importance of standing in unity with Dick in the ministry.

In 1963 God nudged us back to Leesburg, Florida, and another pastorate, Westside Baptist, where we were to stay for 18 years. When we first arrived, we quickly saw that our work was cut out for us. The church had gone through a great shake-up, and the remains were badly scattered. Slowly, through our ministry, God began to heal the wounds, but not without Dick and me facing many days of deep discouragement. Each week for those first two years, it seemed, we battled the desire to call it quits.

We were two very busy people with three active sons. Dick's life became church and ministry. Mine became house, children and church activities. At night, we would fall into bed too exhausted to move, with only enough energy for a gentle pat and a peck on the cheek.

Is this all there is? I wondered. Do we even have a marriage?

Publicly, we presented a united front. "Everything's just fine!" I'd say to anyone who asked. Inside, however, I was mixed up, confused. I wasn't sure I wanted to be a pastor's wife anymore.

Dick was dissatisfied, too. Again, we turned to the Lord for the answer. Our search brought us to the "something more" experience—the baptism in the Holy Spirit. We received the baptism with great enthusiasm in 1967.

Suddenly, our lives and the life of Westside Baptist Church were turned completely around.

At a pastors' conference, Dick was convicted by a message on proper priorities. He came home a changed man. Overnight, I became his number one sheep. I loved it! Why didn't he learn this sooner? In response, I became more sensitive to Dick's needs, and our love for each other was rekindled.

Soon God convicted me about my weak areas—my false goal setting and my proud efforts to be the perfect role model. With the meticulousness of a master sculptor, the Holy Spirit chiseled away large areas of pride, anxiety and my big monster—fear. Over time, I learned to be real. I could say what I really felt, not what I thought I was supposed to say. I could actually disagree with people and still be loved. I could release my children to be children—to get dirty, to have fights, to be less than perfect.

God was changing us. This was all part of His plan to prepare us for what lay ahead.

When word got around about our baptism in the Spirit, Dick began to receive invitations to speak in Full Gospel Business Men's Fellowship meetings throughout Florida and occasionally in other states. When I could, I left the boys with my parents—they lived in a nearby town and were always willing to keep their only grandchildren—and I traveled with Dick.

We became involved in a counseling ministry. As we prayed and counseled people who had all kinds of problems, the gifts of the Holy Spirit manifested themselves in us. We didn't understand what was happening; books about spiritual gifts were not readily available in the late 1960s and early '70s, so we had little to go by. All we knew was that God was touching lives through us with wonderful results.

I admit there were days when I felt I would burst if I listened to one more sad story about marital conflict, adultery, sexual problems, financial disasters or child abuse. To survive, I learned to stop before I was exhausted, get away from the phone and just do something totally unrelated to the ministry—shop (window shop if I was broke), curl up with *Good Housekeeping* or listen to a tape. Then I would refuel through Bible study and prayer. I learned that sharing out of a full cup is much more effective than giving some poor soul the dregs.

God was preparing me.

One evening, when Dick was sharing his testimony in a meeting in Miami, I got my final push. I was seated at the head table, listening intently as my husband spoke. Suddenly, I turned to look at the group. Before me was a sea of faces. But I saw more than that—I saw the needs that were hidden behind them. One person had a specific disease, another had a mental disturbance, another had a deep spiritual problem. I shook my head in disbelief. What was happening to me? How did I know this? Did the Holy Spirit tell people such things?

I slipped out of my chair and told Dick what was happening.

"I think you should tell the people what God is saying," he said.

As I began to minister, the presence of God seemed so real. We prayed for people, and several with a variety of diseases were healed, some instantly.

I was more surprised by what was happening than anyone. Was God really going to use me this way? Why me? I was a wife, a mother, a broom-pusher, a dishwasher with only a high school education. What was God's purpose for me?

I went home that weekend and prayed and diligently studied about the gifts of the Spirit. God had placed a yearning in my heart to receive the gifts and share them with the body of Christ.

Many doors opened to us. Dick gave his testimony, and I was a channel for the Holy Spirit to demonstrate His gifts, especially the "word of knowledge" as God revealed specific areas in people's lives that needed help. Together we would pray for the sick. We were amazed at how God used us.

Later, God impressed on us the need to teach on His order in the home—something we had learned about through our own struggles. Dick taught the men and I took on the role described in Titus 2 of encouraging and teaching the women.

Soon we had more invitations than we could handle comfortably. At home, our church was growing, and the people supported us with prayer and fasting. Life was exciting.

There was one difficulty: the children. Our closest friends, Bill and Mary Holloway, gave the boys a second home, love and oversight when we were away. And, of course, they had their grandparents. Still I knew that no one could take the place of Mom and Dad. I cried on more than one occasion as I took the children's clothes from the closet for another trip to the Holloway home. When I wasn't traveling, it seemed I was spending all of my time in the utility room—washing clothes and preparing us all to "move out" one more time.

Dick and I made every effort to plan our itineraries around the proms, banquets, ROTC parades, award dinners, band concerts and football games the boys were involved in. We weren't always successful. I remember distinctly the night I sat on the bed in a strange hotel room and cried like a baby because I had just missed seeing our youngest son don his first tuxedo. That was not the first nor the last time I felt pulled in a thousand directions.

Our work has continued to grow and change. We backed out of public Christian service for several years. But the desire remained. When we finally returned to the pastorate, the traveling ministry, with all the gifts of the Spirit, reappeared also.

Through it all, Dick has been the stabilizing factor in our work. I have always been ready to fly off anywhere at the drop of a hat. He has lovingly corrected me, shown me more practical ways to proclaim God's word and insisted that I exercise self-control when ministering. I have desperately needed that strong, firm hand.

I've gone places I didn't feel particularly "led" to go. Those meetings usually turned out to be the most powerful ones of the year. I've gone to other places with great expectations, only to fall flat on my face. And it is just as awesome to me today as it was 17 years ago that God heals cancer and other diseases and releases people from sin.

I used to get hung up from time to time by insecurities about how well I prepared. Did I pray enough? Should I fast? A few days before a meeting a voice inside me would say, "You haven't prayed enough" or "You haven't studied enough." This would throw me into a last-minute frenzy. Then the Lord helped me understand "rest." Yes, I pray, I study, I read, I fast, I bounce ideas off my husband and my friends, and I make outlines. But most of all, now, I rest in Him.

"He is the Lord, mighty in battle...." He will do the work. I must only be available. By this, I don't mean an unprepared, backslidden, lazy availability, but an availability that allows me to be a real person. The vessel is earthen, but the contents are a treasure from the Father. My release is in yielding the vessel and giving the glory to Him who fills it. I no longer ask, Did I do well? Were my words clear? How was the response? My question now is, Does it glorify Him?

Without a doubt, the joys of our traveling ministry— past, present and future—far outweigh the disappointments of uneventful meetings; the weariness of long, multi-legged trips; the frustration of knowing we can't get home to a sick child any faster than the plane will fly. Long nights of ministry and short nights of sleep, disagreements, criticisms—these seem as nothing when balanced against the things we've seen God do through us.

We've watched a 75-year-old man weep with thanks to God after receiving a particular gift of the Spirit "at last!" We've seen a 9-year-old boy shout for joy because his crossed eye was instantly straightened—the years of teasing from peers and failure in school finally over. We've stood in amazement as a woman wracked with pain for 10 years miraculously received three brand new vertebrae and a new lease on life. We've seen homes and relationships restored as husbands and wives learned about God's divine order.

Is it worth it? It sure is to me.

Today, Dick and I are involved in a "genesis" project in Raleigh, North Carolina. We're starting a new church. That's taking a lot of our time and attention, as it well should. Still we travel.

In one way, it's easier now to pick up and go. All three of our boys are grown and are walking with the Lord, along with their wives and our four grandchildren.

Someone once said, "You'll know what you taught is true if it reaches the third generation." I'm seeing that now, and it is one of my greatest joys.

I still sit in lonely hotel rooms and pray that my children and grandchildren are all right. I still leave addresses and telephone numbers. I still make a lot of long distance calls. Motherhood never ceases!

What would I say to a pastor's wife who feels led by God to a traveling ministry alongside her husband? My advice is this: Start small. Build a solid base. Bloom where you are planted and let God open the doors. Share your ministry with those who love you most—your family, your friends, your church. These are your testing grounds. If it works at home, it will work anywhere. Then go and be a blessing to the body of Christ at large.

It has been my privilege to be sent out by God with my husband. I have always had Dick's blessing and full support. Our children have encouraged us, and our local churches have supported us with prayer. God has blessed.

It's worth it.

Minnie Coleman was born in Wildwood, Florida, in 1932, an only child in a middle-class home. She and her husband, Dick, knew each other most of their lives, since their mothers were also friends from childhood. The couple began dating in 1947 and was married the next year.

Minnie and Dick have traveled extensively over the last 20 years, usually as a couple, but not always, teaching biblical principles to families. Dick has also pastored churches during this time and is now pastor of the Triangle Community Church in Raleigh, North Carolina.

The Colemans have three sons, all married. Two work as engineers for the PTL ministry in Charlotte, North Carolina. There are four grandchildren.

Chapter Twenty-Eight
Picking Up Where He Leaves Off

———

by Freda (Mrs. Gordon) Lindsay

One of the most devastating experiences a pastor's wife—or any woman for that matter—can face is the sudden death of her husband. There can be no greater loss than that of having to give up the one who has been her lifelong companion and decision maker, the one who has provided financial support as well as emotional strength and stability, the one who has been the guiding force in her life under God.

Only another widow can share the sorrow she feels, and say, "I understand."

I married Gordon Lindsay on November 14, 1937. From the very beginning, there was no doubt that our lives would be spent in service to the Lord. We settled in San Fernando, California, where Gordon was starting a new church and I was able to complete my studies at Life Bible College. From there, we moved on to pastor a church in Tacoma, Washington. Later, we pioneered another church in Billings, Montana.

When the work in Billings matured enough for us to leave, we set out in a direction of true faith—we became traveling evangelists. Those were exciting years—but tough. On most nights, the offering we received barely paid for the gasoline we needed to drive to our next preaching engagement.

In 1948, Gordon, along with Jack Moore of Shreveport, Louisiana, started a new work. Together they founded a magazine called *The Voice of Healing*, which reported on the great miracles and healings that were taking place in the evangelistic campaigns of the late 1940s and '50s. Over the years, circulation soared to over 100,000. People were hungry to hear about the power and grace of a miracle-working God.

But as important as the magazine was to Gordon, it became secondary over the next 15 years to his widening ministry in writing books (he authored 250 of them during his lifetime) and his work with world missions. In 1967 we took on the name "Christ for the Nations." That title seemed to best describe the scope and intent of the organization that had grown up around Gordon's ministry.

In September 1970, the Lord impressed on Gordon the need to start a Bible school in Dallas, Texas. We began to work toward that goal. All seemed to be going well until April 1, 1973. On that Sunday afternoon, Gordon and I were sitting on our auditorium stage at the Christ for the Nations Institute. The congregation before us was singing:

"Jesus, Jesus, Jesus—
there's just something about that name....
Kings and kingdoms shall all pass away,

but there's something about that name!''

In that moment, just as those words were being sung, Gordon Lindsay died.

I did not realize it at first. When I looked over at my husband, he appeared to be asleep. A doctor came immediately to the platform and began administering aid, but he could not revive him. We offered up prayer. But Gordon had gone to be with Jesus, almost in the twinkling of an eye.

At that time, Christ for the Nations was deeply in debt. The Bible school's seven apartment complex dormitories were not yet paying for themselves through student enrollment. We still owed three years of payments on the new ministry headquarters we had just built. We were also in the midst of constructing a 1,400-seat auditorium on which we had already borrowed $450,000. It would take five more months and many thousands of additional dollars to complete the project.

Even when Gordon was alive, I would think to myself, "How in the world are we going to remain solvent?" On the first of every month, it seemed we had to scrounge around to get just enough money to pay the mortgages on the dormitories alone. Now Gordon was gone. What would happen to the ministry? What would happen to me?

As I got out of bed the Monday morning after the funeral, I was startled to find I hadn't the strength even to stand. For several nights, I hadn't slept. I was overwhelmed by the responsibilities that faced me. Someone had to continue the missionary work that was reaching into 100 nations; complete the Bible school auditorium; help build the 300 native church projects to which we were already committed; edit the monthly *Christ for the*

Nations magazine.

How would I manage? Gordon had always been the one in charge. I had stayed in the background. What was I going to do?

That morning, it seemed as if my legs just gave way. I had no strength at all. I called out to my daughter, Shira, who was in the adjoining room. She had returned from Israel two days before her father's death.

"The board of directors has asked me to succeed Daddy at Christ for the Nations," I told her, my voice cracking. "It's just too much for me...." I began to weep.

Shira was silent for a moment. Then, softly, she said, "Mother, let's pray and ask God to give you just enough strength for today."

I laid myself prostrate on the floor and called on the Lord, weeping bitterly. Suddenly, He began to speak to my heart.

"This is not *your work*; this is My work," He said. "I founded it and it shall continue."

Instantly, my burden was lifted. The tears stopped flowing and I began to rejoice. Together, Shira and I praised the Lord. With great joy, we confessed that our God is faithful and would see us through.

"Mother, you do have enough strength for today, don't you?" Shira asked.

"I do!"

And I did. I agreed to succeed Gordon officially at Christ for the Nations.

But soon Satan launched another attack. One night, around 3 a.m., I awoke, filled with an unexplained panic. A flow of negative thoughts pushed through my mind. It was as if the devil himself was sitting at my shoulder, whispering in my ear: "You had 250 students last semester, but you still didn't have enough money to pay for the seven dormitories. Even for Gordon, keeping the school afloat was a constant struggle. Now that he's gone, the attendance will probably drop by half. How are you possibly going to make those payments?"

The argument sounded logical. How would I keep the school from going under? But suddenly, I realized this was doubt, not trust, speaking. I was under satanic attack.

"Devil, you are a liar!" I cried, jumping out of bed. "This fear and doubt is not from God. I refuse to accept it!" Immediately as I spoke, the attack subsided.

Then the Lord brought to mind that many years before, He had been faithful to give me two significant words of prophetic counsel regarding an increase in my responsibility in the ministry. In the mid-1960s, during a Christ for the Nations annual seminar, evangelist John Osteen spoke to me "through the Spirit." He said that although my ministry had been submerged in Gordon's, God was going to give me signs and wonders, and one day my ministry would come forth in its own right. I wondered about this message. I could not imagine myself launching out in my own ministry. My work, I felt, was to be a helpmate to Gordon.

The second "word" had come in 1968 through Clara Grace, a woman with the gift of prophecy. "You have been a Martha; oh, how you have been a Martha!" she said. "But all the time, the Mary in you has been crying out. This cry has entered into the ears of Jehovah of hosts, and your ministry will change from a Martha to a Mary." These precious words of spiritual direction and counsel took on a new importance for me as their meaning became clear. I approached in faith the task that lay ahead.

To my great surprise, enrollment at our Bible school jumped the following semester from 250 to 425 students—nearly double, not the half that Satan had prophesied. Several large cash donations were pledged. Amazingly, other benefactors—some of whom barely knew of our work—gave us large parcels of land, including one piece that was 41 acres in size. By selling some of this new property, we were able to retire our massive debt and even enlarge the campus.

God was and is faithful! Today, the progress of the ministry and the growth of the Christ for the Nations Institute show no signs of slowing. Over 1,700 students are enrolled in our Bible schools in Dallas and New York. We've helped establish other schools in Finland, Germany, Nigeria, Thailand, Zimbabwe, South Africa, Peru, Ecuador, the Philippines, India, Sri Lanka, Zambia and Indonesia. In 1985 alone, we constructed 7,000 native churches in Third World countries. We are publishing the gospel in 68 languages. In all, our work is touching 120 nations across the globe.

In 1983, we were able to purchase the 10-story Sheraton Hotel located across from our Dallas campus. The giant red, white and blue lights that proclaim "CHRIST FOR THE NATIONS" are visible for miles around. For me, this new building symbolizes victory over adversity.

Not too long ago, a friend came to me and said, "Everyone knew that the work would grow. But the fact that it has grown even more rapidly with Gordon gone gives all the more glory to God. A woman could never have done it."

"You're right," I said, "especially not this woman!"

To what do I attribute the growth? It's simple: faith and prayer. Gordon Lindsay was the greatest man of prayer I've ever met. The answers to his prayers did not cease with his passing. Rather, they seemed to gain momentum.

I give God all the glory. At the same time, I recognize that the Lord works through individuals. One such individual was my husband. And now I carry on where Gordon left off.

Visiting Christ for the Nations today, it might be difficult to imagine the many days of heartbreak and uncertainty. I've been called a "woman of steel." Perhaps it is no particular credit to be called that, but it certainly has taken great strength to run an organization of this size and scope. We're not a ladies' aid society meeting once a month for socials. We've got a definite call and a real business to do for God. It isn't easy. When I have to make difficult decisions, I do without flinching. I take my work very seriously.

At the same time, I still have my gentle side. For example, I love flowers. God has taught me many lessons through this hobby of mine. For several weeks, I nursed one little plant that didn't seem to respond to any of my efforts. I thought it would never survive. I almost threw it away. But one day it began to bloom, and now it's the prettiest one I own.

People are a lot like that little plant. I may look at someone and think: "What a mess." But God doesn't see them that way. And eventually, they bloom. I've often been amazed as I've watched some of the most unlikely students at our institute turn out to do the greatest works for the Lord.

As for me, my work is far from finished. There are still a few debts to clear. We have a number of projects to complete, and some ideas for some new ones.

As long as there is one man or woman, one boy or girl living without Christ, I will push on. One day, I want to be able to say with Paul, "I have fought a good fight. I have finished my course, I have kept the faith: henceforth there is laid up for me a crown of righteousness, which the Lord, the righteous judge, shall give me at that day, and not to me only, but unto all them also that love his appearing" (2 Tim. 4:7,8).

Freda Lindsay was born in 1914 in Burstall, Saskatchewan. Her family later moved to Oregon where, at the age of 18, Freda was converted at a revival meeting which a young evangelist, Gordon Lindsay, conducted. She married Gordon five years later.

The Lindsays pastored several churches throughout the Northwest and pioneered an evangelistic association and publishing enterprise, *The Voice of Healing*, before founding Christ For The Nations in 1967. CFN is now one of the largest full-gospel missionary societies in the world.

After Gordon's death in 1973, Freda was named president of CFN, a position she held until her resignation in late 1985. Her son, Dennis Gordon, one of three Lindsay children, has succeeded her. Freda continues to be chairman of the board and chief executive officer. She is also publisher and editor of CFN's monthly magazine and, with Dennis, heads the Christ For The Nations Institute, a two-year Bible school.

Chapter Twenty-Nine
Dealing With Problem People

by Anita (Mrs. Gil) Reno

People! Ministry! That's what my life is all about. As a pastor, my husband is constantly involved with people. As his wife and helpmeet, I am involved with people too—daily, and sometimes hourly.

Years ago, Gil and I determined that we have a message and a calling. It is found in 2 Corinthians 5:18-20: "All this is from God, who reconciled us to himself through Christ and gave us the *ministry of reconciliation:* that God was reconciling the world to himself in Christ, not counting men's sins against them. And he has committed to us the *message of reconciliation.* We are therefore Christ's ambassadors, as though God were making his appeal through us. We implore you on Christ's behalf; *be reconciled to God.*"

Taking the wonderful news of salvation to people is a privilege, but we are not promised a life without difficulty. In fact, the more the Lord works in our lives and in the lives of those we see come to Christ, the more opposition we are bound to face from the enemy. Satan would like to see us out of commission, our ministry crippled.

For ammunition, he rarely has to look very far. Since we are involved so irrevocably with people, and people have problems, we will have problems, too.

There are two different aspects to this in my own experience. There are people with problems, and there are problem people. The first are those we are called to minister to. If they did not have problems, they would not need a Savior. Dealing with these people takes a measure of superhuman grace, patience and at times, firmness.

Problem people are a different matter. Oh, they have problems, too. But these are those who name the name of Christ. Often they are the hardest workers in the church, even leaders. But they cause trouble for the pastor and his wife wherever they go.

Problem people do not perceive themselves as problems. They almost always feel that they are serving the Lord with all their might. Yet, mostly through direct verbal assaults or words spoken behind the pastor's back, they cause dissension and pain. In his book *Well-Intentioned Dragons: Ministering to Problem People in the Church*, Marshall Shelley says it well: "The distinguishing characteristic of a dragon is not *what* is said but *how* it's said. Even though these people are well-intentioned, sincerely doing what's best in their own eyes, they aren't quite with you." How true!

Criticism, sometimes thinly veiled, seems to come with the territory when your husband is a pastor. Comments are jettisoned at me, my husband, my children.

Often, I am dragged into the middle of disagreements over Gil's policies, the content of his sermons, or even the disciplining of my children!

When we went into the ministry—and I am as much in the ministry as my pastor-husband—I was automatically placed in a vulnerable position. "Open season" was proclaimed on me and my family. But the way I see it, this is the price I pay for the privilege of leadership. Going into the ministry is not unlike going into politics. In either situation, people feel a freedom, even a responsibility, to voice their opinion concerning anything about my life.

Criticism hurts. I am human and want the approval of others. When some problem people criticize under the guise of helping or giving suggestions, I cannot help but feel personally attacked.

The important thing is how I deal with each assault. Again, I've seen it stated best in Shelley's *Well-Intentioned Dragons*: "No encounter with a dragon is a complete failure unless one fights venom with venom. No victory is worth winning if it forces us to become bilious."

As the pastor, Gil is usually the major target of criticism. In many ways, I find this harder to deal with than having the unkind words directed personally at me. I am particularly defensive of those I care about most. I've found, however, that I can serve in diffusing the situation if I let the Holy Spirit guide. I can be a sounding board for my husband. He needs to communicate the problem to someone who will not escalate it, someone he can trust completely. I try to be that someone. I then have the opportunity to help him work it through.

Our church is a loving family, the people supportive.

Still, criticisms do come. One of our church leaders, Bill, would lash out at my husband periodically over his sermons. It was always the same complaint: the messages were too negative. Bill would get so angry that at times he would go to one or more of the elders to express his displeasure.

At first, I reacted defensively. I was tempted to tell Bill—in a tone that would have sparked a whole new round of criticism—that he was just plain wrong. I knew Gil prayed over his messages. They were biblical and we believed they were from the Lord. Instead, I resisted the temptation to react and acted instead in the way I felt the Lord wanted me to. Gil and I prayed about the situation.

One day, the Holy Spirit revealed something to me about Bill's criticism. Excited, I shared it with my husband.

"Gil, have you noticed? The sermons Bill always seems to get upset about are the ones with motivational themes, the ones in which you encourage the congregation to become more active in some way."

"Hmmm. You know, you're right," he said.

Gil has the gift of evangelism and exhortation. At times in our growing church, he has preached about the need for every Christian to become more involved in the ministry, to help share the load of Christ's commission. Usually, these messages were given at a time when he was feeling spread too thin; too many of the people were sitting back and expecting the pastor to do it all. Undoubtedly, frustration spilled over into his voice at these times.

Bill, however, was one of the hardest workers in the church. He was skilled in many areas and probably felt many of the same frustrations my husband did. He took Gil's challenge to become more involved personally. Since he felt he was already doing everything he could, he became angry and resentful.

With this realization, my husband went to Bill and asked his forgiveness, explaining that he certainly was not referring to Bill in his sermons on Christian involvement and responsibility. He praised Bill for all the good work he had been doing in the church and thanked him for his input on his sermons. Now Gil makes a concerted attempt to be more positive in his exhortations. The results have been rewarding, not only in the cooperation we have gotten from Bill, but from the whole congregation as well.

What could have been a "bilious" scene was a success because we applied the scriptural principle found in Romans 12:17: "Do not repay anyone evil for evil. Be careful to do what is right in the eyes of everybody. If it is possible, as far as it depends on you, live at peace with everyone."

Gossip is another characteristic of a problem person. As the pastor's wife, I deal most often with the women of the church. And unfortunately, women can be the worst gossipers.

I remember attending a ladies' Bible study shortly after becoming a Christian. When the leader asked for prayer requests, one woman spoke up. "Please pray for Sadie Jones. Poor thing. Her marriage is falling apart."

"The Peter Smiths' are having a terrible time with their teenagers," another woman said. "They even found some marijuana cigarettes in their 16-year-old's room. We should really pray for them."

In a matter of weeks, I found myself looking forward

to the Bible study, not because I would be fed from
God's Word and uplifted by the fellowship, but because
I knew I would catch up on the latest gossip. As I grew
in maturity, however, the Holy Spirit convicted me
about this. He showed me that gossipers are truly "problem people" with tongues that can destroy God's people and tear a church apart. I determined that if I ever
led a Bible study or women's group, I would be careful
to keep gossip under strict control. God eventually gave
me the chance to test that determination. In the ladies'
Bible study I lead today, I have made it my personal
responsibility to keep the time from becoming a gossip
session, particularly when it comes to discussing prayer
requests. It's one thing to confess your own sin, but quite
another to confess someone else's problems. I try to set
a positive example and never allow myself to be a party
to gossip. Sometimes I have had to go to individual
"problem" women to quell rumors, gently and lovingly.
Proverbs 26:20 says, "Without wood a fire goes out;
without gossip a quarrel dies down." This is preven-
tive medicine.

As the pastor's wife, I must also deal frequently with
another kind of problem person—the one who does not
have the courage to tell Gil something to his face but
wants me to deliver the message. More often than not,
these are overbearing women who feel that something
is not being done as it should be. I admit that I have
often let these people intimidate me, and I have ended
up being the reluctant go-between. No more.

The best advice I have ever received on how to handle
such situations is from Mary L. Phillips in her book
Reaching Women. She writes, "Nowadays, when someone comes to me with 'I think you (or the pastor, or

the church) should do something about this,' I level my most righteous look at her and say, 'God has evidently laid that burden on your heart, and I have no doubt that He wants YOU to pursue it. I'll pray with you that you'll know how to fulfill this concern. I would be robbing you of a reward if I tried to perform that ministry. If I can give you any advice, let me know.' We then take hands and pray. If perchance the idea is of God, the woman will pursue it. If not, I haven't lost a wink of sleep because of it.''

Try it. It works! Not only does it get more people involved in the ministry, but when people feel they are an integral part of an exciting, living fellowship, they are much less likely to cause problems.

Of course, problem people are not always what they seem. I may think that someone is a problem person—but the problem is really in my understanding.

When our church was still quite small, Mrs. Fry began to get on my nerves. She had a particularly irritating habit which I first blamed on her self-centeredness. At that time, we had only one restroom in the church building. Sometimes I would need to use it between Sunday school and the worship service. Since I played the piano during the service, I liked to be in and out in short order and at the piano by 10 minutes to 11:00.

But no matter how hard I tried, Mrs. Fry always beat me into the restroom. She would stay there interminably. Many Sundays I had to forego using the restroom and suffer through the service. I found myself becoming very resentful toward Mrs. Fry, whom I labeled a ''problem person.'' I figured she was using my restroom time to primp!

Imagine my shame and chagrin when I learned that

Mrs. Fry had a severe kidney problem! Now before I conclude that someone is a "problem," I make sure I know all the facts.

In 20 years of ministering with my husband, I've learned some basic principles in handling problem people. I've learned them through great difficulties and a few failures, too. I have not yet "arrived." I still react sometimes in the flesh rather than in the Spirit. In those times, it helps to have some guidelines on which to fall back.

When attacks, complaints, criticisms and problems come, I say to myself, "OK, Anita. Slow down. Here's another challenge." I try to give the Lord control of my initial feelings of anger or rejection. This is crucial—otherwise I will react and escalate the problem.

I then take the matter in prayer to the Lord, asking Him to show me if there is validity in the criticism or a deeper message behind the attack. I ask Him to give me the discernment and strength to change anything that needs changing. I acknowledge that I am still "in process." God is still working on me to make me more usable for His glory. Sometimes He can use problem people and the situations they create to prune me, to make me more fruitful. I may not like it, but I can be yielded to it.

If the Lord assures me I am on track (or that my husband is, if he's the one under attack), I pray for the courage to go ahead as He leads to ignore or deal in some positive way with the problem.

I always pray to experience God's love for the problem person. I am honest with Him about my feelings. He knows anyway, but it helps to verbalize them. "Lord, I am angry with ____." Or "Right now, Lord,

I don't even want to be around ____." Then I ask the Lord to extend His supernatural love through me to that person.

Through this process, something miraculous almost always happens. The walls of anger or resentment or pain are torn down, and I come to the renewed understanding that problem people are mostly just people with problems.

I can minister to them.

Anita Reno was born in 1931 in Hemet, California, the youngest of three children in a well-to-do family. She was raised as an "only child," however, since her brother and sister were 15 and 17 years her seniors.

Anita attended a boarding school for her last three years of high school. At the age of 16, while home for Christmas vacation, she met her husband, Gil. They were married almost three years later in 1950.

From 1967 to 1979, Anita and Gil served as rural home missionaries for what is now the American Missionary Fellowship. In 1979, Gil took on his current position as pastor of the Peaceful Valley Church in Elk, Washington.

Anita has held a number of professional positions, including dean of women for two years at Inland Empire School of the Bible. The Renos have 10 children, five of whom are adopted from Korea. They have 14 grandchildren.

Chapter Thirty
Helping Hurting People

---

by Letha (Mrs. Jack) Mathews

It was 10 p.m. when the phone rang. Here we go again, I thought.

Jack and I had been married for two months. We were working with troubled teenagers on the streets and in state institutions. Jack had been gone all day and into the evening, like most of the days thus far in our new life together. Was he going to have to go out again?

It was Karla. "If you don't come right now...I'm going to walk out into the four-lane highway in front of my house...and throw myself in front of the first car that comes along!" she cried hysterically.

I fought back the tears as Jack put on his coat. I thought we had gotten married to be together. But all he seemed to be doing was leaving.

Once he was gone, I did the only thing I was capable of doing at the time. I threw myself on the bed and cried—not for Karla, but for myself.

This was my profound entrance into ministry at the age of 18.

Why do I consider that moment to be my beginning in ministry? Because on that bed, amidst those tears, I had an encounter with the Spirit of Christ. During the next few moments I was set on the road to maturity.

The Holy Spirit reminded me that Jack and I were called to a life of ministering together, not just being together. He gave me a choice. "Letha, you can be on the outside or the inside of the ministry to which you and Jack have been called. Which will it be? Right now you're on the outside. Do you want to be on the inside?"

"Yes, I do, God," I cried. I didn't have the skills needed at that time to go with Jack to help Karla. But I *could* quit feeling sorry for myself, and I *did* know how to pray. For the rest of the night, I interceded for Jack as he ministered to that 16-year-old girl.

Karla celebrated her 40th birthday recently. Jack and I celebrated it with her. During the past 24 years we have seen God do countless miracles of healing in her life. We have watched as she has become an active change-agent in our church and in her world. She has grown from a hurting young girl to a dynamic Christian woman with a purpose.

At 18, I was a very self-centered person. Through Karla, I was provided an opportunity to change, to become a vital part of people's lives. But you know what? God didn't ask me to stop being self-centered for the sake of being others-centered. He asked me to quit being self-centered so I could learn to be Christ-centered.

Amidst the challenge of helping hurting people over the past 24 years, I've been learning to live a Christ-centered life. And being Christ-centered has had implications for how I view hurting people, how I relate to my husband and family, and how I view my own role in ministry.

I used to see hurting people as interruptions rather than as opportunities to show Christ's love. My happiness at the moment was more important to me than their well-being. Being Christ-centered means that while their happiness is not necessarily more important than my own, their immediate well-being is.

Along the way, to deal with the ''I-gotta-go-nows,'' Jack and I have learned to take time out to nurture and encourage one another. We have had to do it to survive, for except for God, sometimes we have only each other. In the struggle to balance the needs of others with my family's needs, I've learned to respond as Christ did to the hurting. At times that means being with people; at times that means getting away from them.

I've finally come to a sane evaluation of myself. I've learned it took only one life on the cross to attain the salvation of mankind. God isn't seeking to use me up but to fill me up, as I make Christ the center of my life.

Each pastor's wife has her own ideas about being involved in the lives of hurting people. My involvement has both excited and frightened me. In human terms, I have felt ill-equipped. I have no degrees in psychology or religion, no experience in social work. But in spiritual terms, I'm well-equipped because I am in a covenant relationship with God. Everything He is in wisdom, power, strength, compassion and mercy is available to me in my need through His indwelling Holy Spirit.

All of this is available to any Christian. Yet, in times of suffering, it's surprising how often we forget, or feel unable, to draw upon the resources of the One who lives within.

Through study and personal experience, I've discovered that God and troubled times go together. Because we so easily forget to rely on God and because people more often than not spell trouble, I have given my life to these simple endeavors: loving God, loving people—and getting the two together in troubled times.

One Sunday morning, Jack and I tarried longer than usual after the worship service. Finally, as all our conversations ended and the last stragglers left, we gathered our things to leave. Before we were out the door, the church phone rang. It was for Jack.

"Please come," cried the distraught caller. "I've just backed over my three-year-old son with a trailer-load of wood. He's dead."

Jack and I jumped into the car and got there in time to see the little boy's body still on the grass, the medical examiner bending over to put his brains in a small plastic bag. I was horrified.

Oh, God, what good can come from this, I thought as we entered that sorrow-filled house.

Bob sat on the couch with his elbows on his knees and his face in his hands. "My son is dead...I killed him. My 6-year-old daughter saw it happen. Oh, God, I hurt...but right now I'm most concerned about my daughter. She can't get the picture of his crushed face out of her mind . . . . What are we going to do?"

"Do you have a current picture of Brett?" I asked.

"Why, yes. He just had a birthday."

"Get the picture for me, would you?"

Six-year-old Sara found the picture with ease. Brett was all smiles, surrounded by cake and birthday balloons.

I put my arm around Sara as we sat on the couch and said, "Sara, would you like to make a trade with God?"

"What kind of trade?"

"Let's give God the bad picture we have of Brett in our minds just now and trade it for the smiling face in this photograph."

"Okay," she whispered quietly.

We made the transaction in prayer. I asked God, according to His mercy, to erase the painful picture of Brett's crushed face and to remove any guilt Sara might be feeling for not having been able to prevent the accident. I asked Him to fill her mind with Brett's "Happy Birthday" face. Then I told her mom and dad to have her put that photograph on her nightstand when she went to bed. Later, I was to learn that Sara made it through that very difficult time with a peaceful mind.

We also prayed with Bob and his wife, Lynne. Lynne's grief and the tremendous guilt Bob was experiencing also needed a divine transaction. As we held one another, mourned together, talked and prayed, God healed Bob of the guilt that very day. It took time and the support of loving friends to heal their grief.

I have come to understand that our faith is in peak action when we minister God's loving nature in the middle of life's darkest moments. In that time of seeming helplessness and hopelessness for Bob, Lynne and Sara, I did what I sensed the Holy Spirit would have me do. I knew He would heal a little girl's mind and set her father free from guilt.

My most faith-stretching times have come in walking with people through the death of a member of their family, or through the process of their own death. In such times, I've found that people are struggling to hold on to the hope that in their helpless situations, God hasn't removed Himself. It is at this point that I set aside my feelings, walk in a faith born of God's Word, and apply a great deal of love.

I've asked God a lot of questions concerning the death of people before they get to an age of maturity in human terms, primarily because we have had 10 such seemingly premature deaths in our church family within a two-year period. We've been with our church family for more than 20 years. Those who died were my friends or members of their families.

As a Christian who believes in the healing manifestations of the Spirit in our day, I have gone to the wrestling mat with my covenant God over these excruciatingly painful experiences when all our collective faith hasn't produced happy endings in my eyes. It has been a growing process for me to understand and accept that God is as interested in faithful endings as He is in happy endings.

At one time I would have thought that to help the hurting was to make them happy. I've learned that God has more than happiness in mind for His children.

Nancy came to the altar for prayer one Sunday morning. Her face was stoic and tense.

"What do you need prayer for, Nancy?" I asked.

"I'm angry at God," she said.

"Tell me about it."

"I don't understand why God has me working at night in a job I don't like, in an environment where all the dust aggravates my allergies. I'm tired, I'm lonely and I'm mad because I've prayed. You'd think God would find me a way out."

"Nancy, if God delivered you from that job, what would you like to be doing?"

"I want a daytime job so that I can have time to help other people with their problems."

I paused for a moment, then said, "Nancy, have you ever considered that God grows us up according to our desires?"

"What do you mean?"

"The trials and tribulations you are going through right now are proving the bent of your spirit toward God," I explained. "If you want to bring hope to others in their time of need, you must learn to be a person of hope in your own time of need."

"I never thought of that," Nancy said. "Maybe God has something to teach me right where I am."

Several years ago, I probably would have prayed for God to deliver Nancy from this terrible situation so that she might have greater opportunity to serve Him. After all, that would have made Nancy happy. In those days, I would have liked to place a bow of happiness around the neck of every person as I finished praying with them. I would have prayed for them to be through with their struggles and happy forever, from that moment forward.

Have you noticed how easy it is to feel happy and hopeful when life is going great? But I'll tell you, it's been during the deaths, the disappointments, the unresolved relationship problems and the times of personal need that I've had to learn to walk as one who is full of God.

Like Nancy, during these battles I've seen whether I was full of a powerful God—or a confused self. At these times, I've had to exchange my own confusion for a divine transfusion of God's wisdom, clarity and hope. I've had to learn to live rightly and lovingly, despite the circumstances.

Never again will I rescue anyone from a painful situation for the sake of their immediate happiness. It is in the context of struggle that we realize what it is to live as one who is holy—a person full of God.

Through all my difficult times, when I've trusted God despite my unanswered questions, I have learned to hear His voice. No greater happiness could I know than to hear His voice in the midst of my struggles!

Last fall I led a group of our church women on an out-of-town retreat. I found myself in a small group with a woman whose husband had just been invited to be an elder of the congregation. She and her husband demonstrate a deep love for Christ, and their family witness to the church had been impeccable.

Within a few minutes of conversation, she was in tears. "I feel so unworthy to be a part of this group with you, Letha. How can I even share a room with you this weekend?"

I was at no great height in the ranks of Christian leadership for her to feel unworthy in my presence, so I asked her a question. "Mary, what has been your previous experience with church leadership?"

What a painful tale this woman related. She and her husband had grown up in a very strict sect in which no one was allowed to read the Bible except the church leadership. But the couple had an experience with the Holy Spirit in college that led them to read the Word of God for themselves. Because of this, they were excommunicated. Not only did they lose the fellowship of the congregation, they lost the fellowship of their families, for both sets of parents were church leaders.

Can you imagine the pain you would feel if you were put in front of your congregation and your own parents led the way in a standing vote to excommunicate you— because you were growing spiritually?

Mary didn't know what to do with our leadership's love and acceptance of her and her husband. She cried. With gentleness, we held her and prayed she would be cleansed of her hurt and unforgiveness. We prayed that the Holy Spirit would fill those clean areas with His power for ministry.

Power for ministry—that is what she and Bill, now an elder, are demonstrating. As a couple, they are teaching a new members' class each week. Our 18-year-old daughter is attending the sessions and is being blessed by their gift of teaching.

Mary had already forgiven her parents and had been reconciled to them. Yet her sense of self-worth had been deeply injured by her experience and needed to be healed. God's "divine accident" of placing her in my room and my small group provided me an opportunity to be the loving arms that held her as we prayed for her. Our associate pastor's wife was in this group, too. Mary had been hurt by leaders, and by God's grace, through leaders she was lovingly restored.

For me, spiritual ministry is not a lot of "razzle-dazzle." It's being a conduit for God's love, acceptance and forgiveness at a particular point of need in someone's life. I may have once thought that people needed my words; now I see they need my love.

Of course, sometimes what I can do for a person is not enough. I've had to learn to recognize those times. For example, a woman named Penny once called my home asking for Jack. Often, as the pastor's wife, I am but a gate people need to go through to get to my husband. That's fine with me; I just try to love them a little as they pass through.

"Hi, Penny. I'm sorry, but Jack is gone for the day. Is there something I can do for you?" I asked.

"I really need someone, Letha. There are spirits in my house that are bothering me. But I can handle that. That is, I could if I could just let go of my dog. I can't let go, though, because if I do my life's energy will drain out of me."

I should have known then that I was out of my league. But my compassionate nature won over what little wisdom I possessed, and I told her I would be right over.

Her last words to me on the phone were as bizarre as the first. "Oh, Letha, don't worry about me. God is taking me through a 'Noah experience.' I don't expect that you will understand what I'm going through. I just need to touch a living person today. Trust me."

It only took two hours of Penny holding on to me, the dog and the children, and talking about my being surrounded by rainbows for me to get the picture. I needed help! I took Penny up to the church. The staff members who were on hand agreed she had a problem, but none of us knew exactly what it was or how to fix it.

Because I couldn't find my husband, and Penny's husband was on a rafting trip in another state, I called in a couple who worked as Christian therapists. Finally, at midnight, the couple, Jack and I admitted Penny to the local hospital for mentally traumatized people. She was having a psychotic breakdown.

I am full of all sorts of imperfections and immaturities. My faith, hope and love are still growing. Sometimes I just don't know what to do for a hurting person.

The experience with Penny took place about eight years ago. If she were to come to my door today in that condition, I'm sure I would call for help again. It is important for me to know my limitations in knowledge and ability. These days, when I sense I'm in over my head, I always look for help from someone with expertise in the trouble area.

I spent a year sick in bed after the string of deaths in our church. I had tried to be involved with too many difficult situations at one time. It took that year to focus completely on Christ again. That was my year of resting and wrestling with God over my unanswered questions about hurt that doesn't get healed in a lifetime.

I've related these experiences because they brought me the most insight into God's desires for people—especially me—in difficult times. He wants me to walk in faith in the dark times, hope in the hard times, and love at all times.

But the year in bed, the loss of 30 pounds, and what I thought was the nearness of my death stripped away the need to have answers to my whys—why people hurt so bad before they get better, why they die when we pray sincerely for them to live, why the church as a whole seems so broken.

Finally, I have come to peaceful terms with this: I may not know why, but I know who; and if I know who, I don't need to know why. As our covenant-keeping God, He will see us through anything this life brings.

Born in 1944 in Denver, Colorado, **Letha Mathews** lived her childhood years in pain and poverty. Her father was an emotionally disturbed alcoholic who battered her mother. Her parents divorced when Letha was 12.

Letha committed her life to Christ in a mission church in Portland, Oregon, which had reached out to her penniless mother after the separation. Letha continued to live with her mother until her own marriage in 1962 to Jack Mathews, whom she met through a local Youth for Christ ministry.

From 1962 to 1965, Letha and Jack worked with Youth Adventures Inc., a non-profit ministry for troubled teenagers which they co-founded with another couple. Currently, Jack is lead pastor of Bethlehem Baptist Church in Lake Oswego, Oregon, where Letha directs the women's ministries. She has also served as secretary of the American Baptist Charismatic Fellowship for five years.

Letha and Jack have two daughters, ages 21 and 19.

Chapter Thirty-One
We're Heading for the Mission Field

by Edith (Mrs. Dick) Hugoniot

"Dick, I will *not* resign as a missionary just because you're feeling low and depressed!"

I was adamant. Normally, I submitted to my husband's leadership in the home. His decisions were godly ones and I accepted them with little argument. But now Dick was suggesting that we throw in the towel on our short careers as missionaries in India. To make such a decision when we were both emotionally and spiritually exhausted, I knew, would be a horrible mistake.

We were—and are—missionaries with Wycliffe Bible Translators. In Wycliffe, both husband and wife sign up together for service. Dick couldn't withdraw without me, and I was determined to wait until we had clear direction from the Lord before deciding to do something as drastic as leaving the mission field.

The same scene was repeated many times over the 10-month period of our first furlough. We had been working in India for three years. It had not been easy. We were tired and discouraged. Resignation seemed the only answer. The furlough rejuvenated us, however. When the 10 months were over, our depression had lifted and we were ready to go back to the field.

It wasn't glamour or excitement or a life of ease that drew us back to India. On the contrary, living as we had been in a thatched clay hut among people who had no way of understanding who we were or where we had come from was difficult, sometimes painful. What drew us back was the Lord.

After the furlough, Dick and I and our two young sons, Kenny and David, went to live among the Tharu people in Santpur. The Tharus were rice farmers. The landowners among them enjoyed a comparatively good standard of living—at least they always had enough food, clothing and other essentials. The poorer families eked by on the work they did in the fields for their richer neighbors.

We lived in two small rooms near many of the poor families in the village. Our challenge in Santpur was three-fold. First, we were to establish our home among the Tharus as a living example of the power of the gospel. Second, we were to learn to speak their language and try to understand their beliefs, world view and culture. And finally, we were to lay a foundation of friendship and mutual respect to prepare for the day when we would know them and their language well enough to tell them about Jesus Christ.

Getting to know and love the Tharus was not easy. We were an oddity. From the crack of dawn until we put out our little kerosene lamp at night, 30 to 40 pairs of curious eyes—most of them belonging to children—

keenly observed our every move. I couldn't even put my 2-year-old on the potty without being aware of the stares.

Since the Tharu language, Bhojpuri, was related to two other languages Dick and I had learned, we could understand a good bit of what our neighbors said, even though we couldn't form good Bhojpuri sentences to respond to them. In those first weeks in Santpur, their comment was almost always the same—"Look at all the things those people have!"

Hearing the same comment day after day made me feel guilty. Did we really have so many more "things" than they did? What could we eliminate? Our kitchen consisted of two little kerosene wick burners for cooking and two plastic basins for cleaning up. I had only brought enough dishes and pans to serve our family of four one meal at a time.

We slept on army camp cots with cheap lengths of cotton cloth for sheets. We used mosquito nets, but they were a necessity. We had splurged on two galvanized tubs so both Kenny and David, ages 4 and 2, could have fun splashing and taking their baths together.

We didn't really have more things than the Tharus; we just had different things. But there was no way I could help them understand this until I could speak the language better. The stares continued.

One day, as the boys and I took a walk and the usual "Pied Piper" parade fell into step behind us, Kenny stopped in his tracks.

"Mom, do those kids have to follow us *everywhere*?" he asked, exasperated.

I stood still and breathed a silent prayer for wisdom. I was struggling with my own attitude toward the Tharus and didn't want to convey any critical thoughts to my sons.

"You know, Kenny," I finally answered, "when Jesus lived on the earth there was always a large crowd of people following Him, and He never told them to go away. He just loved them."

Kenny and David both thought a moment and then smiled, satisfied. I knew I had said the right thing.

A few days later, however, just after lunch, I laid down on my cot, the curtain drawn tight across the window to give me a reprieve from those ever-present Tharu eyes. I wept.

"Lord," I prayed, "I don't love these people. In fact, I can hardly tolerate the way they always stare at us. They turn me off with their inconsiderate ways and their coarse manners. I know You sent me to bring Your love to them, but I just can't."

As I wept with shame, God spoke very clearly to me in that "still, small voice" I have come to know and trust.

"The fruit of the Spirit is love. Fruit takes time to grow."

That was all He said. But those few words spoke volumes. The Lord knew my heart. He knew I wanted to be a vessel of His love. He also understood my human frailties. But given time, if I would allow it, He would cause love to grow in my heart—even for the Tharus.

I did grow to love the Tharus, and the Konda Doras, and each of the other remote tribes and peoples Dick and I worked among in the field. But learning to love is not just a lesson for missionaries in far away places. Other Christians face these same problems and need to learn the same lessons.

Another one was how to overcome fear and simply trust God. We had moved to Nepal and I was pregnant again. I lived for months dreading the upcoming delivery of my third child. Our first son, born in India, had come into the world without the aid of medication and it had been a beautiful experience for both Dick and me. Our second son, however, was born in the United States by caesarean section. At that time, the doctor warned me that any future children should be birthed in an operating room, since I might need emergency surgery and a blood transfusion.

I told my new missionary doctor my history and my former doctor's recommendation. She was from New Zealand, fresh out of medical school. She was spending a year with the mission hospital for experience before setting up her own practice back home.

"Oh, don't worry. It won't be necessary to use the operating room for a simple delivery," she said. "Besides, we'll have at least 15 minutes to get you there if something goes wrong."

Her words did nothing to assure me. I had been in that hospital, which was housed in an ancient mansion. I knew that to move me from the delivery room to the operating room would require locating a couple of men and a stretcher—no simple task—and being carried downstairs and across the grounds to the second floor of another building. My previously arranged blood donor would have to be notified to come to the hospital— and this in a city with few phones. We were going to do all of this in 15 minutes?

I struggled for weeks with my fear. I had visions of myself dying while giving birth.

Then, coming home from the doctor's office one day,

I heard God's voice.

"Your fear did not originate with Me," He said.

I pondered His words. If God said my fear didn't come from Him, then it had no place in me, I decided. For the first time in months I felt calm. If God hadn't given me the fear, then it was unfounded. Everything would be all right.

And it was. Within a few weeks, I was holding a beautiful baby girl in my arms. She was born easily, with no complications.

Many times we had to trust the Lord and an unsophisticated medical community with our health care. We suffered through our share of tropical maladies, such as amoeba and malaria. But the illnesses that caused us the greatest concern and spiritual torment were those we could have just as easily contracted in the United States.

Our daughter, Melinda, had tonsillitis about 30 times during the first three years of her life. On several of those occasions, the Lord intervened in answer to prayer and healed her quickly. Other times, He seemed to be saying, "I have given you antibiotics. Use them."

Our oldest son, Kenny, had a chronic ear infection that lasted four years. In 1977 we moved to Irian Jaya, Indonesia, one of the most primitive regions in the world. There were only three medical practitioners available, and one of them was frequently out of the country. They did their best to treat the infection, but it kept returning. We prayed as a family, asked for special prayer from a visiting minister and had friends anoint Kenny with oil and lay hands on him. Someone even prophesied that he was healed. I clung to that word in a desperate effort to believe it was done.

But the physical evidence of infection remained until we returned to the United States on furlough. American doctors had to perform two operations, the first to clear out the infection and the second to help restore some of Kenny's lost hearing.

I struggled within myself to understand why God had not healed Kenny before so much damage had been done. Hadn't we been on the mission field, doing the Lord's work, depending totally on Him? Finally, I felt the Lord say to my heart: "Trust in Me. My love for you is infinite. Don't trust in prayer, spiritual people, spiritual gifts, or even in faith itself. Don't sell yourself short by seeking merely my gifts—seek *Me*."

"I trust You, Lord," I answered. "Without You I have nothing." The peace which accompanied my relinquishment has remained to this day.

I also have had to balance my wife, mother and career roles. Seasons are inevitable in the life of any married woman with children, even one who is on the mission field.

During our early years as missionaries, Dick and I lived in a tribal village with our small children. Despite my interest and training in the linguistic work, my homemaker role had to come first. I fit in language learning and analysis as I could. Occasionally, I was able to fill more than one role at a time.

For example, while living among the Konda Doras in Sapa Guda, India, I set out to learn how the tribe's verbs worked. Kenny, my only child at the time, was napping. Dick was out in the millet fields with the men of the tribe, learning how to harvest millet—or more precisely, how to *talk* about harvesting millet.

I had a pile of dirty clothes to wash. I marched out

to the back of our hut with the clothes, a bucket of water and detergent. In a few moments, the usual crowd of children gathered around me.

I put a little girl's hands in the bucket and helped her wash clothes. "What are you doing?" I asked (it was one of the few Konda Dora phrases I had learned).

"I am washing clothes," she answered in her native tongue.

I maneuvered the other children around her, putting their hands in the bucket until I had learned all the possibilities: "*We* are washing clothes." "*She* is washing clothes." "*They* are washing clothes." "*You* are washing clothes."

Dick was proud of me later when I told him what I had done. Not only had I gotten the clothes washed, but I had learned an important aspect of the Konda Dora language. And it was fun!

Later, when Dick became associate director and then director of Wycliffe's work in Indonesia, we moved from our jungle base to an office in the capital city of Jayapura—and into a small house which had running water and electricity for at least part of the day. There I was able to make other kinds of contributions.

As long as we had at least one pre-schooler, I only took jobs that could be done at home, fitted around homemaking and mothering. There were always small tasks, some short-term, some longer, that could be done that way. It was rewarding to devote myself mainly to my home and children, yet feel that I was of some help to the mission. Then, as the children grew and went off to school, I became more active, learning bookkeeping, secretarial work and computer operating.

Sending the children away to school was by far the

hardest thing we had to do as missionaries. We did this for the first time when Kenny was in fifth grade and David in third. The school for missionary children was a half-hour drive from where we were living—not very far, except that we had no transportation for a daily commute. Most of the other students boarded full-time because their parents lived and worked one hour to two days away, accessible only by small aircraft. We, at least, could arrange to bring the boys home on weekends.

I had mixed feelings about sending them away during the week. To be honest, a part of me was relieved to have one less responsibility. Adjusting to the intense heat and humidity of the tropics as well as a different living situation drained me. I was worn out by late afternoon. Had the boys come home each day, I would have had nothing to give them. But I wept with tears of guilt and sorrow during those first hard weeks of weekly separations.

Three semesters later, several other missionary families moved into the area, so we chartered a car together, sharing the cost. Kenny and David lived at home once again and commuted to school. By that time, they had gained a greater appreciation for home, and I was coping much better with my new life.

The boarding experience stood both boys in good stead later when the time came to go to high school—a 700-mile flight away. Their infrequent letters took about two weeks to reach us. Dick and I had to commit not only their physical safety but also their spiritual development to the Lord during the long months between school vacations. God was faithful and watched over them.

In 1985, because of Dick's expanding work as direc-or of Wycliffe's Summer Institute of Linguistics in Indonesia, we moved to Jakarta, one of the largest cities in the world. Here, my nest is empty. Kenny, a high school graduate, went to England to enter an intensive Bible study and training program and to get a little closer to the American culture he knows only from a distance. David, a high school junior, and Melinda, a seventh grader, are at Faith Academy in the Philippines—the best and most financially feasible school for them, despite its distance.

At times I feel this part of my life has been thrust on me prematurely. If we weren't missionaries—if we were a normal American family in a typical pastorate—David and Melinda would still be with us at home. But that is part of the package Dick and I bought when we volunteered as missionaries.

There are great benefits, too. In many ways, the Lord has assured me that everything is working for our good. Everything is part of His plan. Our children have continued to develop the values we taught them from the cradle. We see good results from the input of godly teachers and dorm parents in their lives. While we miss them achingly, we know God is forming them into the men and women He always intended them to be.

And He is forming me into the woman He wants me to be, too.

Edith Hugoniot was born in Arkansas in 1941. The eldest of three children, Edith became a Christian at the age of 13 and prayed daily for her parents' salvation. They accepted Christ six years later.

Edith met her husband, Dick, at Central Washington Bible College near Yakima, Washington. They married in 1961.

Dick was pastoring a small church in Washington when he and Edith felt a call from God to go to the mission field. Trained with Wycliffe Bible Translators, the two have worked as linguists/translators in India, Nepal and Indonesia. Dick is director for the Summer Institute of Linguistics in Indonesia and a member of the international board of directors for the Summer Institute of Linguistics and Wycliffe Bible Translators.

The Hugoniots have three children, ages 18, 16 and 13.

Chapter Thirty-Two
Supporting One Another

by Jean (Mrs. Jack) Coleman

Is there anyone lonelier than a pastor's wife? Certainly she is a unique species. In most cases, there is only one per church. She is called to be an example—and the perfection of Christian womanhood. Her children are to be angelic, her house spotless, her disposition sunny. She is never to get discouraged or angry or tired. She is constantly on display. If she has problems (but of course, she isn't supposed to have problems), she learns to keep them to herself.

Pastors' wives are often victims of the Elijah syndrome. They feel so isolated and alone that eventually they cry out, "I, even I only, am left!" There seems to be no one who understands, no one who can appreciate her unique problems. It is tempting to sit down under a juniper tree and give up!

I am reminded of the two little boys with the terrible "aging disease," one from South Africa and the other from the United States. When they met for the first time at Disneyland several years ago, they looked at one another with amazement. After years of wondering if there was anyone else like them anywhere, they had found each other. I understand they became friends immediately.

Obviously, there is a multitude of pastors' wives somewhere. But the big question is, How do they find each other?

In this area of Maryland, a group of pastors' wives found each other for the first time at a pastors' breakfast held in our church. A well-known, out-of-town speaker was coming to share, and the invitation had gone out encouraging the pastors to bring their wives with them to the gathering. Twelve wives attended, and all of us were very quiet and on our best behavior. It was, after all, a men's breakfast, and the women were content to listen to the conversation across the table. The wives were together in the same room, but we were still far apart. Our lives didn't touch or intermingle. At best, each now had an awareness that there were others of this strange breed, even if we didn't know the others' names.

Shortly before breakfast came to a close, the group was called to prayer. As everyone formed a large prayer circle, one of the wives spoke up. "I believe the women are to pray together. We can go to the other side of the room." She strode off. The other wives, hesitant at first, followed.

The "feminist spirit" I thought was long dead rose up within me. Why should the women be separated? Memories of pre-salvation parties where the men were in the living room and the women in the kitchen (I hated that!) came rushing back.

But—praise the Lord—I put down the old thought patterns and joined the other women for prayer. No sooner had we joined hands than one of the wives began to weep—deep sobs welling up from her innermost being.

"I've been so depressed lately that I don't know what to do," she confessed. "I've been to doctors and counselors, but I don't seem to be able to come out from under this terrible cloud of darkness. Please pray that I be delivered and set free. I've got to have help. Oh, God, help me!"

In that instant of time, we became one. We gathered around her and prayed, our tears mingling with hers. Walls of separation were broken down as we lifted our sister before the throne of grace. Rivers of love flowed from us to her. God had supplied her need through others who were able to say, "We understand! We understand!"

It was one of those times when heaven comes right down to earth and the presence of God is so very real. We all recognized it as a sacred moment, born of God.

In the depths of my heart I heard God speaking: "I want you to bring these women together on a regular basis. This is the beginning of a new thing, and I hold you responsible for bringing it to pass."

My spirit bore witness to the words I heard, and with tears streaming down my face, I told the others what the Lord had revealed to me.

I felt like a midwife in the delivery room as God brought forth His will. How can I describe the excitement, the anticipation of what the Lord was going to do in us and through us? No man or woman had conceived this idea, but the Lord Himself. There was a chorus of "Amen" and "Thank You, Jesus" as we reached out to one another in love.

The entire atmosphere had changed. We were no longer strangers, but friends. No longer separated by suspicion and competition, we were sisters. We were truly family—not only in word but in deed. It was the Lord's doing, and it was marvelous in our eyes.

"I'll write you," I told them, "and let you know all the details as soon as possible. We'll get together sometime early next month, and we'll make it a luncheon."

Quickly, names and phone numbers were exchanged, and final hugs given. The one who had such a short time before told us of her despondency was now glowing with the love of the Lord. Her healing was a confirmation of God's desire to bring us together and make us truly one.

That was the start of the Helpmates' Luncheons. Nearly two years have passed since the morning we joined together for prayer. Although we have not yet reached all the pastors' wives who are out there, some 36 in our area are now regularly involved in these gatherings.

And how simple it was to bring these lonely women together! Let's be honest. All it really takes is one person who is willing to take a step of faith and do some organizing and legwork.

It wasn't difficult to make a list of pastors' wives in the area. Of particular interest to me were the wives of those men who pastored independent churches. These were the women who were really isolated and seemed to have the greatest need for fellowship. There were no denominational ties holding these wives together, no hierarchy of senior wives to go to for advice, no special programs. The independents had no shoulder to cry on, no hand to hold.

A pastor's wife has access to a great deal of administrative help if she will take advantage of it. My part was not complicated or involved. I compiled the list, drafted a letter, contacted the woman in our church who is in charge of meal preparation and then handed the whole thing over to our capable secretary. She ran copies of the letter, addressed the envelopes and made follow-up calls the week prior to the luncheon.

I spent my time on my knees seeking the Lord for a format for the gathering. It seemed that what we needed more than anything else was simply an opportunity to communicate with one another. It was not the time to bring in a speaker, but rather a time to share across the table in an informal way. What I really wanted was for the Holy Spirit to be in charge. I wanted Him to direct the flow of our conversation, to pick the topics, to orchestrate the entire luncheon. I was to be the hostess; He was to act as moderator. I wanted everyone to feel free to say what was on her heart.

My part was easy—the battle took place with the individual wives. There were many fears that had to be overcome. Pastors' wives can be very timid women. So many are used to staying in the background and not really taking much initiative. Driving alone some 15 or 20 miles into new territory presented a real challenge to many of the wives. Walking into a room where they would probably know no one at all was another stumbling block. Even mixing with charismatics and those from denominations other than their own was a mighty mountain to move.

It was easier to make an excuse and relax in the security of the dark cave than to walk across the water. But God was in it, and the Holy Spirit was drawing us together. He has a way of making confetti out of our excuses when He wants to build His body together in unity.

For our first luncheon, 26 women met around four tables, breaking bread as well as breaking down walls that had separated us for so many years. I'm not saying there weren't some awkward moments. I had made it a point to put a woman who was a strong, dynamic leader at each table to act as hostess. It was her responsibility to draw each woman out and to be sure that everyone took part. But there were times when we ate in silence, praying inwardly that someone would say something—anything—to get the conversation going.

I had anticipated that our first gathering would be somewhat superficial. The miracle was simply that we were together. We had found each other. It was a time to get acquainted, to ask questions: Where is your church? How long have you been in the ministry? How old are your children? We needed to touch lightly before we could cling.

After the tables had been cleared, I asked each helpmate to stand, introduce herself and share something the Lord was teaching her. "Patience" and "how to wait on the Lord" seemed to be the almost unanimous learning experience of the group.

The first breakthrough came when one wife told us how her husband had recently been released from prison after serving three years for extortion. With complete openness and honesty, she told of the humiliation, the separation, the loss of friends and ministry. He was currently overseeing the construction of a church in the area, where they were accepted and loved by the congregation. She asked for our prayers as they began to build anew.

There were some tears on her part—and some tears on ours. We were discovering that we could be ourselves, we could share hidden hurts, disappointments and failures, and still be accepted. We discovered that being vulnerable didn't mean being rejected. We came into the knowledge that love is stronger than our weaknesses. We could encourage one another and pray for one another. Acceptance wasn't conditional—we were loving one another with the love of the Lord.

Perhaps the highlight of the luncheon came when the woman who had received prayer the previous month for depression testified that the cloud had lifted from the moment we had prayed together for deliverance.

"I love you all so much!" she proclaimed. "Only God knows how important your fellowship and love are to me."

She told of the many letters, cards and calls she had received since we were all last together. Many of the wives had responded in love to her heartcry and served as the hand of God. In the midst of her darkness had come light—words of comfort, strength and encouragement. She was healed.

Surely this was one of the main purposes in the mind of God when He called together the pastors' wives in our area—that we might minister to one another. I have never had to "organize" ministry between the wives. It has always been something spontaneous, prompted by the Holy Spirit alone.

We decided to continue meeting every other month

on a Monday. Monday seemed the ideal day, since it is traditionally the pastor's day off and thus provided a baby-sitter for many of the women with small children.

I was certain we would quickly grow in number to 50 or more helpmates. Instead, our second luncheon was attended by only 16 wives. At first, I was tempted to give in to the natural impulse to "generate" a larger turnout, but then I realized the hand of God was on our numbers. With such a small group we were able to push two tables together, and everyone could fellowship over the meal as well as afterwards. God was not seeking large numbers, but unity and friendship between us. Large numbers can equal a multitude of strangers. Small numbers bring intimacy.

One day I received a call from one of the wives. "I won't be able to attend the Helpmates' Luncheon this month," she informed me. "There's a denominational gathering the same day. How I hate to miss seeing all my new friends! Our time of fellowship is so precious to me." She paused as though pondering her next statement. "If only there was a newsletter, I wouldn't feel so left out when I can't come."

Obviously, it was the voice of the Lord. Following that month's luncheon, I mailed out our first newsletter—just a few friendly, chatty paragraphs that reviewed the topics of conversation, prayer needs among the women, praise reports and news of general interest. Since then, this simple little letter has served to bind us together in a miraculous way. Even if a helpmate has to miss several meetings, she isn't left out of what's happening. She still feels very much a part. She can congratulate a new mother the next time they meet, or express appreciation over a testimony that was shared. One helpmate has saved all her newsletters and put them together into a prayer journal. She lifts up each wife, her pastor husband, their children and their church by name daily.

My part in putting the newsletter together is so very simple. All I have to do is take a few notes during each gathering and spend a short time at the typewriter within the next few days. Again, I draw upon the church staff to mail the newsletters out.

Some of our most memorable luncheons have been those in which we have openly ministered to each others' needs. One in particular that I remember revolved around a rebellious teenager.

"Perhaps you will pray for my daughter," the woman began, choking up. "I just don't know what to do about her."

It was the familiar story of a child raised in the church, an early commitment to Christ that waxed cold, worldly friends and worldly ways. It was also the story of trying to shield the church members from the knowledge of a wayward teen who seemed to have turned her back on everything in which her parents believed.

It was a mother weeping over the prodigal, a mother with a broken heart. It was a mother crying out, "Does anyone understand?"

We understood.

One pastor's wife at the luncheon related how her son had run away from home at 16 with his 15-year-old girlfriend. She hadn't wanted anyone to know and hoped to keep his escapade a secret. But the Lord had instructed her and her husband to inform the body of Christ so that intercession might be made on their son's behalf.

God heard and answered the prayers of the saints on

the boy's behalf. He came home. But that wasn't the end of his rebellion. A few years later when he was in college, he began taking drugs and wandered far from the Lord. But the family continued to believe God, and today their son is the youth pastor of their church.

Our hearts were encouraged as one after another the women shared testimonies of God's miraculous intervention in the lives of their children. Some women revealed things about their children that had never been told publicly before. They were willing to expose themselves to help each other.

Yes, we understood. And we also understood the importance of keeping a confidence. Each woman's "secrets" were safe in this group. We understood.

It was important for us to learn that the children of pastors are not little gods that never tarnish. One wife told us how she had always referred to her son as her "golden boy." He had been saved at an early age and had never given them any trouble at all while he was growing up. But then in his late teens, he began to do his own thing. She said she watched her "golden boy" crumple and break into a million pieces.

It was a heavy meeting that day: golden idols, hidden things brought to the light, failures admitted. But over and over these words were spoken: I understand. I know how you feel. That happened to me too. I understand. I understand.

There was a long session of prayer at the close of the afternoon. Together, we carried our children before the heavenly Father.

It was good. It was healing. There were long embraces, and children's names were added to prayer lists. There were smiles. Someone had understood.

Another time one of the helpmates shared how a church split had recently occurred in her congregation. Over half of the people left and began attending another church. There were tears as she talked about the empty pews on Sunday mornings and how she missed the familiar faces of those who had been her friends.

Again, we understood.

Everyone, without exception, talked of hurts she had also experienced at the hands of members of her congregation. Some told of betrayal by friends and of unwarranted criticism from those they had tried so hard to please. Others shared about church cliques and gossipers who dropped "weed seed" into the ears of anyone open to receive. These deep hurts had been buried for years, but they were still there. They needed to be brought into the light for real healing to take place.

That day we also talked about forgiveness—and in many cases forgave those who had trespassed against us. There was something about knowing that our circumstances weren't so unique after all that seemed to bring freedom to confess them and leave them behind.

All of our gatherings are not "true confession" sessions or times of weeping or dredging up ghosts of the past. On one occasion, we spent the afternoon discussing what we saw as major weaknesses in the charismatic movement. Another time we spoke at length about what we anticipated in the next move of God in America. Once we talked about a book that the majority of us had read and enjoyed.

And there are always testimonies of victory and the overcoming power of God in our lives.

As a rule, we avoid politics and controversial issues in our discussions. We have never experienced any doctrinal conflicts. We are not coming together to discuss doctrine, rather to demonstrate the love of God to our sisters. Our approach is simplistic—let's build up one another in the Spirit.

With the exception that we are all married to pastors, we have little else in common. Some are young, some are old. Some are quiet, others very outspoken. Some have large congregations, others only a handful of faithful. Some are in denominations, some are independent. Some have been in the ministry for years, others for just a few months. It doesn't make any difference. We love one another.

One of the helpmates is somewhat fiery and tells it like it is, but we appreciate her honesty—and appreciate *her*. She's our sister, and we love her. Another is very shy, content just to sit and listen. We love and appreciate her too. We are not coming together to judge one another, but to love one another.

Several of the women expressed a desire to bring along a friend to the luncheons. We have always encouraged the helpmates to invite other pastors' wives, but this was different. They were requesting to bring personal friends who were not married to pastors. It wasn't easy to say "no," but as I sought the Lord I became convinced that the luncheons needed to be restricted to pastors' wives only. I didn't want the freedom of conversation that had been established to be jeopardized—the choruses of "we understand" that had brought release to so many. If everyone brought a friend, before long the luncheon would not be a pastors' wives gathering. My decision may have lost us one or two helpmates, but I have peace that we remained in God's perfect will.

Perhaps you are saying, "I could start a luncheon right where I live."

Then do it!

It's not enough to believe you can do it. Faith without works is dead. We need to become action people who will dare to move out in faith.

Discuss the idea with your husband over dinner and win his support. He will get the overflow from these luncheons because husbands automatically draw closer to each other when their wives become friends. Be honest with him about your need to come together with those who are also pastors' wives. His greatest desire is to see you happy and fulfilled.

We do not charge for our luncheons but consider them to be an outreach to the body of Christ. If the Lord would lead you to begin a helpmates' gathering in your area, I know He will also direct you in how to handle the monetary aspect.

There's no reason to sit under the juniper tree any longer. You may be a unique species—but you're not as unique as you might think. There may not be hundreds of pastors' wives right in your own backyard, but I guarantee you can find some. Seek and you shall find. You shall find understanding friends who will support you and encourage you. You shall find the blessings of God through the outpoured love of your sisters.

All it takes is a simple step of faith on your part.

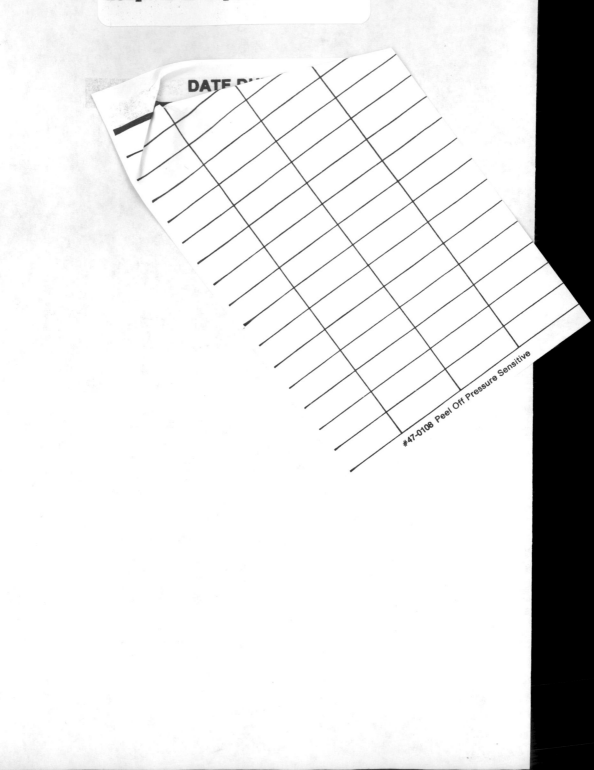

DATE DUE

#47-0108 Peel Off Pressure Sensitive